What is Religiou

What is Religious Ethics? An Introduction is an accessible and informative overview to major themes and methods in religious ethics. This concise and lively book demonstrates the relevance and importance of ethics based in religious traditions and describes how scholars of religious ethics think through moral problems.

Combining an issues-based approach with a model of studying ethics religion-by-religion, this volume examines pressing topics through a variety of belief systems—Hinduism, Buddhism, Jainism, Judaism, Christianity, Islam, and Sikhism—while also importantly spotlighting Indigenous communities. Engaging case studies invite readers to consider the role of religions with regard to issues such as:

- CRISPR
- Vegetarianism
- Nuclear weapons
- Women's leadership
- Reparations for slavery

What is Religious Ethics? is a reliable and easily digestible introduction to the field. With chronologically structured chapters, discussion questions, suggestions for further reading, and interviews with scholars of religious ethics, this is an ideal guide to those approaching the study of religious ethics for the first time.

Irene Oh is Associate Professor and Chair of the Department of Religion at the George Washington University, USA.

What is this thing called?

The Routledge Religion *What is this thing called?* series of concise textbooks have been designed for use by students coming to a core area of the discipline for the first time. Each volume explores the relevant central questions with clear explanation of complex ideas and engaging contemporary examples.

Available in the series:

What is Mormonism?
A Student's Introduction
Patrick Q. Mason

What is Antisemitism?
A Contemporary Introduction
Linda Maizels

What is Religious Ethics?
An Introduction
Irene Oh

For more information about this series, please visit: https://www.routledge.com/What-is-this-thing-called-Religion/book-series/WITTCR

Made in the USA
Middletown, DE
21 August 2020

What is Religious E   s?

An Introduction

Irene Oh

Routledge
Taylor & Francis Group

LONDON AND NEW YORK

Designed cover image:

First published 2023 ingdon, Oxon OX14 4RN
by Routledge
4 Park Square, Milto

and by Routledge rk, NY 10158
605 Third Avenue the Taylor & Francis Group, an informa business

Routledge is an i

British Library Cataloguing-in-Publication Data
A catalogue record for this book is available from the British Library

ISBN: 978-1-138-39268-7 (hbk)
ISBN: 978-1-138-39359-2 (pbk)
ISBN: 978-1-003-35063-7 (ebk)

DOI: 10.4324/9781003350637

Typeset in Bembo
by codeMantra

Dedicated to James, Robert, and Ellie

Contents

Acknowledgments

I am beyond grateful for all the people who have provided me with their wisdom, humor, time, patience, encouragement, food, and drink during this long, long journey. My proposal for *What is Religious Ethics?* was accepted just prior to the pandemic. Needless to say, my hopes for completing this manuscript in a timely manner were waylaid by life during a global pandemic. For many months, I made little progress on this manuscript as I helped my children with their virtual schooling, learned how to teach courses online, and survived for more than a year in a kind of existential fog. What helped tremendously was the kindness of family, friends, colleagues, and students along the way. I would like to thank Elizabeth Bucar and Grace Kao for their years of friendship and wise counsel throughout this process. I could not ask for better colleagues in the Religion Department at the George Washington University; they have been wonderfully supportive of my teaching and research: Eyal Aviv, Kimisha Cassidy, Rob Eisen, Mohammad Faghfoory, Ryan Halloran, Xiaofei Kang, Noelani Kelly, Derek Malone-France, Eli McCarthy, Kelly Pemberton, and Allison Taylor-Adams. I would especially like to thank my colleague Paul Duff, who not only provided feedback on an entire draft of this book, but who has also been a generous and sage mentor to me since my arrival at GW. My GW writing group, formed at the start of the pandemic, encouraged me throughout this process: Katrin Schultheiss, Jennifer Tobkin, Phillip Troutman, and Daqing Yang.

Writing, despite its reputation as a solitary endeavor, is the product of many hearts and minds. I am indebted to numerous friends, colleagues, and mentors: Lisa Sowle Cahill, Diana Fritz Cates, Jim Childress, Jonathan Crane, Shannon Dunn, Nichole Flores, Laura Hartman, Sohail Hashmi, Terrence Johnson, Aline Kalbian, Martin Kavka, John Kelsay, Suejeanne Koh, Rollie Lal, Chuck Mathewes, Nadia Oweidat, Andrea Scardina, Abdulaziz Sachedina, Michael J. Smith, Aaron Stalnaker, Barney Twiss, Diane M. Yeager, and many others. I have had the privilege to work with many brilliant thinkers through scholarly organizations such as the Society for Christian Ethics, the Society for the Study of Muslim Ethics, the Christian-Muslim Studies Network, and the Comparative Religious Ethics group of the American Academy of Religion.

The panels and informal discussions that I have participated in through these associations have all informed my approach to this book. Thank you to the editors and staff at Routledge, who have uniformly been a pleasure to work with: Rebecca Clintworth, Amy Doffegnies, Iman Hakimi, Ceri McLardy, and Emma Yuan.

My friends from beyond the walls of academia bring me tremendous joy and are absolutely essential for a full life: Susannah Adler, Nicole Anzia and Michael Davies, Adrienne and Stu Biel, Audrey Choi and Bob Orr, Heather Fath, Anabel and Christian Genetski, Alexandra Gianinno, Alicia and Sean Glover, Stacey and Jeremy Grant, Alison Grasheim, Nicole Jassie, Selene Ko, Kitty Lin, Tali and Dickon Mager, Maeva Michelis, Amber and Warren Romine, Dana Sade, Jenny Silversmith, Suann Song and Eugene Hong, and Kira and Claude Vol. Sandra Ventura, who has cared for our children and our home for nearly a decade, deserves a tremendous amount of credit for allowing me to achieve a semblance of work–life balance.

I am so fortunate to have the constant and unwavering encouragement of my family. My mom Jean, my sister Jen, and my brother and his wife, Will and Paige, have been incredibly supportive throughout this long journey. Finally, to my husband James Koukios, and my children, Robert and Ellie— thank you for bringing so much happiness and meaning to my life. The brightest light throughout the darkness of the COVID pandemic has been spending time at home with you.

Introduction

What is the value of religions in understanding moral problems? While it is true that many of our most urgent problems can be solved using perspectives that are not religious, the fact of the matter is that people will often turn to religious beliefs to guide decisions, direct and inform policy, and interact with others. Religious beliefs are important not only for understanding why each of us thinks or believes as we do, but also about how our actions impact others. Sometimes religious beliefs are explicit; other times, they inform our ethics or morals in implicit or indirect ways. Some of us may be acutely aware of how religions inform our worldviews. Others prefer to leave the role of religion in their lives unexamined. I assume as a reader of this book that you are up for the challenge of examining how religions may shape what you believe and how you live.

I have studied and taught religious ethics for over two decades. Most of this time has been spent teaching and researching in secular university settings, and for the last dozen years or so I have been a professor at the George Washington University in Washington, DC, where I teach a course called "Ethics and the World Religions." This course forms the basis of many of the chapters of this book. The title of the course, like the title of this book, focuses on the intersection of two fields of study: ethics and religion.

Although there are multiple definitions of ethics, a basic working definition would describe ethics as a sense of goodness or rightness. From here, we may branch out intellectually and consider what it means to "sense" the good and the right; question whether goodness is opposed to something like evil; or note the differences between rightness and concepts such as justice. For now, however, this definition works reasonably well for a wide variety of situations.

When using the word "ethics," scholars often mean the study of moral beliefs or moral codes. Ethics, therefore, is "meta" in that it analyzes and compares the specific ways of understanding right and wrong in various organizations and communities. Practically speaking, however, the difference between "ethics" and "morals" is semantic. In colloquial and even professional contexts, the two words are interchangeable. In this book, "ethics" and "morals" are used interchangeably.

DOI: 10.4324/9781003350637-1

Many of us associate "religion" with traditions such as Hinduism, Buddhism, Judaism, Christianity, and Islam, as well as the smaller sects that belong to each of these larger traditions. Some of us might be familiar with Sikhism and Jainism, in addition to various Indigenous traditions. Unlike ethics, however, which was understood as an area of study as far back as the ancient Greeks, religion is a relatively new category of scholarly inquiry. The formal study of religions emerged with colonialism, when European Christians sought "equivalents" to Christianity and the Bible in Asia, Africa, the Americas, and Indigenous lands. The category of religion—and the comparative study of religions—emerged out of attempts to convert colonized peoples away from their own traditions, which European imperialists pejoratively classified as primitive, uncivilized, or savage. Kathryn Lofton, a professor of American religious history, notes that religion "as a description of human behavior was created through colonialism and its governments, its sciences, and its theologies. To be trained as a scholar of religious studies is then to practice a postcolonial methodology of a profoundly colonial subject."[1] Many of the traditions of the peoples in Africa, Asia, Australia, and the Americas were wiped out because Indigenous populations were killed, died from diseases brought over by European Christians, or were forbidden from teaching future generations about their traditions and languages when they were forcibly converted to Christianity. When we study religions today, we are reminded of this legacy and pay particular attention to the ways in which we might avoid perpetuating imperialist practices. At the most fundamental level, this means refusing to place any one particular religion on a pedestal above others.

At secular universities, the purpose of religion departments differs in some respects from their counterparts at religiously affiliated schools. The purpose of the study of religion at a secular college or university is not to reinforce the religious beliefs of students; rather, it is to study the beliefs, practices, and histories of persons and communities defined as religious. Indeed, the labeling of such departments as "religion" or "religious studies" as opposed to "theology" is often indicative of their differing purposes. Theology departments at, for example, Catholic universities may take the ideal of "faith seeking understanding" as the basis for their teaching and research. Many religiously affiliated colleges and universities require students to take a theology course in order to graduate, whereas at most secular schools, religion courses are considered electives. Seminaries, yeshivas, and other explicitly religious institutions of higher learning moreover train students to become ministers, rabbis, and leaders of religious communities, whereas religious studies departments do not. The core of theology faculties, seminaries, and yeshivas teach from within their own faith. At secular institutions, faculty members' personal religious commitments do not necessarily play a role in their teaching or research.

In secular religion departments and in larger theology departments, students will find faculty with expertise in multiple religious traditions (e.g., Hinduism, Buddhism, Judaism, Islam, Christianity), a range of historical periods (e.g., ancient near east, early modern Europe, new religious movements), and diverse regions (e.g., East Asian, Latin American, African). In some departments, students may also find faculty trained in anthropology, sociology, or ethics, as well as faculty with expertise in specific texts such as the Bible or Qur'an. The study of religion is an area of academic inquiry that necessarily draws from the work of scholars in adjacent fields, including archeologists, historians, linguists, and philosophers, as well as other scholars of the humanities and social sciences.

In this book, the religions that are most frequently referenced are Hinduism, Buddhism, Judaism, Christianity, and Islam. If a substantive body of literature about ethics in Sikhism and Jainism was readily available, those religions were also included as appropriate. Indigenous communities are discussed in the book in a chapter on the environment and as part of the history of the spread of Christianity. I am hopeful that in the decades to come there will be greater attention paid in religion departments to Indigenous traditions.

Why Study Religious Ethics?

I assume that the reader of this book, like most of my undergraduate college students, has not had any prior college-level coursework in religion or ethics. My hope is that the reader of *What is Religious Ethics?* leaves with a greater appreciation of the diversity and complexity of ethical perspectives grounded in religious traditions, whether of our own or of others.

Some readers who have grown up in a particular religious tradition may be familiar with that religion's beliefs and rituals; increasingly, people are not affiliated with any particular religious tradition or find themselves seeking spirituality rather than adhering to an already established organized religion. Regardless of our personal faith commitments, many of us are already familiar with popular texts like the Ten Commandments of the Bible, which are often understood as an ethical code. Some readers may have a passing familiarity with professional codes of ethics, such as the Hippocratic Oath taken by physicians.

Finally, we are almost all aware of social and informal codes of ethics. We have a sense, for example, of appropriate behavior for different contexts and what the right thing to do might be in certain situations. When we find a lost wallet on the street, we know that the right thing to do is to attempt to return the wallet to the owner, and that the wrong thing to do would be to steal the credit cards and cash. The way we dress, the volume and tone of our voices, and the thousands of ways in which we regulate our social interactions are all guided by social determinants of proper behavior. These everyday examples of ethics provide a foundation for understanding the more complex religious and ethical reasoning found in the chapters of this book. When we analyze why we believe certain actions, behaviors, and ideas to be appropriate and right, we begin to comprehend the factors and circumstances that shape ethics.

What kind of student or reader would benefit from studying religious ethics in greater depth? College students take classes in ethics and religion for a wide variety of reasons. Pre-med students who plan to go to medical school and become doctors want to learn about biomedical ethics; budding journalists and political science majors want to learn more about religions and war; historians realize that mastery of their discipline requires knowledge about religious traditions; philosophers study religious approaches to shared questions about meaning and truth; business students are interested in socially conscious entrepreneurship, and so on. Anyone who wants to understand value systems, human motivations, and belief communities would benefit from the study of religious ethics.

Models for Studying and Teaching Religious Ethics

Assuming the desire to learn more about religious ethics, what might be the best structure for learning about religious ethics? Truth be told, there are many, many ways to learn about religious ethics. Generally, however, I have found two dominant pedagogical models. One model attempts to cover the field religion-by-religion. The benefit to this method, assuming one covers many religions, and not just say, the Abrahamic traditions of Judaism, Christianity, and Islam, is its relative comprehensiveness. This method allows the teacher to review, however cursorily, the major tenets, beliefs, and practices of each religion. The major downside to this approach is that it assumes that ethical problems are weighted equally across religions. This is simply not the case. Take the case of abortion. This is an important concern for many Roman Catholics, but not as much for Hindus. When Hindus are concerned about abortion, they are concerned for different reasons. Or take the ethics of war. In the early twenty-first century, this topic has become uniquely urgent for those studying Muslim ethics, but less so for other religious traditions. Scholarship on the ethics of war as it relates to other religious traditions certainly exists, but there is an immediate exigency to the study of just war as it relates to Islam in our post-9/11 world.

The second dominant model is to study religious ethics issue-by-issue. This approach avoids the problem of assuming that every ethical issue is similarly weighty across traditions. One can draw into the discussion only those traditions that have much to say about the issue at hand, and point out which traditions do not find the issue of ethical significance. Studying religious ethics based on issues also lends itself to the use of case studies. Case studies are concrete, relatable, and provide footing for understanding more abstract theories. The problem with this approach, however, is that it works best when students already have a foundational understanding of multiple religious traditions. Having a discussion about *ahimsa* and the avoidance of eating animals has little meaning for students who have no background in Hinduism or Buddhism.

I have taught *Ethics and the World Religions* in different formats and have found through much trial and error that a mixture of the two pedagogical methods, which combines the religion-by-religion approach with issue-based case studies, to be the most effective way of reaching my undergraduate students. It is admittedly imperfect, but reasonably effective in orienting students to the study of religious ethics and enough to enable further research if so desired. Based also upon my classroom experiences, I frequently draw upon recent events and contemporary case studies because these tend to be more relatable than events and case studies from the distant past. That being said, many of the texts important to the field are old, even ancient. Despite their age, these texts provide insights still relevant today about the human condition. These commentaries on power, wealth, and sex, for example, are universal and timeless. The texts also touch upon issues that humans have long been concerned about, such as the environment, health, and governance.

Moral Expertise

Given that these are broadly shared concerns that many people have thought about for a very long time, the question arises as to why we might even want to turn to scholars trained in ethics to think through these issues. After all, many people have intuitive responses to moral questions and have an innate sense of what they think is right or wrong. Why should anyone want to turn to specialists in moral thinking when one has a conscience?

The moral philosopher Peter Singer has argued that there is, indeed, such a thing as moral expertise that comes about through proper intellectual training over a period of time. The "problem is not so much to know 'the difference between right and wrong' as to decide what is right and what wrong."[2] Coming to conclusions about moral issues requires the ability to conduct research, distill relevant information, apply multiple analytical frameworks, and reach a defensible conclusion. Each of these steps requires skill and, presumably, people who have been trained and practiced in these skills are more likely to reach a sounder conclusion than people who have no such training. Professors of ethics and others whose job it is to think about ethics also have invested significant amounts of time and energy in pursuit of this craft. Like many other skills, such as playing the piano or baking bread, moral reasoning arguably improves with years of dedicated practice.

Experts in ethical reasoning also are helpful resources when sorting through the vast options of social media. Holocaust deniers, members of the Flat Earth Society, and conspiracy theorists post their missives in various corners of the internet, where people can go down deep rabbit holes and find themselves unable to distinguish fact from fiction. The proliferation of false information, made possible by the internet, unfortunately lends itself to moral relativism. This has been especially egregious during the COVID global pandemic, when misinformation has proven deadly. I say with confidence that there are no highly regarded ethicists in the field of religious studies who would make arguments based on, for example, the claims of Holocaust deniers or theories that the COVID vaccines contain microchips. As I explain to students, while the idea of moral relativism, or the idea that there are no moral absolutes, is worth discussing, we would all agree that slavery, genocide, and racism are morally abhorrent. Experts who have spent a lifetime studying these subjects can help to evaluate the accuracy of data, reveal the weaknesses of arguments, and dismantle dangerous theories.

We live in a world populated by people who hold different ethical beliefs. Reasonable people can differ with regard to how closely they bind themselves to these beliefs, and people may change their views with age, experience, and circumstance. Polls suggest that religious commitment, even more so than religious identity, determines moral values. Extremely devout Muslims, for example, have more in common with extremely devout Roman Catholics than with non-practicing Muslims when polled about their views on issues such as abortion, gay marriage, and euthanasia. Likewise, liberal Jews have more in common with liberal Hindus than with orthodox Jews about these issues. And, of course, sometimes a person's views about politics or economics or race may not be informed by religion at all. The demographic growth of "spiritual, but not religious" people and "nones," or people who have no affiliation with an organized religion, is an important trend that will undoubtedly have an impact on the future of religious studies.

With regard to religious diversity, we are more and more likely in our globalized world to meet people who come from different religious cultures. Often to know these cultures is to appreciate them, and therefore to be more likely to engage in dialogue with their adherents about moral dilemmas. John Rawls, a giant in twentieth century philosophy, asserts that we should try to make decisions for the community as if we lived behind a veil of ignorance. That is, we should decide on public policy as if we had no knowledge of our own gender, age, wealth, religion, etc. Because under the veil of ignorance we are unaware of our own personal advantages or disadvantages, we will presumably make decisions with the public interest as our first and foremost priority. Rawls's thought experiment is important in showing how intellectually we ought to decide upon the public good, but is most useful when considered alongside the reality of the existence of our personal biases and our tendencies to make decisions in our self-interest. Assuming these biases and tendencies, we are faced with the options of either learning more about others in our community or remaining ignorant about them. Although some might choose the latter option, many of us believe—including, presumably, readers of this book—that educating ourselves about the world's diverse peoples, cultures, and traditions is the preferable option. With this information and a willingness to learn more, we can then make better informed choices about issues that affect us all.

Strands of Religious Ethics

Scholars of religious ethics are typically trained widely in the areas of religion and ethics as graduate students, but then specialize in sub-fields as they progress toward the completion of the doctoral degree. The topics that engage scholars of religious ethics are quite varied in subject area. Scholars may focus on influential figures and their works, delve deeply into specific issues, or research particular historical periods, among other topics.

This book will explore what I refer to as "strands," or the multiple sub-fields, of religious ethics. Each chapter focuses on upon a particular area within religious ethics and, collectively, the book covers a fairly wide swath of the discipline. This means, unfortunately, that specificity has been lost in order to accommodate breadth. I hope, however, that readers will be able to use this book as a springboard to further research that can provide the depth that this book necessarily lacks.

Strands of religious ethics are often interwoven because the problems we grapple with are complicated. The parsing of religious ethics into sub-topics is a practical way to research an issue more deeply, even if in reality, complex issues like climate change or racism rarely exist independently from issues such as economic inequality and gender. Various case studies in this book highlight how sub-fields within religious ethics never quite stand alone. They will help the reader to delve into ethical dilemmas, to see when religion matters and when religion might not matter so much, and to consider the applicability of a wide variety of religious and ethical resources. In order to comprehend and begin to solve these cases, we must view them as multi-faceted. The cases are based on actual events and are of broad enough interest so that every reader can participate in discussions of the cases. Readers might have an initial reaction to, experience with, or even fully developed opinions on these topics.

The majority of chapters of the book examine specific strands within religious ethics. The opening chapter surveys foundational ideas, narratives, and texts within the religions discussed in the book. The last chapter includes responses from colleagues in the field of religious ethics about why and how they do the work of creating knowledge. This chapter is meant to dispel any mystery behind how books and articles in religious ethics are written; religious ethics is a product of humans and their institutions.

The middle chapters of the book focus on recognized sub-fields within religious ethics. These constitute areas by which we categorize religious ethics research. As noted above, these categories have blurry edges, even though they are useful as an initial means of organizing complex issues.

Chapter 1 provides an overview of sources of moral authority and moral influence. Although most of the chapters of the book can be read in any order,

I would recommend that readers who are unfamiliar with different religious traditions begin with this chapter. The content of this chapter orients readers to important sources and references within various religious traditions that are essential to understanding the remainder of the book.

Chapter 2 on biomedical ethics surveys religious traditions with regard to their stances on issues ranging from abortion to stem cell research. Healers historically assumed that the divine bestowed upon them the knowledge, skills, and responsibility to care for the ill. Religious traditions have also often established rules regulating the body and its functions. Indeed, the notion that human life is worthy of special care and consideration has often been tied to belief in a God that created human beings. More recently, rapid advances in medical technologies have demanded responses from religious leaders to questions regarding the appropriate use of these tools. The case study for this chapter looks at the ethical challenges posed by CRISPR, a technology that enables changes to genes, including genes that can be passed onto future generations.

Chapter 3 tackles the problem of climate change and the environment. Because global warming by definition affects us all, regardless of our religious identities, nationality, race, ethnicity, age, and gender, this is a topic of concern for religious institutions and leaders around the world. Many religious traditions have resources regarding the purpose of creation, the proper use of plants and animals, and the place of humans in the universe. Additionally, religious traditions often have narratives involving the treatment of non-human animals and the environment. Although many of these resources developed prior to the current climate crisis, they nonetheless serve as foundations for developing ethical stances toward the planet and living creatures. The case study for this chapter looks at the question of whether, given the climate crisis, religious believers ought to adopt vegetarian diets. Studies have shown that reducing meat consumption would benefit the environment; however, religious traditions have varied views with regard to consumption of meat, ranging from its complete eschewal to its centrality in important ritual feasts.

Chapter 4 examines the issue of poverty and wealth disparity. A number of religions have seemingly contradictory views on poverty and wealth. On the one hand, we find in traditions such as Buddhism and Christianity the elevation of asceticism and lifestyles that eschew even basic creature comforts; on the other hand, we observe gilded shrines and architectural masterpieces constructed for those very same religious traditions. Such differences may be attributable to distinctions drawn between monastic traditions and lay followers, but there is in actuality little consistency with regard to the religious classes and their levels of wealth. Economic conditions have changed dramatically in the centuries since the founding of these religions, and along with these changes have come shifts in the way in which we understand the place of wealth in societies. In the twentieth century, the idea—even if not the practice—of a basic level of economic security took hold alongside the acceptance of human rights. More recently, the problem of the wealth gap has worsened. The richest members of our society hold a tremendous amount of the world's wealth, while the vast majority of the population shares a disproportionately small amount. This imbalance is evident both within nations such as the United States, as well as among nations, with a few nations holding the bulk of global economic resources. This chapter's case study takes the specific example of measures to increase economic opportunity among the lowest castes in contemporary India. Although India has outlawed discrimination based upon caste, the high poverty levels among low caste Indians point to the intractability of prejudices, historically supported by religious traditions, even in modern democracies.

Chapter 5 focuses upon the ethics of war and violence in religious traditions. As with the issue of wealth and poverty, religions hold seemingly irreconcilable views toward war and violence. Although multiple religious traditions evince strong presuppositions against violence and the taking of life, religious leaders have sanctioned wars, authorized torture, and tolerated abuse within their own institutions. Christian communities were complicit in the colonization of territories that brought about the deaths of millions of Indigenous peoples. To this day, we find groups, such as ISIS, that justify violence and terror using religious reasoning. At the same time, many religious organizations advocate peace-making and reconciliation; some religious communities have long histories of radical non-violence. The case study in Chapter 5 explores Jewish debates over the possession of nuclear weapons by Israel. The obligation of Israel to protect Jewish life following the Holocaust makes for a strong case in favor of the possession of nuclear warheads as a means of deterrence. Although Judaism does not forbid war outright, the tradition also makes clear that wanton destruction, particularly on a scale as large as one that would be caused by nuclear weapons, is immoral.

Chapter 6 introduces ethical issues in religious traditions concerning sex, gender, and feminism. Religions have justified the exclusion of women from positions of authority based upon biological, cultural, and theological reasoning. Heterosexuality was normative, and homosexual acts were widely considered immoral. Today we find a wide variety of views toward sex and gender equality. A number of religious sects now include women in positions of leadership, perform same-sex marriage and commitment ceremonies, and welcome transgendered and non-binary persons into their communities. This chapter examines several of these shifts in thinking about sex, gender, and feminism, while noting that many religious communities continue to maintain traditional views about gender roles based upon biological sex. The case study in Chapter 6 uses the example of Amina Wadud, a leading Muslim scholar of Islam, to think about the role of women's leadership in religion. Wadud led a highly controversial public, mixed-gender Friday prayer in New York City. While some lauded her leadership, others found her act to be immoral and in violation of Islamic values.

Chapter 7 differs a bit from the previous chapters in that it focuses on one particular religion, Christianity, and its role in the creation and perpetuation of racist social and economic structures in the United States. As the murder of George Floyd and the consequent intensification of the Black Lives Matter movement occurred during the writing of the book, I felt a particular moral obligation to include a chapter on racism in the United States. Moreover, aside from the COVID pandemic, the topic of racism has been the leading issue in the lives of the youngest generations of Americans. Part of the reckoning of Americans with the evils of our past includes recognizing the efforts of some churches to create a society in which Whites are privileged and Black Americans deprived of fundamental rights. These acts reflect a combination of cultural, theological, and economic self-interest. The case study examines the response of Georgetown University, a Jesuit institution, to its own past involvement in the slave trade and its current efforts to compensate for the benefits the university derived from the sale of human beings.

Chapter 8 functions as an epilogue of sorts in that it shares the stories of the people who make possible the research and ideas found in the previous chapters. Although religious ethics has traditionally lacked gender, racial, and ethnic diversity, there has been a gradual effort to make the discipline more inclusive. This diversification brings into the discussion scholars who can contribute significant perspectives that have for too long been overlooked. A plurality of religions, races and ethnicities, genders, geographies, and economic and social class backgrounds bring both richness and greater accuracy to the work that we do. The closing chapter aims to show readers this burgeoning and welcome diversity of voices in religious ethics. Each of the scholars profiled has succeeded in academia with publications, positions at institutions of higher learning, and well-regarded reputations among peers. My hope is that readers may recognize themselves in the profiles of these scholars. I am deeply indebted to my colleagues for their generosity in sharing a part of themselves to make religious ethics a little more approachable for readers and students.

As noted previously, the separation of ethics into strands is important for the work of categorizing and analyzing vast amounts of information. Ethical issues in real life, however, do not fall into neat containers. Although each of these chapters concerns a discrete aspect of religious ethics, the chapters can also be read "across" each other such that insights gleaned from one chapter apply to analyses of topics found in other chapters. Readers of this book might, for example, think about the intersection of poverty and the climate crisis; or gender and biomedical ethics; or violence and racism. Indeed, recognizing the complexity of ethical dilemmas gives rise to important questions and research needed to ameliorate and circumvent the problems that plague humanity.

Notes

1 Lofton, "Religious History," 384.
2 Singer, "Moral Experts," 117.

Bibliography

Lofton, Kathryn. "Religious History as Religious Studies." *Religion: The Study of American Religions: Critical Reflections on a Specialization* 42:3 (July 1, 2012), 383–94.
Rawls, John. *A Theory of Justice.* Cambridge: Belknap Press of Harvard University Press, 1971.
Singer, Peter. "Moral Experts." *Analysis* (Oxford) 32:4 (1972), 115–17.

Chapter 1

Moral Authority and Moral Influence

What are our sources of moral authority and moral influence? In other words, who or what determines how we evaluate goodness or the lack thereof? When I teach courses in ethics, in particular, my Ethics and the World Religions course, undergraduate students will often name sources such as the Bible, the Qur'an, parents, churches, synagogues, priests, rabbis, imams, coaches, teachers, friends, and, increasingly, social media. All of these sources teach us, directly and indirectly, which persons and actions are worthy of moral praise and which are worthy of moral condemnation. Less obvious, however, are answers to the questions of how we come to those judgments and why reasonable people can sometimes have strong moral disagreements. Indeed, we will find that even within religious traditions, believers will disagree among each other as to the most important sources of moral authority, how these sources ought to be evaluated relative to each other, and the best way to interpret and apply these sources to a given situation.

When religious believers claim that their source of moral authority is God, they typically do not mean that they hear God talking to them, telling them what to do, and demanding how they should think. For most religious believers, God's moral authority is explained through the guidance of religious leaders, whether it be the Pope or the head of their local religious community. Religious moral authority is also found in religious texts, like the Bible or the Qur'an. Some religious believers hold that human rationality, or our ability to reason and use our intellect, is an important source of moral authority that God endowed to human beings at creation. When evaluating issues and making arguments in the field of religious ethics, we take into account a diversity of sources of moral authority.

If we define authority as a legitimate or authorized source of power, then we can see that religions draw upon multiple sources of moral authority. Authority is conferred by people, tradition, or sometimes self-proclaimed. Furthermore, we ought to be cognizant of the context of moral authority. Why are certain people or texts considered to be authorities in particular religious traditions? How is that authority claimed, and how is that authority given? How does authority change over time and place?

DOI: 10.4324/9781003350637-2

The most immediate source of moral authority for many religious believers is the leadership of their religious community. Oftentimes, religious leaders have had special training or education or display special talents that followers accept as proof of authority. Sometimes, a charismatic leader becomes authoritative by virtue of an unusual ability to draw followers. Priests, rabbis, imams, the Pope, nuns, ministers, monks, shamans, and other leaders serve as interpreters of sacred knowledge for the larger lay community. These experts of the sacred translate texts, symbols, natural phenomenon, or any other type of data to relate information about the sacred. They may also be responsible for performing sacred rituals. Because of these responsibilities, religious leaders may have access to specially designated sacred spaces where they might perform rituals or carry out their work.

There are typically restrictions placed upon who can hold positions of authority in many traditions due to sex, age, and family lineage. For much of history, women have been—and still sometimes are—prevented from holding high-ranking positions in religious communities. Also, in many traditional communities, elders have more seniority than younger members. And in some communities, the family into which one is born can determine whether or not one may enter the ranks of religious leadership. Religious leaders, however, are not the only source of moral authority.

Texts that are foundational to particular traditions often have the backing of generations of religious believers. These texts may have a special origin story or be authored by founding members of the religion. These texts, referred to as sacred scripture, may hold a special status relative to other texts associated with the religion. While sacred scripture is often quite old, other sources may be more contemporary and still carry the weight of authority. Papal encyclicals, or essays penned by the Pope of the Roman Catholic Church, are influential and often address pressing ethical issues of the day. Here, we have an example of a text written within a particular tradition authored by a person of authority. These texts may acquire stature over time and become part of an official or unofficial canon, or collection of texts that are considered authoritative of a particular tradition.

Scholars of religion have looked to religious texts as sources of moral authority. When we look at the Hindu Vedas, the Torah, the New Testament of the Christian Bible, or the Qur'an, we are looking at texts that have been transmitted through time and have held special meaning to particular groups of people. One reason why texts have held such an esteemed position in religious scholarship is because texts can be assigned to particular groups of people as representing their religion. Books and texts—although they are occasionally edited or redacted—tend also to be relatively static, making them ideal objects of research.

The reliance upon textual authority, however important, has its flaws. Defining a religion primarily by association with sacred scripture makes the assumption that a religion must center around literature in order for it to be taken seriously as an object of scholarly study. Indeed, the very idea of "religion" as a distinct aspect of culture cannot be understood without acknowledging the European colonial enterprise that construed analogous belief systems in foreign countries for the purposes of comparison—and conversion—to Christianity. In other words, the comparative study of religion, for however valid and nuanced this academic field may have become, remains the creation of Christian imperialists.

Although many Indigenous cultures transmit knowledge through oral storytelling, rather than through written language, the privileging of the written word in the academy has meant that oral religious traditions have been neglected by scholars. Many of us would be fortunate to have had a single class, or even part of a class, during our graduate education dedicated to Indigenous religious traditions. This omission is unfortunate because the religious experiences of large swaths of the human population are overlooked.

In many communities, only a few select scribes and religious leaders may have been literate enough to be able to interpret sacred texts. For much of religious history, the majority of believers were not literate, or not trained in the literature of sacred scripture. This does not mean, however, that their religious experiences should be considered somehow less significant. The religious lives of women, for example, many of whom were denied opportunities to learn how to read and write, would also be discounted if we focused only on written religious texts as sources of moral authority.

In thinking critically about the nature of religious authority, we ought also to take into account the ways in which historical events, revolutionary movements, or scientific breakthroughs lead religious believers to reconsider the meaning or relevance of sacred texts, ideas, or traditions. These events and developments are not authoritative, but certainly have been influential in the development of religious ethics. As mentioned above, the impact of colonialism around the world left an indelible mark on Indigenous cultures, assuming, of course, that they even survived the diseases transmitted by Europeans that eliminated countless native populations. The trans-Atlantic slave trade and the enduring legacy of racism have thoroughly changed the way in which scholars understand, for example, American Christianity. White Americans used Christian scripture to defend the subjugation of Africans and Black Americans for centuries. During the Civil Rights era, the lack of support among predominantly White churches for racial equality reflected an ambivalence towards the struggles of Black Americans. In the present day, membership in evangelical Christian churches correlates strongly with the denial of structural racism. Likewise, the scientific theory of evolution has had a dramatic impact upon the ways in which many people understand the Biblical creation narratives found in Genesis. The theory of evolution, in other words, changed the way in which we interpret an authoritative source. Perhaps one of the most influential shifts in Christian ethics in the last century has been the emergence of liberation theology, a Roman Catholic justice movement that arose in the twentieth century in Latin America as a response to crushing poverty and corrupt political regimes. Acting on behalf of the poor and the oppressed, liberation theologians utilized Christian texts and teachings to support the disenfranchised in their struggles.

Because authority must often be interpreted by believers, the process of interpretation, sometimes referred to as hermeneutics (after the Greek god of messages, Hermes), becomes critical to our understanding and implementation of ethics. In other words, what we do with the pronouncements of authoritative leaders and texts depends upon how we interpret that content. Major shifts in ethics that lead us to interpret—or re-interpret—authoritative language may be linked to revolutions like the abolition movement to end slavery, the fight for women's suffrage and gender equality, the civil rights movement, the signing of the Universal Declaration of Human Rights, and, most recently, environmental protests.

These examples show us that while we ought to take very seriously religious authority, we must also consider the ways in which authority has been and might be challenged over time and in different contexts. We need to ask: who claims authority; how is authority claimed and wielded; and how is authority checked? Religious authority, in other words, is not static. It changes throughout history and differs from context to context.

Although there are multiple sources of authority found in every religious tradition, there are some texts and leaders that have become standard sources of reference. Also, certain major historical events—whether within a tradition or global in reach—have been critical in the development of the tradition's ethics. Knowing who and what these are proves extremely helpful when learning about religious ethics. Because they are referenced with regularity by religious leaders and believers, as well as scholars of religion, these resources provide valuable insight into ethical beliefs and practices.

In the sections that follow, I provide very brief overviews of what I have found, when teaching courses in ethics and world religions, to be several of most influential ideas, people, and texts in religions such as Hinduism, Buddhism, Judaism, Christianity, and Islam. Given the necessity of brevity, these sections are not nearly exhaustive, but rather will give readers a basic idea of religious resources from which believers of different traditions might draw when thinking through these complex problems. Mention of a few major historical events that weigh heavily on ethical deliberations, especially contemporary ones, is also made. At the very least, this section will provide readers guidance in the happy case that they want to learn more.

Hinduism

There is no central authority figure or set of beliefs that unites all Hindus. The religion finds its origins not in any specific scripture or individual, but rather in the geographic region demarcated by the Indus River. The practices of classical Hinduism are intensely varied depending upon the region of India (or diaspora community), as well as age, gender, and socio-economic status of the individual believer.

The texts that form the foundation of Hindu ethics were historically the domain of the elite, priestly class. Hindus today consider these to be historically significant, but they are not always considered to be normative for the twenty-first century. Classical ideals regarding sex, gender, and caste have been examined critically and generally replaced with more egalitarian concepts of citizenship and opportunity, although sexism and caste-discrimination still exist. Notions about duty (*dharma*), the moral consequences of actions (*karma*), and belief in reincarnation (*samsara*) remain relevant, as well.

In terms of religious ideas, there are both monotheistic and polytheistic elements found in Hinduism. On the one hand, practitioners hold that there is a single supreme entity, typically understood to be Brahman. Brahman reigns as the supreme deity, the ultimate reality, or God of all things. On the other hand, there are a multitude of lesser deities to whom Hindus might direct their worship. Gods such as Brahma (the creator, not to be confused with Brahman), Shiva (the destroyer), and Vishnu (the preserver), as well as Ganesh (the elephantine remover of obstacles) and Saraswati (the consort of Brahma and the goddess of wisdom and the arts), are frequently the object of veneration by Hindus. While there is debate over whether Hinduism is a monotheistic or polytheistic, it is clear that in both belief and practice these traditional categories for characterizing religion do not neatly apply to Hinduism.

There is no central text, akin to the Bible for Christians or the Qur'an for Muslims, that plays a similar role among Hindus. The Vedas (c. 1200 BCE), a collection of sacred hymns written in Sanskrit that are attributed to ancient sages and considered divine revelation, serve as the primary source of Hindu ritual and philosophical wisdom. Most Hindus, however, do not read the Vedas, much less keep copies in their homes. Understanding and interpreting the Vedas fell under the domain of the scholarly elite, the brahmins (sometimes spelled "brahmans"), who stood at the top of the caste pyramid and exclusively controlled ritual traditions. The Vedas date back to the second millennium BCE and consist of a large variety of materials, ranging from the hymns of the *Rig Veda* to the philosophical tracts found in the *Upanishads*. Although the Vedas represent the concerns of the elite male priests, the impact of the Vedas can be felt among Hindus of all segments of society, both men and women. From the prescriptive societal stratification that became the caste system to the recommended stages of life for men of the upper classes, the Vedas played a role in shaping many Hindus' views of the good life.

The Vedas refer not infrequently to the concept of *dharma*, translated roughly as righteousness, law, or duty. *Dharma*, however, is not merely law or even jurisprudence; rather, *dharma* refers to the orderliness of a cosmic law that incorporates moral and social propriety. The *dharmasutras* and the *dharmashastras* are texts that describe the duties of Hindus according to one's station—dependent upon sex, caste, and life stage—and the rules that govern social conduct. The most prominent of the dharma literature, the *Manusmriti*, asserts that in addition to the Vedas, highly regarded customs and traditions, as well as a person's conscience, all serve as guides to righteous conduct. Thus, while there are no strict rules that determine Hindus' proper conduct, there is a sense that Hindus ought to keep in mind the multiple factors that determine appropriate behavior and relationships according to the situation at hand.

Both class and life-stage, as well as gender, determine much of what would be considered appropriate behavior according to *dharma*. In the highest classes—the castes consisting of priests, rulers, warriors, and merchants—Hindus lived according to what was considered normative according to one's age. A boy of the upper castes was expected to be a conscientious student; as an adult, to be married and to support his household economically; and, as an elder, to retreat from the pursuits of the householder and to live the life of the contemplative ascetic. A girl, on the other hand, was expected to be under the control of her parents, and then, upon marriage, under the control of her husband. The members of the lowest castes, the peasants and the *shudras*, or those who worked in spiritually polluting jobs and handled corpses, waste matter, or slaughtered sacred cows, were not expected to receive an education, or to become philosophers in the later days of their lives.

While most Hindus do not consult the Vedas or the *dharma* literature given that they are considered to fall under the domain of elite scholars, they do admire the heroic figures found in the ancient epics, the *Ramayana* and the *Bhagavad Gita*. The *Ramayana*'s hero, Rama, and his wife, Sita, are considered by many Hindus to be moral exemplars, exhibiting qualities worthy of emulation. In the epic, the unjustly exiled prince Rama saves his wife Sita from the evil Ravana. Rama is loved for his courage, wisdom, and bravery; Sita is regarded as the epitome of virtue and female purity. Similarly admired is the hero of the *Bhagavad Gita*, Arjuna, who exemplifies moral fortitude. In a famous dialogue with Krishna, Arjuna realizes that he must above all uphold *dharma*, even if it means that he must fight against his own family. Although these epics do not offer specific advice to Hindus with regard to how they ought to live righteously, they offer the moral lesson that one must carefully maintain *dharma* despite the various challenges that emerge throughout one's life.

In Hinduism, context determines the extent of a person's authority. One's teacher and mentor, a *guru* is considered an important influence in the life of a student. Because a *guru* is responsible for both the intellectual and moral development of a pupil, the expectation is that a *guru* will be a model of good behavior. Similarly, a ruler, or *raja*, who holds authority over many subjects is expected to demonstrate his capacity for both justice and bravery. Viewed as a paternal figure, the ruler is expected to protect his subjects from external threats and to maintain an orderly society. On the flip side of authority is deference or obedience. Because hierarchies exist in traditional Hindu families and societies and because Hindus generally accept these hierarchies as normative, the duty to behave according to one's rank is assumed.

When those in power abuse their high rank, there is a sense of cosmic retribution. In the case of a weak ruler, one expects popular protests, internal uprisings, or the usurping of power. One's *dharma* is linked to *karma*, or the notion that any moral act has consequences. An ethical life and good conduct may improve one's status in the next life. Ultimately, one may obtain release from earthly life (*moksha*) after numerous cycles of reincarnation.

While he did not explicitly identify himself as Hindu, Mahatma Gandhi (d. 1948) invariably emerges in discussions of ethics and India. The leader of the non-violent movement to gain Indian independence from the British Empire, Gandhi employed a philosophical approach to the interplay of power, truth, and non-violence. Using the Sanskrit term *satyagraha* to describe the forcefulness of truth, Gandhi successfully mobilized millions of Hindus to employ non-violent methods such as marches, boycotts, and media exposure to force the hand of the British government. His example inspired and continues to inspire other colonized and oppressed peoples to attempt to gain their freedom from imperialists using non-violent tactics. In the post-Gandhi era, the rigidity of caste and gender roles has softened, but class hierarchy and gender inequity continue to exist.

Buddhism

Like Hinduism, Buddhism has no centralized authority that governs over all Buddhists. Even the Dalai Lama does not assume a position of authority that holds sway over a majority of Buddhists. Rather, Buddhists determine for themselves the appropriate *dharma* teachers for their religious paths. In many Buddhist communities, these teachers are monks or nuns, who are considered religious exemplars and knowledgeable in the tradition's teachings.

Founded in Northeast India in the fifth century BCE, Buddhism developed out of the experiences of a prince who renounced his comfortable life and family to seek a solution to the problem of suffering. After years as a religious mendicant, Siddhartha obtained enlightenment, or *nirvana*, by following a path, not of extremes, but of moderation and meditation. Siddhartha became known as the Buddha, or the "enlightened one," and became an itinerant teacher. His loyal followers spread word of his teachings and, upon his death, continued to establish schools throughout Asia. Because the Buddha did not leave a successor or clear directions for how his teachings should be disseminated after his death, variations of his teachings developed over the following centuries. The most complete record of the Buddha's teachings to survive is the canon of the Theravada school of Buddhism, found primarily in Thailand and parts of Southeast Asia. The canon, known as the Pali Canon for the language in which it was recorded from the oral tradition, consists of three parts: (1) discourses or conversations of the Buddha; (2) rules for monasteries; and (3) scholarly treatises.

Because Buddhism grew out of the same region in which Hinduism developed, it should come as no surprise that several of the prominent concepts that ground Hinduism also find a home in Buddhist teachings. *Dharma* in Buddhism refers to a kind of cosmic ordering that encompasses not just physical laws, but also moral laws. In this sense, *dharma* might be understood as a kind of natural law that ascribes principles that govern both the physical world and the moral one. The Buddhist notion of *dharma* also includes Buddhist teachings insofar as they provide an explication of the natural ordering of things and instructions on how to live in harmony with this natural ordering. *Karma*, as in Hinduism, refers to the theory that all moral actions have repercussions that affect the ability of the actor to attain release from cycles of rebirth. The Buddha viewed life as suffering, so release from reincarnation would release one from perpetual suffering. Attaining *nirvana* requires that a person live her life in such a morally perfect way that no negative *karma* accumulates to prevent her from escaping reincarnation. In order to live a morally perfect life, one must first have mastered the teachings on *dharma*. In this sense the notion of rebirth in Buddhism is closely tied to both *dharma* and *karma*.

The Pali Canon functions as a source of moral authority because it relays the teachings of the Buddha. In the Discourses, the first basket of materials that make up the canon, the Buddha provides a version of the so-called "golden rule"—"you should not inflict on another what you yourself find unpleasant"—and analyzes the harms that accrue from thoughtless actions, the necessity of kindness, and the importance of mindfulness.[1] The *Kalama Sutta*, one part of the collected teachings of the Buddha, emphasizes the necessity of using reason and experience to determine the morality of a situation. The *Sigalovada Sutta*, described as a code of discipline for householders, describes the obligations of the (male) head of the household towards different members of his family and larger community. As such, it stipulates the proper relationships between the householder and his wife, children, and parents; his servants and employees; and religious figures. The *Dhammapada*, a collection of the Buddha's teachings, summarizes the whole of the teachings of the Buddha in this way: "To avoid all evil, to cultivate good, and to purify one's mind—this is the teaching of the Buddhas."[2]

Many consider the Buddha's formulation of the Four Noble Truths and the Middle Way to be the foundational teachings of the tradition. The Four Noble Truths are insights into the causes of human suffering and the means of ending suffering. The Four Noble Truths are as follows:

1 Life is suffering
2 The cause of suffering is desire
3 Nirvana ends suffering
4 The Noble Eight-fold Path shows the way to nirvana

The Noble Eight-fold Path provides guidance on how to attain *nirvana*. It does not call for austerity, which the Buddha rejected after his experience as a wandering ascetic, but rather a moral life that considers balance in one's thinking and actions. The Noble Eight-fold Path is divided into three sections. The teachings on right view and right attitude concern the cultivation of wisdom. Moral conduct focuses on speech, action, occupation, and effort. Tranquility of mind and soul rely upon right mindfulness and meditation. The components of the Noble Eight-fold Path, with brief descriptions of each component, are:

Wisdom

1   Right View: Accepting the teachings of the Buddha
2   Right Attitude: Committing oneself to the teachings of the Buddha

Moral Conduct

3   Right Speech: Speaking truthfully with compassion
4   Right Action: Refraining from immoral behavior (killing, stealing, lying, avoiding alcohol and drugs, etc.)
5   Right Livelihood: Rejecting employment or work that will harm others
6   Right Effort: Asserting control over one's will to commit to the teachings of the Buddha

Tranquility

7   Right Mindfulness: Developing a full and rich awareness of one's thoughts and actions
8   Right Meditation: Focusing the mind through the practice of special techniques

The Noble Eight-fold Path is not to be understood as a linear road heading towards *nirvana*. Rather the components of the path are best viewed as interlocking aspects of life, where each component exists in relationship to the others. Indeed, to complete the Noble Eightfold Path, one must also understand the role of virtue in moral development. The Noble Eight-fold Path functions not merely as a checklist whose completion leads to the award of *nirvana*. One must cultivate the ability to comprehend properly a situation and also to develop a practice of habituating the correct response to any situation with wisdom and compassion.

The role of deities in the practice of Buddhism may be to help believers in their own path to enlightenment. Unlike in Hinduism, there is no concept of Brahman, but Buddhists in communities around the world worship deities and *bodhisattvas*, or beings who are on the path towards enlightenment. These deities and *bodhisattvas* play a role in the moral lives of Buddhists in that they can help humans in their efforts to understand the Four Noble Truths and live according to the Noble Eight-fold Path.

Traditional Buddhist communities emphasize respect for elders and for those who have obtained high levels of knowledge. In this sense, older members of the community, as well as the monks and nuns of the *sangha* (the religious community, sometimes specifically referring to monasteries and nunneries) are considered persons of moral authority.

The Buddhist monk most well known throughout the world is the Dalai Lama. Although he technically holds authority over Tibetan monks, and not monks in other parts of the world, his widespread influence essentially makes him a representative of Buddhism writ large. The plight of Tibet for freedom from oppressive Chinese rule invariably plays a role in discussions of Buddhist ethics and politics.

Jainism

Jainism arose in the same region and historical period as Buddhism and now claims approximately eight million followers. Jainism developed as an alternative to the brahminic rituals of sacrifice, caste system, and elaborate liturgy. At the same time, Jainism preserves certain Hindu concepts such as *dharma*, *karma*, reincarnation, and perhaps most significantly, *ahimsa*. The tradition traces its lineage to 24 sages, referred to as Tirthankaras ("creator of fords"), or those who found a path to overcoming *samsara* (indefinite cycles of rebirth) and attaining *moksha* (release from cycles of reincarnation). The most well-known and recent of these sages is Mahavira (d. 527 BCE), who led an ascetic life committed to the ideal of *ahimsa paramo dharma* (non-killing as the supreme way). These moral exemplars serve as authorities in the tradition.

The sacred texts of Jains, the *Agamas*, existed for much of the religion's history as a purely oral tradition and were generally reserved for monks and nuns, rather than lay people. The *Agamas*, which are believed to be the teachings of Mahavira as handed down through successive generations of his disciples, consist of treatises and discussions on a range of topics including cosmology, philosophy, and astrology. Over time, the provenance of the *Agamas* came under dispute by different sects of Jainism. Other writings that are important to the tradition include writings by mendicant scholars, *acharyas*. The *Tattvartha Sutra*, attributed to the scholar Umasvati sometime between the second and fifth centuries CE, stands out as a comprehensive overview of the tradition and is considered authoritative by both major sects of Jainism, the Svetambara and Digambara. Most recently, the major sects of Jainism collaborated to produce the *Saman Suttam* (1974), a text meant to describe the shared and foundational teachings of the tradition.

Although sacred literature plays an important role in Jainism, the emphasis in the tradition lies in its comprehensive commitment to a non-violent lifestyle. Distinctive to Jainism is the ethical practice of non-violence that stems from an acute awareness of suffering. Rather than attempt to eliminate violence throughout the world, Jains find that the cessation of one's own movement, mind, and speech is the primary way to avoid harm to others. In order to eliminate suffering, one must commit to reducing suffering by having both the correct mindset and by living the correct lifestyle. *Karma* for Jains exists as an unavoidable reality. In order to free oneself from negative *karma*, one must live as pure a life as possible. For most Jains, accumulating negative *karma* is inescapable. Simply by engaging with the world and partaking in activities such as working, preparing food, or having children, a person gathers negative *karma*. There are, however, ways of living even as a householder that minimize negative *karma*. For the ascetic, who aims to eliminate all traces of negative *karma*, Jain ethical practice is quite difficult and requires extreme commitment.

The spiritual goal of many observant Jains who have not taken monastic vows is not extreme asceticism, but rather non-interference. For the lay practitioner, negative *karma* can be minimized by engaging in practices such as maintaining a vegetarian diet, fasting, reducing the consumption of material goods, reducing travel, and otherwise limiting one's engagement with the world to only that which is necessary for the survival of oneself and one's family. Lay persons may also support monks and nuns through the ritual of giving, *dana*, so that they may undertake the fasting, meditation, and religious study required to attain *moksha*. The ritual of giving embodies the principle of *ahimsa*. When laypeople offer food to monks or nuns, they prepare the food carefully, even straining the water used in preparation for the food, to ensure that the smallest insect will not be unintentionally consumed by the ascetic. Living one's life in this manner reduces the amount of negative *karma* that will be carried into the next life.

Jains hold that in order to avoid reincarnation and to be released from this life, one must take monastic vows. The *mahavratas* are the five vows to which a Jain commits upon becoming an ascetic: *ahimsa* (no harm), *satya* (truth), *asteya* (no stealing), *brahmacharya* (no sexual activity), and *aparigraha* (no attachment). These are radical vows that ask the renouncer to avoid harm to water, fire, and earth, in addition to plants and animals, whether they be microscopic animals or human beings. Because of this vow, ascetics are not to make their own food, which would inevitably harm living beings, such as microscopic insects, during their preparation. Householders, as mentioned above, offer them food that, while carefully prepared, should not be considered a burden on the donors. Renouncers are expected to be restrained not only in their consumption of food, but also in their speech, movement, bodily functions, and even in their dreams. They are perhaps most often recognized for the broom that they continuously sweep ahead of them as they walk, in order to avoid unintentionally stepping on and thereby harming an insect in the way.

In some Jain communities, particularly in the northern parts of India, women are considered spiritual equals to men and are able to undertake the monastic lifestyle, free from the responsibilities and distractions of domestic and family life. Scholarly nuns wrote philosophical treatises and maintained relative autonomy in female-governed nunneries. Generally, however, women hold a lower status than men, even though they may be praised for their asceticism and chastity. Moral authority is in practice held primarily by men in the tradition, and even high-ranking nuns are subordinate to novice monks.

Judaism

A religious tradition that dates back 4,000 years, Judaism stands out for the centrality of scripture in its teaching. Hilary Putnam has argued that the "very special value attached to *study*, indeed, the identification of study and discussion of sacred texts (when conducted in the right spirit and in the right way) with the truest human flourishing, is *the* distinctive feature of 'Jewish ethics'."[3] Although interpretation of Jewish scripture varies considerably among the multiple sects of Judaism, the Torah—the first five books of the Bible—remains central to Judaism.

The written Torah is considered by many Jews to be sacred scripture. The Tanakh, a type of acronym for the three segments of the "Old Testament" part of the Bible, includes in addition to the first give books of the Bible (*Torah*), the books of the prophets (*Neviim*), and historical and wisdom literature (*Ketuvim*). Beginning with accounts of the creation of the universe, the Tanakh describes the rich early history of the people of Israel. These books cover, in addition to the Genesis, the stories of Noah, his ark, and the great flood; Moses and his leading of the people of Israel out of slavery in Egypt; God's giving of the Torah to Moses on Mount Sinai; and dozens of stories of fabled kings such as David and his son Solomon. The Tanakh also includes genealogies, the Ten Commandments, laws, psalms, and proclamations of prophets.

In addition to the Tanakh, Jewish tradition contains a number of important rabbinical texts that capture the cultural, interpretive, and legal nature of the religion. Accompanying the written Torah is the oral Torah, which describes Jewish tradition as it relates to everyday life. The oral Torah was eventually codified and written down as the *Mishnah*, and covers topics such as farming, festivals, women, crimes, temple rituals, and purity laws. The *Gemara* provides commentary on the *Mishnah* and the written Torah. Combined, the *Mishnah* and the *Gemara* form the *Talmud*.

Because so much of Jewish history has been marked by exile, the existence of written scripture helped to unify the Jewish peoples across time and space. Jews could take solace in the familiarity of scripture regardless of where they were forced to live. Thus, the emphasis upon literacy was not merely a means of connecting to the divine, but also a practical concern. The culture of discussion and debate was both a way to connect to the religion, as well as a way to ensure the relevance of the sacred scripture over time. Each successive generation interprets the sacred texts anew.

Across these texts, certain ethical themes emerge. Judaism is often thought of as a legalistic tradition, and classical Jewish religious law (*halakha*) plays a significant role in the development of Jewish ethics. It would be a mistake, however, to fail to see the importance of certain motifs that cut through the legalistic details of the tradition. Key motifs include the idea of universalism, established in Genesis, which describes God as creating not just the people of Israel, but all of humanity and the world we inhabit. This has serious moral implications because it serves as reminder that all humans are created by God and thus connected to each other through a shared divine imprint.

Another motif is the steadfast belief in God's righteousness. This is the flip side to the unwavering commitment demanded by the covenant between the people of Israel and God. Following God's commands assumes complete trust in the power, goodness, and compassion of God. If we consider, for example, the story of Abraham's attempted sacrifice of his son, Isaac, the scene is—objectively speaking—quite horrifying. A father taking his son to slaughter because God told him so would, in today's world, result in a frantic call to the police. But in the context of sacred scripture, the story's surprising ending reveals in dramatic fashion God's ultimately merciful nature.

Social justice is another recurring theme in the Tanakh. God's reminder to the Hebrews that God "brought you out of the land of Egypt, out of the house of bondage" (Exodus 20:2) might be interpreted to mean that relieving the suffering of others is a duty incumbent upon Jews. Just as God released them from the horrors of captivity, Jews have a responsibility to fight on behalf of those who have been treated unjustly. Much of Jewish law concerns the protection of and provision for the poor, and many of the admonishments of the prophets describe the failure of Israelites to care for the weakest members of society.

Although Jewish scriptural traditions assume the highest position of moral authority in the religion, rabbis play an important role in the day-to-day lives of observant Jews. As teachers and leaders of religious rituals, rabbis shoulder the responsibility for leading the members of their synagogues or temples. Rabbis, however, still serve at the request of the lay leaders of the religious community. Moral authority in the hands of rabbis, thus, is not of an absolute nature, but is contingent upon the will of the larger group. The exception to this would be in Hasidic sects where the *rebbe* is often an inherited position and believed to be endowed with special divine insights. This means that the *rebbe* holds considerable power over members of the Hasidic community and is expected even to determine marriage partners, career paths, and other important life-decisions.

When discussing Jewish ethics in the contemporary era, one cannot underestimate the profound significance of the Holocaust. The deliberate and systematic annihilation of over six million Jews by Nazi Germany during the Second World War not only decimated the Jewish population, but shattered any illusions about the progress of humankind. Germany in the twentieth century had appeared to stand at the pinnacle of western civilization, and yet carried out one of the most horrific genocides in recorded human history. Moreover, many Allied nations, including the United States, refused to take in Jewish refugees fleeing from the Holocaust. Jews—and Christians—in the aftermath of World War II were left to question assumptions about the goodness of humanity and of a God that would allow such suffering to occur.

The creation of the state of Israel in 1948, which was intended in part to provide a homeland for Jews following the Holocaust, remains a major topic in Jewish ethics. Because of incessant violence and political turmoil, regional threats to Israel, as well as concern over the plight of Palestinians, discussions of Jewish ethics with regard to politics and just war invariably turn to issues surrounding the Israeli-Palestinian conflict.

Christianity

With over two billion adherents, Christianity is the largest of the world's religions. A religion that is over two thousand years old, Christianity emerged from a small, radical sect of Judaism to become arguably the most diverse and dominant religious tradition in the world today. With believers around the globe and with new variations of Christian practice emerging constantly, Christianity is a profoundly influential and dynamic religious tradition.

Any religious tradition with a large number of adherents will display a tremendous amount of diversity in its beliefs and practices. This is certainly true for Christianity. Indeed, if one observes the worship practices of Christians in different parts of the world, one might question why they all fall under the same umbrella given the highly varied rituals, architecture, languages, and sounds of worship. When we study Christian ethics—particularly in the contemporary era—we must be careful to take into account the tremendous diversity within the tradition. That being said, for many Christians, the focus on Jesus Christ is central to their religious identity. In the development of Christian ethics, the figure of Jesus, the Bible, influential theologians, and key historical events can be seen as authoritative in that they have shaped moral arguments for many—but not all—sects of Christianity. While some texts, people, and events are received in roughly similar ways across wide cultural, political, economic, and social differences, there are also texts, people, and events that have proven deeply divisive among Christians.

The most authoritative text in Christianity is the Bible. In the New Testament of the Bible, we find the earliest narratives about the historical Jesus of Nazareth, the Jewish rabbi whose life and teachings inspired the movement that eventually grew to become Christianity. Most of what we know about Jesus comes from the writings of the New Testament. The New

Testament was composed around the second half of the first century, and thus represents the views of the first generations of the followers of Jesus Christ after his death. Based upon the four short books that make up the Gospels of the New Testament—Matthew, Mark, Luke, and John—and the epistles, or letters, that are attributed to various early leaders of the Jesus movement, Christians believe that God sent Jesus, the son and the embodiment of God, to fulfill messianic prophecy. Jesus's miraculous birth, dramatic death—a crucifixion carried out under the auspices of the Roman government—and his astounding resurrection prove to believers that Jesus of Nazareth is indeed the Son of God, sent by God the Father to die for humanity's sins.

The rise of Christianity from a sect of Judaism took many historical turns before becoming established as a major religion in its own right. The first major church meeting, sometimes referred to as the "Council of Jerusalem," took place around 48 CE. At this meeting, the leaders of the nascent "Nazarene" movement, notably Paul of Tarsus (St. Paul), successfully argued that gentile converts should not be obligated to undergo the most difficult barriers to join their religious community. Namely, gentiles need not undergo circumcision or maintain a strict kosher diet. This flexibility resulted in an increasingly large number of gentile converts to the tradition, which by the second century CE was beginning to distinguish itself not just as a sect of Judaism, but as a distinct religious movement altogether.

As Christianity spread across the Mediterranean region and beyond, the need to standardize dogma, or teachings, about Jesus became increasingly urgent. At the Councils of Nicaea (325 CE) and Chalcedon (451 CE), church leaders eventually agreed that Jesus was, paradoxically, both fully human and fully divine. The Council of Constantinople (381 CE) established the doctrine of the Trinity, or the idea that God is of one essence, but of three persons: the Father, the Son, and the Holy Spirit. Christians insist that the Trinity and Jesus's dual nature affirm the idea of a God that is both present in and transcendent to the world.

Although the numerous Councils are important for understanding the basic theological ideas of Christianity, arguably the most significant event was the conversion of the Roman emperor, Constantine, who converted to Christianity in 312 CE and in the following year, issued the Edict of Milan, which for the first time allowed Christians to worship freely. In 380 CE, the emperor Theodosius declared Christianity to be the official religion of the Roman Empire. In under four centuries, the tiny movement started by Jesus of Nazareth, who was executed by the Roman Empire, became the state religion. This remarkable growth also had profound ethical implications for a religion that initially stood for the marginalized members of society over against the wealthy and powerful. Now the wealthiest and the most powerful were Christians, and the teachings and example of Jesus would have to adapt to the new status of Christianity in the world.

During the reign of Theodosius, Augustine of Hippo (d. 430 CE), perhaps the most influential theologian in the history of western Christianity, penned a number of works that deeply impacted the ways in which the tradition would develop for centuries to come. His views on human nature, free will and sin, sexuality, grace, time, memory, and any and all aspects of theology were expressed in his prolific writings. His autobiographical work, *Confessions* (ca. 400 CE), became a prototype for memoirs. In his *Confessions*, Augustine, in the first-person, recounts deeply personal struggles between desire, faith, and reason. He ties those struggles into his understanding of human nature and, ultimately, of God. *The City of God* (426 CE) examines the relationship between the city of humans and the city of God. Augustine uses the metaphor of the two cities to create an architecture by which the church and the state could co-exist. The city of humans is embedded in historical cycles and rises and falls as civilizations do; the city of God is the destination of humans who seek God and eternal life. For Augustine, both cities have a divine purpose and serve each other. The state makes possible the existence of the church, and the church supplies the spiritual purpose for the state. Augustine's analysis of the two cities is a model by which later philosophers, theologians, and heads of state would approach questions about the nature of religion and politics, including, eventually, the separation of church and state.

The relationship between the church and the state became the most significant factor in the political schism between what are today generally regarded as the Eastern Orthodox churches and the Roman Catholic Church. Whereas the papacy in the Roman Catholic Church remained separate from the head of state, in the Orthodox churches, the emperor reigned over the bishops. In addition to their differences in political structure, the Orthodox churches preached a vision of Jesus Christ that emphasized the mystical union of believers with God and understood sin primarily as a form of ignorance, rather than as a form of corruption.

If Augustine is regarded as the one of the greatest thinkers of Christianity's formative era, then Thomas Aquinas (d. 1274) holds a similar honor for the medieval era. Reconciling faith with reason, Aquinas argued that one can use reason to obtain knowledge about God. Aquinas's magnum opus, the *Summa Theologiae* (unfinished, published 1485), was written in dialogical form and was intended as an extensive compendium of all aspects of theological knowledge, ranging from God to humankind to sacraments. The *Summa* is remarkable not only for its theological breadth, but also for Aquinas's extensive knowledge of Greek philosophy, Islamic thought, and Hebrew texts. For those who study religious ethics, Aquinas' treatments of natural law, just war, virtue, and human nature have remained hugely influential.

Aquinas was able to read Aristotle because his works had been preserved by Muslim scholars. Known as the "Commentator" among scholars such as Aquinas, Ibn Rushd (Averroes) provided detailed analyses of Aristotle, which were translated from the Arabic into Latin. Such intellectual exchanges between Christians, Muslims, and Jews were not uncommon, despite the destructiveness of the Crusades, a series of military invasions from the eleventh through the thirteenth centuries under the leadership of various popes to rid Europe and the holy city of Jerusalem of Muslims and Jews. The legacy of the Crusades is a reminder of the blood-thirsty violence that a corrupt religion is capable of unleashing, particularly when it has military force at its command. This corruption was evident also with the Inquisitions that followed the Crusades and aimed, under the auspices of the Catholic Church, to root out heresy often by torturing and executing Jews and Muslims. Unfortunately, the European colonial enterprise, sanctioned by the Catholic Church, would extend regimes of brutality and death to peoples abroad.

Colonialism, the statecraft of possessing and ruling foreign territory for the primary purpose of enriching the colonizer, was sanctioned by European Christian rulers and given the blessing of the church under the auspices of converting "uncivilized" natives to Christianity. Unfortunately, the arrival of Europeans to parts of Africa, Asia, and the Americas, meant that millions of Indigenous peoples died, either because they were unable to fight off the novel deadly diseases that Europeans carried with them, or because they were killed so as not to interfere with the possession of these lands. The subsequent conversion to Christianity by surviving Indigenous peoples significantly changed the face of the religion. No longer confined to the European continent and parts of the Levant, Christianity became a truly global religion whereby Christian beliefs and rituals mixed with local customs, languages, and traditions. The cost of the growth and diversification of Christianity, namely the destruction and annihilation of numerous Indigenous populations and the erasure of local cultures and languages, plays a significant role in ethical thought today. When we discuss just war theory, for example, the legacy of colonialism becomes a part of the conversation. The same is true for ethical discussions about economics, international politics, and arts and culture.

As Christianity spread to different parts of the globe, the tradition was also experiencing significant change internally. Discontent with the corrupt practices of the popes, bishops, and other high-ranking members of the Roman Catholic Church reached a head when Martin Luther, a theologian and priest, protested in 1517 against the practice of selling indulgences, or the promised reduction of time in purgatory upon death. (With the permission of the Pope Leo X, for example, the Catholic Church sold indulgences to fund the restoration of the grand Cathedral of St. Peter in Rome.) Luther argued that indulgences not only took advantage of the poor, but that the selling of indulgences was theologically unsound. He argued that salvation was not the result of what people did—or bought—but, rather, that salvation came through God's grace, not human works. Justification, or the state of being just and good before God, by faith alone has since become a cornerstone of Protestant theology.

For Protestant Christians, Luther's Reformation extended beyond a critique of indulgences to arguments about the role of the church, the position of the Pope, and the place of scripture. Moving away from an extremely hierarchical tradition towards a religion whereby individual persons could access God through faith alone and guided solely by scripture, the Protestant Reformation has been credited with laying the foundation for democracy and human rights by privileging principles of equality and individualism. No longer dependent upon clergy to serve as intermediaries to God, one could understand how God saves and justifies through God's grace by simply reading the Bible. With the invention of the Gutenberg press, the Bible became accessible to an increasingly literate population.

The instability that the Reformation brought to Europe contributed to the rise of both rationalist and pietistic movements in the following centuries. The Enlightenment, which developed partially out of the Scientific Revolution, stressed the capacity of human reason over what was described as the irrationality of religious traditions. Immanuel Kant (d. 1804), the most prominent of the Enlightenment philosophers, found that there was no rational way to prove the existence of God (although he himself was a Lutheran Protestant) and focused on determining universal ethical laws that could be derived from human rationality.

Pietism, in response to the rationalist argument, attempted to bring emotion back into the understanding of God. Pietists argued that humans were, after all, emotional creatures, and faith in God seemed to develop not because one was able to reason logically God's existence, but to feel it. Too much focus on dogma only divided Christians from one another; the emotional connection to God unified Christians. This emphasis upon knowing God through one's feelings eventually gave rise to forms of Christianity that elevated the experience of God, including some types of evangelical Christianity.

Up until this point, the idea that one would question the existence of God was essentially unthinkable. However, the possibility of the argument that "God is dead," as Friedrich Nietzsche (d. 1900) claimed, emerged after scientific and rationalist movements. In this period, historians, archeologists, and linguists applied to sacred texts, like the Bible, historical and literary methodologies and revealed that sacred texts were likely produced by multiple authors and redacted, or edited, over time. While some fundamentalists still believed that God—or God speaking through someone—authored the Bible, scholarship showed the influence that humans have had over time on the text. Moreover, Darwin's *On the Origin of Species* (1859), the rise of paleontology, and the beginnings of genetics all supplied evidence about the creation of humans, animals, and plants that did not rely on Biblical explanations.

The horrors of the World Wars, particularly the Holocaust and the dropping of atomic bombs in Japan, made the argument about the death of God increasingly plausible. These events led many believers to question seriously the goodness of God and God's omnipotence. Although the faith of many

Christians may have been shaken, the impact of these events was not so great as to decrease the number of believers, but to remind believers that seemingly good people were shamefully content to ignore and even partake in evil when confronted with it. This was a key message that civil rights leader Martin Luther King Jr. (d. 1968) attempted to convey when sitting in a Birmingham jail for participating in one of many acts of civil disobedience. King argued that what was most morally egregious in the fight for civil rights was not necessarily the outspoken segregationist, but the contented White Christian minister who failed to see the teachings of Christ in the struggle of Black Americans for justice.[4] In addition to the civil rights movement, the women's rights movement and the climate change crisis have shifted ethical discourse within Christianity.

Moral authority in Christianity today depends significantly upon which of the thousands of sects we are discussing. For many Christians, the Bible remains a key source of ethical insight, and moral leadership—depending upon which sect or denomination to which one belongs—resides in chosen clergy. Perhaps the biggest threat to Christianity's influence in North America and western Europe is the stark rise in the number of religiously unaffiliated people. Over half of Americans now believe that one need not believe in God in order to be moral.

Islam

Islam, the third of the three Abrahamic religious traditions, began with the reports of a respected merchant and caravan-leader, Muhammad ibn Abdullah, in the city of Mecca on the Arabian Peninsula. In the year 610 CE, Muhammad, then 40-years old, claimed to receive messages from the angel Gabriel. These divine revelations occurred while he was meditating on Mount Hira and continued to come to him over the next two decades. Eventually, these messages were recorded and organized into what we know today as the Qur'an ("the Recitation"). Muhammad saw himself as the last in a line of prophets from the Jewish and Christian traditions. The Qur'an is understood by many Muslims to be the word of God handed down to them through his messenger, Muhammad.

Today, Islam is embraced by nearly two billion adherents, making the religion the second largest in the world. The life of Muhammad and the Qur'an are the main sources of moral authority for Muslims. Given the history and diversity of the tradition, however, many differences exist among Muslims with regard to their beliefs, their leadership, and practices. Sunni and Shi'ite Muslims, who trace their differences to the time period immediately following the death of the Prophet Muhammad, Sufis, and various regional differences among Muslims in different parts of the world, including among Black Americans in the United States, reveal marked variations in the beliefs and practices of Muslims.

After Muhammad began receiving divine revelations, he began to share these messages with his family and close friends. Eventually, as his influence grew, Muhammad attracted the attention of Meccan leaders. Because Muhammad preached against polytheism, his increasingly popular message was perceived as the threat to the economic livelihood of Mecca, which relied upon the industry of religious pilgrimages. As a major trading city, people from many different backgrounds visited Mecca both to engage in commerce and to worship the many gods that had shrines in the city.

By 622 CE, Muhammad felt sufficiently threatened by the Meccan elite that he migrated to Medina, a city that utilized his leadership and diplomatic skills to unify its citizens and to establish basic laws. The date of Muhammad's travel to Medina is so significant in Muslim history that 622 CE became the start of the Muslim calendar—any date afterwards is noted with an *AH*, or "After Hijra." Through a series of successful battles against Meccans, Muhammad eventually established the beginnings of the Islamic empire. Many Meccans converted to Islam, and Jews and Christians in the region were permitted to continue to practice their traditions, protected as *ahl al-kitab*, or People of the Book.

Muhammad had left behind no clear instructions regarding the successorship of the *umma*, or Muslim community, before his death in 632 CE. The division over how the *umma* should continue resulted in the creation of two factions, the Sunni and the Shi'ite. The Sunni, named after the *sunna* or "tradition" that followed the recommendations of the elders in the community, named Abu Bakr the first caliph. Unlike Muhammad, the caliph was not a prophet, but rather the political and military leader of the *umma*. Abu Bakr was not a direct relative of Muhammad; he became his father-in-law when his daughter, Aisha, was married to Muhammad, and was a long-trusted companion and advisor to Muhammad. The Shi'ite (also referred to as the Shi'a or Shi'i) believed that Ali, the cousin and son-in-law of Muhammad, should have been the first caliph and that Muhammad indicated in an earlier sermon that Ali should be his immediate successor. The Shi'ite suffered major blow at the Battle of Karbala (680 CE), where the son of Ali, Husayn, was killed. The Battle of Karbala and the martyrdom of Husayn have since taken on the symbolism of the Shi'ite minority's experiences of suffering and oppression. Today, approximately 15% of Muslims worldwide are Shi'ite, with the remaining 85% majority identifying mostly as Sunni.

The differences between the Sunni and Shi'ite concern religious leadership and historical memory. Muslims of both sects agree about the monotheistic God, the divine status of the Qur'an, and the status of the Prophet Muhammad. However, Shi'ites believe that their leader, or *imam*, should be a direct descendant of the Muhammad. The *imam* is a religious and political leader, and he also has divine status in the sense that the *imam* is infallible and sinless, even if not a prophet. In Sunni Islam, the caliph is a political and military leader, but not one who is divinely inspired or necessarily a direct descendant of Muhammad. In Sunni Islam, the leader of the *umma* is elected or chosen by the elders of the community.

Aside from the question of leadership, the division between the Sunni and Shi'ite can be observed through their distinct takes on Islamic history. For the Sunni, the successful reigns of the first four "rightly guided" caliphs validated God's approval of the *umma*. For the Shi'ite, the early caliphate represented a miscarriage of justice with leadership of the *umma* wrested away from its rightful ruler.

The differences between the Sunni and Shi'ite have also extended into Islamic law, which attempts to clarify how Muslims and Muslim governments ought to conduct themselves in accordance with the Qur'an, the tradition of the Prophet Muhammad (*sunna*), and the reports of Muhammad's life *(hadith)*. *Sharia*, the Arabic term commonly used for Islamic law, metaphorically refers to a straight path that leads to water, thus suggesting that one will be rewarded by following *sharia*. Islamic law developed in the eighth and ninth centuries as a means both to check the power of the caliphate and to clarify the application of religious material to various situations that arose throughout the Islamic empire. Multiple schools of Islamic law developed throughout the empire, each with a different worldview that reflected the perspective of its founding scholar. Despite their differences, the legal schools agreed upon the validity of legal methodologies such as *qiyas*, or analogical reasoning; *ijma*, or the consensus of religious scholars; and for Shi'ite legal jurisprudence found in the *Jafari* school, *ijtihad*, or independent legal reasoning. While the schools differed on various issues, they generally respected the validity of each other's rulings.

In addition to legal jurisprudence, Muslim scholars have looked to material regarding *aklaq* (character), as well as *adab* (civility), when discussing ethics. Tremendous emphasis is placed upon correct behavior, which is assumed to reflect one's character. Someone who embodies the proper virtues displays virtuosity through proper action. In this way, laws that govern behavior, ethics that focus on the development of virtue, and religion, which provides the template for both, are intertwined and practically inseparable from each other. The importance of the five pillars of Islam—the *shahada* (declaration of faith), *salat* (five daily prayers), *zakat* (almsgiving), *sawm* (Ramadan fast), and *hajj* (pilgrimage to Mecca)—testify to the emphasis placed in Muslim ethics on correct action. In Islamic jurisprudence, laws that govern the relationship amongst humans are to mirror the laws that govern the relationship between humans and God. In one famous *hadith*, Aisha, one of Muhammad's wives, describes the Prophet as having a character that mirrors the Qur'an. In this brief statement, Aisha brings together the perfection of human character with divine revelation.

For those Muslims who desired to move away from the legalism of Islam, Sufism developed as a strand of the tradition that emphasized a mystical union with God. Sufis, so-called because of the wool (*suf*) garments they wore, looked to the spiritual practices of the Prophet Muhammad to find religious meaning. The meditative aspects of Sufism were woven into artistic endeavors, such as dance, music, and poetry. Sufis focused on divine love and esoteric knowledge, which they believed was a truer way to knowing God than the formalism of Islamic jurisprudence. Perhaps the best known of the Sufi masters is the poet Rumi (d. 1273) whose mystical masterpiece, the *Mathnawi*, teaches various ways to love God through anecdotes, stories, and descriptions taken from the Qur'an and other Muslim sources. Not surprisingly, given the centrality of the individual's search for divine wisdom, Sufism developed without a central authority figure. Rather, persons who sought a relationship with God through Sufi practices turned to *shayks*, who served as teachers and guides for their students' spiritual journeys.

When discussing modern Muslim ethics, one must consider not only the sect or legal school, but also how historical events may influence particular worldviews. In particular, the rivalry between the Islamic empire and Christendom, the Crusades, and colonialism have influenced modern day perceptions of global politics, religious violence, and cultural imperialism. For the first several centuries following the death of Muhammad, Islam expanded rapidly. The Islamic empire stretched across large swaths of Africa; the Middle East; Western, Central, and Southeast Asia; and the Iberian Peninsula. From the seventh through the eleventh centuries, Islam posed a formidable challenge to Christendom, which, while older, was not expanding nearly as quickly as Islam. Moreover, Christians were converting to Islam, which was viewed as a natural progression following Judaism and Christianity, with Muhammad understood as the next great prophet after Jesus. Islam was in its golden age, having reached its zenith in terms of political, militaristic, and cultural prowess.

Meanwhile, Christendom, under the rule of Pope Urban II, was determined to regain its place as the dominant religion of the Middle East and Europe. The Crusades were ostensibly undertaken by Christian armies to wrest Jerusalem from Muslim rule, but economic and political gains played a significant role in the decision to launch the series of militaristic endeavors. Moreover, there is scant evidence that the Christians (and certainly the Jews) of Jerusalem desired to be "saved" by the Pope and his crusaders, especially as Muslim rulers were generally far more tolerant of religious differences than Christian rulers. The horrific violence unleashed in the name of Christianity during the Crusades is viewed today as a particularly shameful episode in Christian history.

The impact of the Crusades and other foreign incursions into Muslim territories has had a significant impact on collective memory. The experience of the Mongol invasions into the Levant in the thirteenth century, for example, shaped the attitudes of the scholar Ibn Taymiyya (1263–1328), whose writings would be used later to justify the use of force against non-Muslim influences. European colonialism, which reduced the former Islamic empire into colonies that fed the economies of countries such as France, England, and the Netherlands, is viewed as repetition of the Crusades, fueled by the belief of Christian Europeans that they have the right to invade Muslim lands for their own benefit.

In response to these events, Islamic revivalist movements aimed to restore Islam to its former glory. Although these movements varied from region to region and in their strategies to regain Muslims' standing in history, they all asserted that a renewed approach to Islam would be key to successes. Perhaps the most well-known today of these revivalist movements is Wahhabism, which has had a tremendous influence in shaping the political and religious identity of Saudi Arabia. Named after an eighteenth century religious leader, the Wahhabi movement attempted to recapture the Islam of the first generations of Muslims and forcefully suppress forms of Islam that did not comport with his vision of the pure tradition. In addition to its strict interpretation of Islam, Wahhabis also place restrictions upon the freedoms of women based upon their belief that gender disparity and hierarchy accurately reflect the ideals of the first generations of Muslims. The way in which Wahhabis and other extremely conservative Muslim groups, such as the Taliban, treat women and girls has attracted global concern. Although some Muslim communities deny their women and girls' basic human rights on the basis of sex, most do not; and in many Muslim communities, women and girls are treated as equals to men and boys. The stereotype of the oppressed Muslim woman has become a trope in Western media, however, and has undoubtedly contributed to the passage of laws against Muslim women's dress.

In addition to the status of Muslim women, the other major theme that has become synonymous with Islam in recent decades has been terrorism. No moral discussion about war and violence in contemporary Islam escapes the imprint of the 9/11 attacks carried out by al-Qaeda. 9/11 and events in the years following raised questions about the relationship between Muslim theology, just war theory, and international politics. The more recent rise of ISIS—the horrifically violent, extremist Islamist group that arose following the war in Iraq—has meant that the relevance of these questions remains.

Sikhism

With 25 million adherents, including a substantial diaspora community in Great Britain, Sikhism is a world religion. The tradition was founded by Guru Nanak (d. 1539) around 500 years ago in the Punjab region in northwest India. Sikhs believe in the One Supreme Reality or the Timeless Being, referred to as Akal Purakh, and follow the teachings of ten Sikh Gurus and two main authoritative texts, Adi Granth (also called the Guru Granth Sahib) and the Dasam Granth. A more recent text, the Sikh Rahit Maryada, received the approval of the main Sikh governing body, the Chief Gurdwara

Management Committee in 1945, and addresses issues of moral conduct for both individuals and groups of Sikhs.

Not surprisingly given the location of the origins of the tradition, Sikhism has created an identity that shares some of the same qualities but yet distinguishes itself from both Hinduism and Islam, at the time the dominant religions in the region. The founder of the tradition, Guru Nanak, was born into an upper-caste Hindu family but worked for a Muslim nobleman. According to tradition, Guru Nanak disappeared after stepping into a river and then reemerged out of the waters three days later. Guru Nanak's first proclamation following his three-day mystical journey was, "There is no Hindu; there is no Muslim." One of the striking messages of Sikhism is its tolerance of other religious traditions. For that reason, few people have felt pressured to convert to Sikhism; nearly all Sikhs have inherited the tradition through their Punjabi family heritage. In the diaspora community, the terms Sikh and Punjabi are essentially interchangeable.

Sikhism is a monotheistic tradition that believes in the existence of a single God, who represents truth, creation, and eternity. It is the same God that appears in other religious traditions and is both timeless and formless. God, according to Sikhs, is present in the Gurus, as well as the Guru Granth Sahib. Sikhs recall God through the repetition of the Holy Name of God, or Nam. However, Sikhs do not hold that theirs is the only path to God, and Sikh solder-saints are obligated to protect not just the freedom of Sikhs to practice their own tradition, but also the freedom of people of other faiths. In line with this belief, Sikhs believe that all people should be treated equally, and therefore Sikhs reject the Hindu caste system, although Sikhs retain Hindu beliefs in reincarnation and karma.

The *Khalsa*, the order of Sikhs who have shown their commitment to the tradition through an initiation rite known as the *amrit* ceremony, forms the nucleus of the community, the *Panth*. They show their devotion through the donning of five outward symbols of their faith. The Five Ks are:

1 *Kes*, uncut hair to symbolize saintliness
2 *Kangha*, a wooden comb to symbolize an orderly life
3 *Kirpan*, a sword to symbolize courage
4 *Kara*, a steel bracelet to symbolize commitment to the Guru Gobind Singh
5 *Kach*, cotton undergarments to symbolize moral purity

In addition to these five externally-oriented aspects of the faith, *Khalsa* Sikhs recite daily prayers; avoid eating ritually slaughtered meat; and abstain from tobacco, alcohol, and other intoxicants. As a community, Sikhs gather together in a gurdwara, where a copy of the Guru Granth Sahib is held and communal worship takes place. The gurdwara often is also the location of the communal meal, the *langar*, which is typically vegetarian and open to all.

Sikhs have established communities around the world, but nonetheless consider the Punjab to be the center of the faith. The region has been the site of much political strife and violence that can be directly traced to the 1947 partition of British-ruled India. The partition resulted in the division of Punjab between India and Pakistan, which led two million Sikhs to emigrate from Pakistan to India under extremely difficult conditions. In India, violence erupted between Sikhs and Hindus between 1978 and 1982 when anti-Sikh legislation was passed by the Indian government. As a result, Sikhs demanded their own nation state, Khalistan. When Indian Prime Minister Indira Gandhi ordered an attack on the Golden Temple, Sikh's holiest shrine, mass violence between Hindus and Sikhs ensued. In 1984, Indira Gandhi was killed by her Sikh bodyguards, resulting in even greater levels of Hindu-Sikh violence. The quest for Sikh independence remains alive to this day and is often supported by the Sikh diaspora community.

Conclusion

This very brief introduction provides a basic orientation to several prominent religions for the purposes of moral inquiry. Although there are some similarities between and among these traditions—for example, many of the traditions worship a monotheistic God, use scared texts, and begin with an exceptional leader—there are also major differences. Both within and among the different traditions, we see different emphases with regard to ritual practices and belief, the centrality of scripture, and the place of humanity relative to creation. Large-scale historical events have also affected believers in different religious traditions in varied ways, and localized historical events influence religions in particular areas.

One significant issue that requires significantly more consideration when discussing world religions is the interaction between religious traditions. Although we do discuss different religions when it comes to inter-religious warfare, we tend not to discuss as much the more mundane aspects of our lives that involve religious differences. Religious believers do not live in silos, and, in fact, many religious traditions developed out of environments rich in multiple religious traditions. Today, especially in large cities and dense urban areas, people from a diversity of religious traditions live in the same buildings, work together, attend the same schools, become friends, and join families. Let us remember this when we think about religious ethics.

Notes

1 Keown, "Origins of Buddhist Ethics," 289.
2 Keown, "Origins of Buddhist Ethics," 290.
3 Putnam, "Jewish Ethics?," 159.
4 King, "Letter from a Birmingham Jail."

Bibliography

Cannon, Katie G. *Black Womanist Ethics*. Atlanta, GA: Scholars Press, 1988.

Cone, James H. *Black Theology and Black Power*. New York: Seabury Press, 1969.

Cozort, Daniel, and James Mark Shields, eds. *The Oxford Handbook of Buddhist Ethics*. Oxford: Oxford University Press, 2018.

Dorff, Elliot N. *Love Your Neighbor and Yourself: A Jewish Approach to Modern Personal Ethics*. Philadelphia, PA: Jewish Publication Society, 2003.

Ernst, Carl W. *Following Muhammad: Rethinking Islam in the Contemporary World*. Chapel Hill: University of North Carolina Press, 2003.

Fitzgerald, Timothy. *Discourse on Civility and Barbarity: A Critical History of Religion and Related Categories*. New York: Oxford University Press, 2007.

Gethin, Rupert. *The Foundations of Buddhism*. Oxford: Oxford University Press, 1998.

Gill, Robin, ed. *The Cambridge Companion to Christian Ethics*. 2nd ed. Cambridge: Cambridge University Press, 2012.

Grelle, Bruce, and Sumner B. Twiss. *Explorations in Global Ethics: Comparative Religious Ethics and Interreligious Dialogue*. Boulder, CO: Westview, 1998.

Gudorf, Christine E., and Regina Wentzel Wolfe. *Ethics and World Religions: Cross-Cultural Case Studies*. Maryknoll, NY: Orbis Books, 1999.

Harvey, Peter, ed. *Buddhism*. London: Continuum, 2001.

Hourani, George. *Reason and Tradition in Islamic Ethics*. Cambridge: Cambridge University Press, 2007.

Jakobsh, Doris, and Henry Rosemont. *Sikhism*. Honolulu: University of Hawaii Press, 2012.

Kellner, Menachem Marc, ed. *Contemporary Jewish Ethics*. New York: Sanhedrin Press, 1978.

Keown, Damien. *The Nature of Buddhist Ethics*. Basingstoke: Palgrave, 2001.

King Jr., Martin Luther, and Jesse Jackson. *Why We Can't Wait*. New York: Signet Classic, 2000.

Lawton, Clive, and Peggy Morgan, eds. *Ethical Issues in Six Religious Traditions*. 2nd ed. Edinburgh: Edinburgh University Press, 2007.

Lipner, Julius. *Hindus: Their Religious Beliefs and Practices*. 2nd ed. Abingdon: Routledge, 2010.

Lofton, Kathryn. "Religious History as Religious Studies." *Religion* 42:3 (2012), 383–94. https://doi.org/10.1080/0048721X.2012.681878.

Martin, Nancy M., and Joseph Runzo. *Ethics in the World Religions*. Oxford: Oneworld, 2001.

Raboteau, Albert J. *Slave Religion: The "Invisible Institution" in the Antebellum South*. Oxford: Oxford University Press, 2004.

van der Veer, Peter. *Imperial Encounters: Religion and Modernity in India and Britain*. Princeton, NJ: Princeton University Press, 2001.

Chapter 2

Biomedical Ethics

Perhaps more so than any other topic I introduce to my undergraduate students, biomedical ethics is the one most personally relatable. Prior to the COVID pandemic, I would typically talk about common experiences like signing a consent form to have wisdom teeth removed, a rite of passage for many young adults. Even if they are unaware of the ethical reasons behind such documents, students remember bits of the language on the forms they signed, including phrases like "risk of death." We would talk about access to birth control; college students are often shocked to learn that obtaining birth control was once virtually impossible for unmarried persons in the United States. Now that we have lived through a global pandemic, discussions about biomedical ethics have a palpable urgency. Subjects such as mandatory vaccination, equitable distribution, and allocation of scarce resources are all too real. With the 2022 overturning by the US Supreme Court of *Roe v. Wade*, which had guaranteed for nearly 50 years a woman's right to abortion, autonomy and access to healthcare have reemerged as critical ethical issues.

Religious beliefs play an important role in medicine. The most fundamental questions about the beginning and end of life, pain and suffering, and the care of the body have been central to every major religious tradition. Religious laws often deal with the regulation of bodily functions. Caring for the sick in itself is often seen as a common expression of religious commitment. Religious institutions, guided by their values and missions, have long traditions of establishing hospitals and clinics. The earliest providers of healthcare appear to have been Egyptian temple priests. Nursing developed in the first centuries of Christianity as a form of charity that included caring for the sick, hungry, and poor. The first modern-style hospital was established in 805 CE in Bagdad and staffed by Muslim scholar-physicians.

Physicians and healthcare workers, as well as secular governments, today rely on non-religious principles and reasoning to pursue policies that are applicable to a wide swath of people since using ethical reasoning that references just one particular religious tradition might be viewed as discriminatory against those who do not belong to it. For this reason, healthcare workers, who often treat people from a variety of religious backgrounds or

DOI: 10.4324/9781003350637-3

who may be atheist or agnostic, rely upon guidance in biomedical ethics that would be appropriate for all these different patients.

The language of biomedical ethics today often avoids reference to specific religious traditions even though religious beliefs may play an important role in biomedical ethics. This approach to biomedical ethics has practical advantages for healthcare workers and for policy makers who cannot reasonably tailor ethics rules for each individual. And, indeed, there are certain protections that come with guidelines that are meant to apply to all people, regardless of their religious beliefs or lack thereof, race and ethnicity, age, sex, sexual orientation, income, or educational level. The practice of "informed consent," for example, which requires that healthcare providers communicate with patients about their condition and treatment so that patients can knowledgably give or withhold their consent, should ideally protect the autonomy of every patient. The principle of respect for autonomy, from which informed consent is derived, is one of four major principles—along with non-maleficence ("do no harm"), beneficence, and justice—that form a framework by which issues in biomedical ethics can be evaluated. On their surface, these principles appear to be religiously and culturally neutral and couched in the widely-accepted language of human rights.

The non-religious language found in much of contemporary biomedical ethics literature, however, does not preclude the importance of religious beliefs in the field. For patients, religious beliefs may inform decisions about abortion, reproductive technologies, various medical procedures, and end-of-life processes. For healthcare providers, familiarity with how practitioners and patients of different faith traditions consider various issues in medical care is informative and can help to guide policies. The religious beliefs of healthcare providers may also dictate whether they will offer certain procedures, such as abortions, or provide abortifacient medicines to patients.

In the last several decades, scholars with training in religious studies and philosophy have developed ways of thinking through ethical problems raised by the rapid development of medical technologies. Although the language these scholars employed was non-religious, Christian views of virtue and justice often informed their conclusions. Indeed, much of the history of medical ethics has been dominated by the notion that caregivers should possess particular virtues in addition to the necessary knowledge and skills. The Hippocratic Oath emphasizes certain virtues, including loyalty to teachers and to patients. Case-based approaches to biomedical ethics, also referred to as casuistry, were popular among Catholic thinkers.

To this day, famous case studies are still taught in ethics courses at colleges and medical schools around the world to help students to understand how decisions about patient care are made. Two of the most well-known cases include the case of Karen Ann Quinlan, who remained in a persistent vegetative state for nine years, and Dax Cowart, who suffered from life-threatening burns and forced against his will to undergo painful treatment. The Quinlan case has become a classic study of the right-to-die movement; and Dax Cowart's experiences became central to issues of patient autonomy. Tom Beauchamp and James Childress's highly influential *Principles of Biomedical Ethics* (1979), which frames biomedical ethics in terms of the four prima facie principles mentioned above, features qualities such as benevolence and justice that are also prominent themes in Christianity. Notably, both Beauchamp and Childress have academic backgrounds in theology and religious studies.

In the United States, several national biomedical ethics commissions were established by the federal government to determine religious views on controversial technologies such as cloning (1997) and stem cell research (1999). Testimonies from noted scholars, as well as representatives of multiple traditions, including Judaism, Islam, and various sects of Christianity, described religious views regarding these technologies. These testimonies express the ethical struggles, as well as the promises, that such technologies bring to believers. The testimonies also make clear that within the same religious traditions, believers can hold divergent views about the morality of new medical technologies, and that across different religious traditions, believers can share similar views.

The COVID pandemic has raised a number of fundamental issues in biomedical ethics. Highly contagious, lethal, and air-borne, the novel coronavirus has highlighted challenges facing public health, disparities in access to healthcare, and the dangers of politicizing medicine. The global death toll as a result of COVID just over two years into the pandemic exceeds six million. COVID has infected more than 500 million people, many of whom have suffered terribly as a result of this highly contagious virus. Coronavirus has not affected people equally. In the United States, for example, wage-workers in poorly paid service industries, Black American and Hispanic communities, and elderly residents in nursing homes were among the hardest hit by the coronavirus.

In addition to the dead and the sick, COVID-19 was also responsible for a global economic recession, high unemployment rates, the closing of schools, and myriad other negative events. Globally, the summer of 2020 began with a slowdown of the transmission of the virus, followed by an ominous rise of new variants of the coronavirus. The Delta variant ravaged India and the Omicron variants spread rapidly through many countries. Although there are several effective vaccines against the coronavirus, the distribution of the vaccine has been highly inequitable with wealthier countries possessing a larger supply of vaccines relative to poorer ones. Within the United States, the distribution of vaccines has generally favored those least likely to be infected with the coronavirus. White, wealthy, and well-educated people are among those most likely to get vaccinated, while Black and Hispanic Americans are among the least likely. To complicate matters, many people who have access to vaccines choose not to take them for political or religious reasons.

The pandemic has shown that safeguarding health is a communal endeavor. Although the highly contagious nature of the airborne coronavirus makes this plain, the pandemic has also shown that diseases have serious consequences for families and societies, and not just sick individuals. Sickness affects families, communities, political systems, and economies. When parents become ill, children suffer. When schools close, parents, usually mothers, drop out of the workforce to care for children. The inability to contain the coronavirus has bankrupted thousands of businesses, resulted in high unemployment rates, and set back industries ranging from airlines to restaurants. In thinking about biomedical ethics in light of the pandemic, we are instructed to understand the field as applicable not just to the circumstances of individual persons, but of entire societies, as well.

Public health mandates present challenges to the focus of biomedical ethics on patient autonomy, and, specifically, the importance of respecting the right of individuals to make informed choices about their own bodies and well-being. This emphasis on autonomy can be attributed both to European and North American philosophical legacies that stress the rights of individuals and to the historical context of contemporary biomedical ethics as an area of study that developed with the Nuremberg Code and the various political movements of the late 1960s and 1970s. The Nuremberg Code was developed in response to the medical experiments German Nazis performed on Jews against their will and requires, among other things, voluntary consent from human subjects when conducting medical research. In addition, many of the scholars who participated in the formation of biomedical ethics witnessed, if not participated in, the era's movements for civil rights and women's rights. In light of the demands by Black Americans and women for equal respect under the law, these scholars viewed respect for autonomy as a crucial feature of biomedical ethics. Given the paternalism that had characterized many aspects of medical care, the notion that doctors had a duty to inform patients about their treatment and that patients should consent to their medical care was radical.

For Black Americans and for women, the critique of paternalism and the endorsement of self-advocacy in medical care marked a departure from the historical treatment of these two groups. To this day, Black Americans mistrust the American healthcare system as a result of the Tuskegee syphilis study (1932–72) during which healthcare workers intentionally withheld widely available, effective treatment from Black men merely to observe the fatal progression of the disease. The Black men enrolled in the study were never informed that they suffered from syphilis, deliberately stopped from obtaining life-saving penicillin, and misled until their deaths into believing that they were being cared for by the doctors and nurses of the study. Moreover, they were subject to painful, unnecessary, and risky spinal taps for no plausible reason. In exchange for their participation, the men were given occasional hot meals and $50. Historian James Jones's *Bad Blood* (1981), which bioethicist Arthur Caplan describes as "the single most important book ever written in bioethics," details the Tuskegee syphilis study and leaves the reader to ask how this nightmarish experiment was able to carry on for decades in clear public view despite its horrific cruelty and repeated violations of the men's rights.

Well into the 1970s, it was not uncommon for women to be "protected" from unwelcome medical diagnoses by their physicians and their family members. It was also not uncommon for courses of treatment to be determined unilaterally by doctors who assumed what would be in the best interest of the patient, without regard for what the patient actually desired for herself. This attitude was at odds with the push for greater sex equality by the women's rights movement. Moreover, the arrival of the birth control pill in 1960 promised an unprecedented level of reproductive autonomy for women. In reality, however, women, even married women, faced tremendous legal and cultural obstacles when attempting to acquire the pill. Married couples were forced to turn to the courts to access the birth control pill; the Supreme Court in *Griswold v. Connecticut* would eventually rule, in 1965, that the constitutional right to privacy, extended to married couples, covered the right to use birth control. Unmarried women would not be given the same constitutionally protected right to access birth control until 1972 with *Eisenstadt v. Baird*. The assertion in principled approaches to biomedical ethics that women's autonomy ought to be respected rejected commonly accepted practices of paternalism.

The focus on autonomy in biomedical ethics has come under critique by anthropologists, sociologists, and historians, who have pointed out the biases of such an approach. While the historical context in which biomedical ethics developed as a discipline in the second half of the twentieth century explains the emphasis on autonomy, the priority placed on the individual over the social unit is less appealing in cultures in which the family unit is as relevant as the individual when making medical decisions. Indeed, in many religious traditions, the concept of duty—whether to God, community, or family—is far more prevalent and historically rooted than the concept of rights. Having obligations and responsibilities would not, however, obviate the contemporary development of rights-based ideas within religious traditions. Many religious believers and institutions today, for example, support the basic notions behind human rights articulated with the Universal Declaration of Human Rights (1948).

More than two years into the COVID-19 pandemic, the privileging of individual autonomy over the well-being of the social group has revealed its high cost during a public health crisis of this magnitude. The rise of new variants and the resurgent waves of cases can be attributed in part to low initial vaccination rates. In the United States, where COVID vaccines are plentiful, people who hesitate to get vaccinated or are anti-vaccination often assert their freedom and right not to be vaccinated.

Despite the fact that the coronavirus is highly contagious, and new strains appear to be even more so, the idea of individual choice for the vaccine-hesitant and anti-vaxxers continues to override concerns about transmission of the potentially fatal virus. When the Centers for Disease Control (CDC) strongly advised people to wear masks before vaccines were available, some Americans equated "mask mandates" with infringements on personal autonomy and freedom. During its first crucial months, the pandemic was also politicized such that the seriousness of the coronavirus was downplayed by political leaders in countries including the United States, Great Britain, Brazil, and India. Rather than relying upon non-partisan medical authorities, such as the CDC and the World Health Organization (WHO), people turned increasingly to preferred online media outlets for information about the coronavirus. Masking and vaccination quickly became equated with liberal politics; and anti-masking and anti-vaccination attitudes became equated with traditional views and conservative politics. White, Christian evangelicals in the United States linked patriotism and libertarian values with the rejection of the expertise of medical scientists, whom they viewed as anti-religious.

The rationale employed by these White, Christian evangelicals to avoid vaccinations was often accompanied by attitudes that downplayed the seriousness of COVID, beliefs that the novel coronavirus was a hoax, or suspicions about the safety of the vaccine. Widespread misinformation about the coronavirus could be attributed largely to the popularity of social media and reliance upon internet sources to obtain information about healthcare. Because social media utilizes algorithms to reinforce pre-existing biases, misinformation about COVID was and remains difficult to dispel. This worldview poses challenges to vaccination efforts, which require a large majority of the population to be inoculated in order to be maximally effective against the coronavirus. Black Americans, who initially had lower vaccination rates compared to most other racial and ethnic groups, are understandably suspicious of vaccines due to the legacy of Tuskegee and other abuses by the medical establishment. In order to increase vaccination rates among Black Americans, a number of local governments and healthcare providers have teamed up with Black churches. These churches and their leaders, as trusted sources of authority, help to reduce levels of vaccine hesitancy and provide a logistically convenient place to obtain vaccinations.

Biomedical ethics, as an interdisciplinary field, relies upon the knowledge of practitioners and scholars in multiple areas of study: medicine, epidemiology, anthropology, sociology, philosophy, religious studies, theology, and others. Moreover, biomedical ethics has rapidly evolved to meet the challenges of advancing medical technologies. The focus on such technologies has come under criticism by biomedical ethicists working in poorer countries, where problems like hunger and access to vaccinations are far more relevant issues to their patient populations. Technologies like cloning and stem cell transplantation are problematic in "first-world" countries that can afford to develop these extraordinarily expensive procedures, but not relevant in developing countries where meeting even basic healthcare needs proves challenging. This gap in wealth is especially troubling when researchers from wealthy countries conduct medical research on people living in low-income countries. Cultural differences, lack of informed consent, lower standards of care, and threats of exploitation plague such relationships.

The practical applications of biomedical ethics are likely to expand as we learn more about the role of the environment, genetics, and other factors that play a role in health. The environmental crisis, in particular, will become an important topic that should ideally involve the input of multiple religious traditions. Unlike some topics in biomedical ethics, the environment and climate change are factors that will affect people across the globe, regardless of their religious affiliations or their own particular ethical commitments. If there is anything that the COVID pandemic has revealed to us, it is that in our globalized world, we inextricably bound to each other.

In the section below, several religious traditions are described and analyzed with regard to biomedical ethics. The formative texts and teachings from ancient religious traditions, however, do not directly address issues arising from cutting-edge medical technologies. Instead, scholars look to concepts, ideas, and practices that may help to inform a framework for understanding the morality of controversial issues in biomedical ethics today. In other words, a tradition might draw upon certain texts, persons, and ideas in analyzing various issues in biomedical ethics, even if issues like stem cell research or human cloning are not mentioned directly.

Notably, not all issues are equally important across traditions, although certain themes can be found across multiple religions. Abortion, for example, may be an important ethical issue for some Christians, but ranks fairly low in importance for Buddhists as a topic of moral concern. Or, the same issue may be important, but for different reasons. Devout Roman Catholics may abhor abortion because the act is viewed as the taking of innocent life; whereas Hindus might be concerned about abortion because of the disproportionately high number of female fetuses that are aborted compared to male fetuses. Within each of these traditions, believers may hold differing, even opposing, views on this and other controversial issues. There are, of course, issues of concern that are shared across traditions. There is common concern, for example, about the value of women and girls relative to men and boys. Gender inequality and gender discrimination are found in most, if not all, of the world's religions, but whether they are considered ethically problematic varies. Generally, the world's major religious traditions agree in theory on the principle of non-maleficence, or do no harm. There is also general consensus about the importance of beneficence, or doing good. The interpretation and application of these principles, however, vary tremendously both within and among traditions. The following section visits these issues and highlights sources in various religions as they apply to biomedical ethics.

Hinduism

The tremendous diversity within Hinduism makes the application of principled approaches to biomedical ethics challenging. Hinduism covers a large swath of beliefs, god and goddess traditions, and populations. Moreover, ethical norms in Hinduism are highly situational; what is considered appropriate behavior depends upon a number of factors, including sex, age, and caste. Because of the responsiveness to situational context, consensus with regard to controversial issues in biomedical ethics, such as abortion or stem cell research, is unrealistic. S. Cromwell Crawford describes the Hindu approach as a "contextual orientation of moral reasoning." With this situational sensitivity in mind, there are nonetheless a number of sources within Hinduism that can provide some guidance when faced with dilemmas in biomedical ethics. Concepts such as *dharma*, *ahimsa*, and *karma*, as well as the notion of reincarnation, can all inform biomedical ethics in Hinduism.

Dharma, which generally refers to duty, but also has connotations of virtue, responsibility, and law, helps to guide one's priorities. For a healthcare provider, *dharma* demands a holistic awareness of patients. Attention is paid to meeting appropriate physical, intellectual, and social needs of patients. *Dharma* asks that medicine be understood not just as the repairing or restoration of physical health, but as concern and recognition of the humanity of patients. Along with *dharma*, the concept of *ahimsa*, or no harm, suggests care that minimizes pain and suffering of patients. *Ahimsa* does not mean avoiding physical pain, as many medical procedures are indeed painful, but rather the ability to recognize the suffering of patients and utilizing knowledge and skills to minimize it. Certainly, *ahimsa* would also require the elimination of any unnecessary pain and suffering. *Karma*, the notion that actions have moral consequences, determines whether one is reborn into the cycle of *samsara*, or whether one is finally released from cycles of reincarnation and attains *nirvana*. Like *dharma*, *karma* carries moral weight for observant Hindus. Earning good *karma* requires situational awareness and sensitivity to the harm and suffering of other sentient beings.

Traditional Indian medicine, *ayurveda*, which dates back to the earliest foundational Hindu scriptures and is associated with the god Indra, is the science of living to old age. The traditional approach to health is comprehensive and holistic, and takes seriously the mandate of medicine to alleviate suffering. While the core of *ayurveda* is technical knowledge about the curing of disease and the preservation of health, this approach to well-being also stresses the importance of happiness and purpose in life. Furthermore, *ayurveda* approaches health and sickness as a social phenomenon. Disease and wellness dictate not just the longevity of individuals, but also of communities' political, social, and economic stability.

Although traditional Hindu approaches to medicine and wellness are theoretically inclusive, in actuality, discrimination based on sex or gender, class, and caste remains a problem. A priority in the biomedical ethics literature regarding Hinduism concerns the problem of sex-selection of fetuses. Reproductive technologies enable parents to know the sex of the fetus early in pregnancy, and female fetuses are aborted at a much higher rate than male fetuses even when there are no severe medical conditions that would warrant pregnancy termination. This practice has contributed to the phenomenon, famously described by Nobel-prize winning economist Amartya Sen, of missing girls and women in India; there is a population imbalance in the country with some 60 million more men than women, despite several laws that have attempted to ban the practice of sex selection. Arguments in favor of these bans cite the need to stop sex-based discrimination and to prevent even greater sex imbalances into the future. Arguments against the bans claim that sex-selection procedures will continue but be driven into the unregulated black market. Moreover, these bans ultimately harm mothers because they will be pressured into giving birth to more and more children until they give birth to a boy. This is harmful to pregnant women and also potentially to the girls who are brought into this world as unwanted disappointments.

Absent a major cultural shift, which would include dealing with Hindu sources that privilege men over women, changes are unlikely. *Manusmriti* 9.81, for example, is one of a number of classical Hindu texts that value women solely for their procreative capabilities. The text states that infertile wives may be replaced by other women if they are infertile, if their children die, or if they produce only daughters. At the same time, *Manusmriti* 3.55 states that women should be "honored and adorned" by the men in their families, and that when women are so honored, the gods rejoice. As with the scriptures of other religious traditions, the dharma literature is full of inconsistencies.

Like girls and women, Hindus belonging to the lower castes and the "scheduled castes" have also faced discrimination in healthcare. Members from these castes suffer poor health outcomes, which correspond to higher rates of poverty and political disenfranchisement. However, counties in India that have high literacy rates also have low rates of sex imbalance. For example, Kerala has one of the highest literacy rates among women, as well as one of the most balanced ratios of women to men in India. The correlation between women's educational levels and low evidence of female death is unsurprising, as both point toward the equal value placed on both females and males in this region. Kerala is also notable for its excellent "cradle to grave" healthcare that encompasses well-being from prenatal to palliative care. Over half of Kerala's population is Hindu, with sizeable Muslim and Christian communities. The long history of widely available education and high rates of civic participation seem to mitigate the lack of economic growth in the region.

One commonality that binds the members of all Hindu castes is the idea of reincarnation. Life is understood not in linear time, but rather in terms of cycles. Birth and death represent points along the cycle of multiple reincarnations, and each soul returns in a different life form based upon the amount of *karma* earned in previous lives. Death is not viewed as a permanent end to life, but is seen instead as a transition to a different form of existence. This does not mean that death is taken lightly; indeed, *ahimsa* requires great care be taken to avoid unnecessary pain and suffering. Physicians in the *ayurvedic* tradition are trained to avoid disclosing imminent death to the patient without the patient's consent for fear of hastening death. Extraordinary measures are also to be avoided, as death is understood as the natural and expected end to life. Death in Hindu cultures ideally comes about in the presence of family and loved ones, rather than alone. The *ayurvedic* approach to death thus requires that a physician be sensitive and attentive to the symptoms of the patient so that family can be summoned at the appropriate time.

Buddhism

The Buddha himself is regarded as a healer. Like many in the healing professions, the Buddha sought to end suffering. Indeed, the Four Noble Truths and the Eight-fold Path employ a methodology not unlike that found in medicine that begins with a diagnosis of the problem of suffering, pinpoints the source of suffering, offers a remedy, and recognizes the resolution to the problem (*nirvana*). For Buddhists, suffering encompasses both physical and psychological pain. The treatment for suffering, likewise, is both physical and psychological in nature.

Considered one of the Five Great Sciences, the science of medicine was one of the fields that *bodhisattvas*, enlightened beings who help others on their path to nirvana, were to master. Concepts central to Buddhism, such as compassion and *ahimsa* can aid in determining Buddhist responses to controversies in biomedical ethics. As with Hinduism, the formative texts in Buddhism do not deal directly with contemporary medical technologies, but there are nonetheless certain Buddhist ideas that are relevant to several of the profound questions at the heart of biomedical ethics. The tremendous diversity within Buddhism translates into a variety of approaches and conclusions to issues in biomedical ethics, but there is much agreement about the central tenets of the tradition.

Because the work of physicians involves treating illness and alleviating pain, the Buddha regarded the medical profession as one of great compassion. The Pali Canon contains significant amounts of material dealing with medicines, sicknesses, and healthcare. Buddhist monasteries have traditionally provided both medical and spiritual resources for lay people, served as health clinics, and offered hospice care for the dying. Ideals of compassion, no-self, and *ahimsa* guided the provision of medical services by monks and nuns.

Although there is no direct parallel to the framework of principles to guide biomedical ethics, concepts in Buddhism share some similarities to principles such as non-maleficence, beneficence, justice, and respect for autonomy. *Ahimsa* can be understood as a comprehensive take on the notion of non-maleficence, in that one must take care to avoid harming the patient, as well as to all living entities. Concern for family members, loved ones, the community, and even animals and nature, are included in the concept of *ahimsa*. Compassion can be understood as a type of beneficence. Both *ahimsa* and compassion are relevant to a sense of justice, or fairness. The idea of no-self, also, that encourages generosity and empathy is an important motivator for establishing justice. Respect for autonomy is perhaps the most challenging of the principles to derive from Buddhist teachings. The very idea of no-self, which on the one hand is useful for establishing the urgency of justice, on the other hand, contradicts the concept of autonomy. There is, in a sense, no individual to assert one's autonomy. At the same time, however, it is clear that the notion of the individual exists in Buddhism, and there is respect for allowing individuals to follow their own paths toward nirvana.

The progression of time in Buddhism follows a circular path. Life is not understood as having a finite beginning or end, but rather participates in cycles of reincarnation. Although the notion of reincarnation might suggest that life holds less value, the first of the Five Precepts in Buddhism states that one ought not to kill or injure living beings. The sanctity of life extends beyond humans to all living creatures, who are, too, reincarnated beings. At the same time, compassion and moderation are important principles that, along with the First Precept, help to develop a framework for resolving ethical dilemmas. Abortion, while understood as a violation of the First Precept, is permissible to save the life of the mother. In Japan, where abortion is legal, Buddhist rituals have been developed for women who have abortions. Abortion is viewed as a temporary return of a child to a liminal state until a more auspicious time, rather than as the outright killing of a fetus, as William LaFleur describes in his classic study of abortion in Japan, *Liquid Life: Abortion and Buddhism in Japan* (1992). In any case, compassion and moderation are also important Buddhist principles to apply to the case of abortion. Even though abortion is generally outlawed in Sri Lanka and was only recently legalized in Thailand, abortion is permissible to save the life of the mother, as well as in cases of rape out of compassion for the victim.

Buddhists view death as a transitory state; indeed, cycles of reincarnation mean that one dies many deaths before attaining nirvana. Although one's death should not be hastened, extraordinary measures that allow one to barely cling onto life are to be avoided. Attachment, which Buddhists believe lies at the root of suffering, can also manifest as an undue attachment to life. When death, traditionally defined as the cessation of heat, vitality, and sentience, approaches, one should accept it as an inevitability. Assisted suicide and euthanasia, or the deliberate hastening of death whether initiated by the patient or not, are problematic because they intentionally accelerate death, which does not necessarily end karmic suffering. However, as with abortion, compassion and moderation are also important principles to consider. If a patient is suffering from chronic pain, assisted suicide may be understood as an act of compassion.

Buddhist teachings do not necessarily oppose technologies such as stem cell research and cloning. However, such technologies are evaluated in terms of their intention and whether or not they will increase suffering. The intent of such research should not be financial gain, but to decrease human suffering. If people harness these technologies in an attempt to "recreate" a deceased loved one, for example, a concern might arise about excessive attachment. These technologies in and of themselves are not viewed as morally suspect, but the purpose and consequences of such technologies need to be analyzed through the lens of Buddhist teachings.

Judaism

In Jewish thought, scriptures, including the Tanakh, the Talmud, and *halacha*, or Jewish law, are among the most important resources for ethical analysis. Some of these texts are quite ancient, dating as early as the sixth century BCE. They do not anticipate many of the ethical dilemmas that have arisen because of contemporary advances in medical technologies. There are, however, a number of ideas and principles derived from these texts that can be applied when deliberating upon ethical problems from Jewish perspectives. Moreover, Jewish law remains an ever-evolving field. Organizations such as the Rabbinical Council of America, which represents Orthodox Judaism, and the Rabbinical Assembly's Committee on Jewish Laws and Standards, which represents Conservative Judaism, regularly convene to revisit older interpretations in order to meet contemporary concerns.

Within Judaism, the variety of beliefs and practices is reflected in views about controversial topics in biomedical ethics. Orthodox Jews are beholden to *halacha*, whereas Reform Jews and Conservative Jews will consider *halacha*, but are not as tied to Jewish law. Reform and Reconstructionist Jewish communities issue statements about various issues, including those related to biomedical ethics, but these are not binding. Rather, Reform, Reconstructionist, and other liberal Jews take these statements as guidelines. Individual members of the community are entrusted to determine for themselves what would be most appropriate for their personal situations.

Maimonides, the esteemed twelfth century rabbi and philosopher, was also a physician, and he believed that Jews were obligated to care for their physical health so that they would be able to carry out God's will. Failure to care for one's body meant the failure to carry out God's commandments. Doing what is necessary to remain healthy is tied to religious belief and practice. At the same time, this reasoning does not morally permit persons to undergo medical procedures that are elective and not medically necessary. Taking unnecessary risks that could endanger one's life is generally discouraged. There is, however, debate as what constitutes acceptable levels of risk.

Cosmetic surgery, for example, is discouraged by some rabbis, but considered acceptable by others.

Preserving life is an obligation for Jewish physicians. Immanuel Jakobovits, former Chief Rabbi of the United Kingdom who published the ground-breaking *Jewish Medical Ethics* (1975), argues that the physician has a duty to perform life-saving procedures, even when the duty contradicts the wishes of the patient. From this perspective, the responsibilities and beneficence of the physician override respect for a patient's autonomy. Because the human body and soul ultimately belong to God, patients ought not to forego ordinary life-preserving measures.

Jakobovits's application of Jewish teachings to medical ethics, however, is not unchallenged. Rabbi Moshe Feinstein, a prominent twentieth century scholar of Jewish law, disagrees with Jakobovits's views and argues in favor of patient autonomy over rabbinical judgments. Patients, Feinsten observes, know their bodies best, and are therefore in a better position than rabbis to determine how they might react to particular treatments. If suggested treatments could lead to great mental anguish, for example, patients may refuse them, even against the recommendation of their physicians.

Abortion is permissible to save the life of the mother up until the time of birth. Indeed, the *Mishna*, or Jewish oral law, does not permit a mother to sacrifice her own life for that of the fetus, if the choice must be made between saving her life and the life of the fetus. (According to the *Mishna*, half of the child must have emerged from the mother's body in order to be considered a separate and full human being.) Furthermore, acknowledging the mental health of a patient plays a role in determinations of the morality of abortion in Judaism. An abortion for the physical or mental health of the mother is considered legitimate by analogy to a mother acting in obligatory self-defense against a pursuer. In short, Jewish thought has generally deferred to the mother's opinion when deciding on the morality of abortion.

In pursuit of preserving and enhancing life, Judaism embraces medical technologies. The availability of human rationality to discover, create, and utilize God's creation to fight disease and minimize human suffering is a God-given gift. All three major branches of Judaism, for example, permit the use of in-vitro fertilization, even with the use of donor gametes. In Conservative and Orthodox Judaism, so long as the gestational mother is Jewish, the child is considered Jewish at birth. (In Reform Judaism, a child's Jewish identity is determined by having one Jewish parent, regardless of the parent's sex.) Sex selection is not morally permissible, but selection of the healthiest embryos for implantation is recommended.

At the end of life, the use of standard life-prolonging medicine and tech-nologies is broadly encouraged, but there is disagreement over the accepta-bility of shortening the end of life when a patient is suffering and there is no cure. For Jakobovits, killing a dying person was the equivalent of murder. At the same time, he does not advocate for the artificial prolonging of otherwise imminent death. Feinstein takes the view that a terminally ill patient has the right to refuse treatment, and that physicians should withhold treatment if the only purpose is to briefly extend life. Feinstein also eventually accepted the definition of the end of life as determined by brain death, rather than the traditional definition of heart and lung cessation. Currently, the widespread acceptance of brain death makes acceptable organ donation, which becomes possible when the brain has stopped functioning, but the organs are viable. Because of the widespread belief that the human body should remain intact for burial, rates of organ donation remain relatively low, but rabbinical authorities from the three major branches of Judaism agree that organ donation is morally permissible. Because saving human life, *pikuach nefesh*, is obligatory and considered the equivalent of saving the entire world, some rabbis have argued that organ donation is an ethical obligation.

Christianity

All Christians would agree on the sanctity of human life and the creation of humankind in God's image. The Christian Gospels depict Jesus as a healer of the sick and even a reviver of the dead. Likewise, the Acts of the Apostles portray several of the apostles as healers. Furthermore, according to tradition, the author of the Gospel of Luke was a physician. Traditions of caring for the sick and dying were practical expressions of Christian notions of virtue and charity from the beginning. Motivated by faith, Christians established infirmaries, hospices, and hospitals both at home and abroad.

Although Christian scripture, theology, and history suggest a common approach to medicine, there are few, if any, issues in biomedical ethics that garner universal consensus given the diversity within Christianity today. Topics ranging from abortion to euthanasia are met with intense disagreement within Christian communities. Moreover, members of particular Christian denominations may disagree both in theory and in practice with their own denomination's official teachings.

The Roman Catholic Church has issued a number of papal encyclicals—letters written by a pope to the Catholic community—on issues related to biomedical ethics. *Humanae Vitae* (1968), written by Pope Paul VI after the birth control pill became widely available, prohibits the use of artificial birth control even within marriage. *Evangelium Vitae* (1995), an encyclical penned by Pope John Paul II, instructs the faithful about the meaning of a culture of life that is rooted in the Bible and affirmed by church teachings through the ages. The encyclical maintains arguments against contraceptive use, describes abortion as an "unspeakable crime," and finds euthanasia "morally unacceptable." While Pope Francis encourages compassion for those who violate these teachings, he nonetheless reaffirms the immorality of contraceptives, abortion, and euthanasia.

Protestant and Orthodox Christian churches have taken different stances than the Catholic Church with regard to these issues. While all agree that abortion is a tragic choice for many women, Protestant churches do not necessarily equate abortion, particularly in the earliest stages of pregnancy, as having the same moral weight as murdering a human being. Moreover, unlike in Roman Catholic teaching, many Protestant Christians view abortion to save the life of the mother and in cases of rape or incest as morally acceptable. According to Roman Catholic teaching, the only morally permissible reason to terminate a pregnancy would be a situation that satisfies the "rule of double effect." This rule applies to actions having two effects, one good (e.g., saving the life of the mother) and one bad (e.g., causing the death of the fetus). The four conditions of the rule of double effect are: (1) The act must be morally good or neutral; (2) The actor may not intend the bad effect, but may permit it; (3) The act should directly cause the good effect; and (4) The good effect must be great enough to compensate for the bad effect. In a case of a pregnant women's treatment of uterine cancer, for example, removing the uterus would have two effects: directly eliminating the deadly cancer and killing the fetus. According to the rule of double effect, the unintended, but predictable demise of the fetus would be permissible because saving the woman's life through the hysterectomy meets these conditions. Aborting a fetus of a pregnant woman with hormonal breast cancer, however, would violate the criteria of the rule of double effect, even if ending the pregnancy would contribute to saving the woman's life. Because aborting the fetus would not be *directly* treating the breast cancer—unlike removing the cancerous uterus with a fetus—the rule of double effect is violated.

All methods of birth control aside from the rhythm method (i.e., avoiding intercourse while a woman is ovulating) are prohibited by the Roman Catholic Church. In practice, however, a large majority of Catholics admit to having used birth control. The Catholic prohibition against birth control stands in stark contrast to the major Protestant denominations' views on birth control. Since 1930, with a resolution passed at the Lambeth Conference of the Anglican Church that permitted married couples to use contraceptives, a number of Protestant denominations have allowed birth control. The Episcopal, Methodist, and Presbyterian (PCUSA) churches, for example, all permit the use of contraceptives. Many evangelical denominations discourage the use of birth control, but do not explicitly prohibit its use. The Southern Baptist Convention (SBC) permits birth control, but discourages the distribution of contraceptives to minors. The Coptic Church and some Eastern Orthodox sects also allow married couples to use contraceptives.

With regard to end-of-life issues, again the Roman Catholic Church takes the stance that intentionally ending a person's life is not permissible unless it meets the criteria of the rule of double effect. Euthanasia and physician-assisted suicide are, according to Catholic teaching, "intrinsically evil." Most Protestant churches also oppose euthanasia and physician assisted suicide, but agree that palliative care that results in the death of a suffering patient may be done compassionately and with respect to the patient's wishes. With the passage of laws such as Oregon's 1997 Death with Dignity Act, individual leaders within Protestant denominations have cautiously supported such legislation. This tentative approach to euthanasia and physician-assisted suicide in Protestant denominations is found also with regard to technologies such as cloning and stem cell research. The Catholic Church is also open to stem cell research, as long as it does not involve the destruction of human embryos.

Islam

With nearly two billion adherents, constituting a quarter of the world's population, Islam displays much of the diversity concerning biomedical ethics as is found in other world religions. The variety of cultures, traditions, and practices embedded within the tradition guarantees a multitude of views about important issues. Moreover, the lack of a central authority within Islam and the historical acceptability of multiple legal schools of thought contribute to the range of views on topics in biomedical ethics. Although practicing Muslims agree on the centrality of the Qur'an and the virtue of Mohammad, interpretations of the Qur'an and the example of the prophet differ.

Muslim jurists have long discussed and disagreed over issues relevant to biomedical ethics, but the development of new medical technologies has resulted in more conversations about the application of Islamic ideas and principles to these inventions. Because many of these developments have come to Muslim-majority countries from North America and Western Europe, there is caution about how this knowledge and technology should be transferred to cultures that may hold different priorities. Medical technologies that use pigs, for example, are controversial in some Muslim communities. Because many Muslim-majority countries are also poor, the question of access to expensive new technologies takes on a greater significance than in wealthier countries where such technologies may be widely available. In addition to questions arising from new technologies and advances in medicine, commonly accepted American principles of biomedical ethics, such as respect for autonomy, can face significant cultural barriers in Muslim-majority countries where traditional paternalistic norms hold strong.

Islamic biomedical ethics consists of a mix of principles: Muslim social ethics, theology, and *sharia*. The application of these multiple sources to issues such as abortion, reproductive technologies, and end-of-life decisions results in ways of thinking through these difficult topics that can provide guidance, even if not always concrete decisions. As Abdulaziz Sachedina notes, in Muslim societies "praxis precedes search for principles and rules."[1] In other words, although fatwas and legal rulings may prohibit or require certain practices, individual circumstances are also considered and deviations from the generally recommended norm are sometimes permitted in practice. For example, the use of pig tissue in a life-saving medical procedure would be permissible because saving human life takes precedence over the avoidance of consuming pork.

When examining Muslim teachings about abortion, one quickly discovers that the practice is discouraged. However, exemptions can be made based upon individual circumstances. The Qur'an itself does not specifically mention abortion, and so prohibitions against the practice are based on interpretations of when "ensoulment" of a fetus occurs. In the Sura al-Mu'minun ("The Believers"), the stages of embryonic development are described:

> And certainly did We create man from an extract of clay. Then We placed him as a drop of sperm, firmly fixed. Then We made the sperm into a clot of congealed blood, and of that clot We made an embryo; then We made out of that lump, bones, and clothed the bones with flesh. Then We developed another creation out of it. So blessed is God, the best of Creators.
>
> Qur'an 23: 12–14

Based on this passage, Muslim scholars have claimed that the time of conception to ensoulment lasts between 40 and 120 days, depending upon one's interpretation of the sura. As the pregnancy continues, abortion becomes increasingly problematic. Whereas abortion prior to ensoulment is discouraged, abortion in the later stages of pregnancy would be impermissible except to save the life of the mother. Prohibitions against female infanticide and the killing of children more generally are also important considerations when weighing the ethics of abortion, especially as medical technologies enable parents to pursue sex-selective abortions. Female infanticide was prevalent in pre-Islamic Arabia, and a distinctive teaching of Islam in the early period was to discourage the practice. Perhaps as a result, there appears to be little evidence in Muslim-majority countries of the practice of sex-selective abortions.

During the 1994 Cairo Population Conference, Muslims initially appeared to ally with Roman Catholics in staunch opposition to abortion. As the conference progressed, however, it became clear that Muslims were unwilling to oppose abortion under virtually all circumstances. Exceptions should be made to save the life of the mother, for example, or in cases where an infant would be born with extreme medical conditions incompatible with life.

Muslims treat the end of life as with the beginning of life with a presumption toward preservation. The Qur'an states that only God should determine the end of one's life: "And no person can ever die except by Allah's leave and at an appointed term" (Qur'an 3:145). With the exception of ending life except for "the course of justice" (Qur'an 17:33), persons are not to cut short their natural life spans. This does not mean that Muslims are obligated to use extraordinary means to prolong life, but rather that persons should be allowed to die without attempting procedures that will only temporarily extend their lives. Patients in persistent vegetative states do not need to be maintained utilizing heroic efforts, as such interventions would be considered merely a temporary delay of inevitable death.

The Qur'an describes death as the point at which the body begins to decay into dust and bones. The Qur'an also recognizes death as a process, including the time of departure of the soul from the body: "The Angel of Death, put in charge of you, will take your soul: then you shall be brought back to your Lord" (Qur'an 32:11). Today, however, a number of Muslim organizations, including the Muslim World League, the Organization of International Cooperation—Islamic Fiqh Academy, and the Islamic Medical Association of North America, among others, accept brain death as a true definition of death. With the acceptance of brain death, vital organs can be kept viable using artificial means and then donated. This acceptance of brain death by several major organizations, however, is not uncontested. There remains uncertainty and debate over the measuring of whole brain death, as opposed to brain stem death, and the standards used to determine brain death. Muslims have traditionally used a heart-and-lung definition of death, noting death as the time when a person stops breathing and the heart stops beating. Theologically, there is no clarity as to the location of the soul in the body, and as such the death of the whole human body becomes the standard for death. Relying upon the death of just one organ of the body is deemed insufficient to determine the loss of the soul from a person.

With regard to the most recent technological developments, including forms of artificial reproductive technologies, stem cell research, and cloning, Sunni Muslim authorities tend to restrict technologies such that no third parties to a married hetero-sexual couple can donate a gamete. The mother's egg may be fertilized in vitro using her husband's sperm, but not donated sperm. Surrogacy is not permitted, as the woman who gives birth to a baby is considered the mother. In Iran, which is a Shi'ite country, surrogacy is allowed. Furthermore, the Islamic government has given permission to allow the donation of gametes. Since 1999, when the Ayatollah Khamenei issued a fatwa allowing third-party sperm and egg donation to increase the nation's birth rate, Iran has become a beacon for Muslims, both Sunni and Shi'a, who seek reproductive assistance.

Human cloning and stem-cell research have raised concerns among Muslims similar to those regarding IVF in that the creation of a human being outside of a traditional heterosexual marriage is suspect. There are addition-ally concerns about the degradation of the family structure and the commod-ification of children. However, because the pursuit of scientific knowledge remains an important Islamic value, research that may lead to cloning will likely not be stopped.

Case Study: Buddhist Views on CRISPR and Gene Editing

The 2020 Nobel Prize in Chemistry was awarded to Emmanuelle Charpentier and Jennifer Doudna for their work in gene editing. Charpentier and Doudna developed a highly precise and efficient method for changing genes using CRISPR (Clustered Regularly Interspaced Short Palindromic Repeat), which is modeled from the "genetic scissors" used by bacteria to disable invading viruses. CRISPR enables scientists to "cut" sections of the DNA of other organisms, including humans, and replace the removed DNA with another set of DNA. This gene editing technology makes possible cures for genetic diseases, improvement of crops to withstand destructive conditions, and the alteration of sperm, eggs, and embryos. By altering germ-lines and thereby affecting inheritable traits, CRISPR has the potential to change humanity for generations.

The announcement of the Nobel Prize was preceded in 2018 by the startling news that a Chinese scientist, He Jiankui, had created the world's first gene-edited babies. He and two colleagues altered genes in three human embryos and then implanted them into two women. The edits He introduced make the children less susceptible to HIV-infection by altering the DNA of a protein that would normally allow the virus to enter human immune cells. But He violated ethical standards. He placed children at risk by using untested technology. It remains to be seen what the future holds for the children, or what the consequences for future generations borne out of these children will be. Given that there was little risk that the children would have contracted HIV, the potential harm associated with He's experiment far outweighed any benefit accrued by the children.

Upon the announcement of the CRISPR babies, scientists around the world expressed outrage at the unethical use of gene editing technology. In addition to using potentially dangerous technology on children, He also failed to obtain adequate informed consent from the parents. Gene editing of embryos is illegal in many countries, including the United States and Great Britain, because of its potentially devastating and uncontrollable consequences, both intended and unintended. There are currently no international bodies that have enforcement mechanisms to stop the unethical use of gene editing technology.

Gene editing of somatic stem cells holds great promise in curing inherited diseases. Unlike edited germline cells, such as sperm and egg cells, edited somatic stem cells do not pass changes in DNA onto future generations. The risks, therefore, of somatic stem cell gene editing are limited to the patient only. In 2019, Victoria Gray, who suffers from sickle cell anemia, was the first person in the United States to receive treatment for a genetic disease using CRISPR. Years after her treatment, Gray continues to produce cells that lack the gene for sickle cell anemia, and she no longer suffers from the debilitating pain caused by the disease. Since Gray, nine other patients have been successfully treated for genetic diseases with CRISPR, and they all appear to be doing well.

Because CRISPR is new and so little research has been conducted using its technology, particularly on human embryos and germ cells, religious authorities have not produced extensive statements about gene editing. Religious groups and scholars, however, have commented on the use of genetic modification of germlines for other organisms, including plants. Generally, the Abrahamic traditions have tended to express caution, if not outright condemnation, of germline editing. Until the possibility exists for experimentation without "disproportionate risks especially in the first experimental stage, such as the huge loss of embryos and the incidence of mishaps," few, if any, Jewish, Christian, or Muslims religious institutions would likely endorse such research.[2]

However, in religious traditions that tend to consider life in a non-linear way but in terms of cycles, gene editing of human germline cells and embryos may be considered ethically permissible. Professor Yong Moon of Seoul National University, in discussing human cloning, describes the research as "a different way of thinking about the recycling of life…. It's a Buddhist way of thinking." According to Buddhist teachings, souls can re-incarnate into any type of living being as a result of accumulated or lost karma, so clones and genetically modified creatures are understood as situated on circular path of reincarnation rather than as life irreversibly ended. Moreover, for many Buddhists, the pursuit of scientific knowledge, particularly when such knowledge can eliminate human suffering, is highly laudable.

Not all Buddhists would agree with Moon and those open to research on human embryos. Although scientists highly value human embryonic stem cells because of their pluripotency, or ability to form into any cell in the human body, for some Buddhists, the principle of *ahimsa* is an overriding concern. From this perspective, embryos are still lifeforms deserving of respect even if not understood as full human beings. It should also be noted that the suffering that could arise during the process of obtaining scientific knowledge might not justify the possibility of a cure for debilitating genetic diseases. The destruction of thousands, if not millions, of human embryos even in the service of medical science may violate strong norms against killing.

Questions:

1   How might the research of He Jiankui be interpreted through the lens of Buddhist teachings?
2   How would suffering be quantified or measured such that the potential cure of genetic diseases could be compared to the destruction of human embryos or risks of human research subjects?
3   Given the diversity of Buddhist thought, should Buddhists nonetheless attempt find common ground with regard to establishing guidelines about gene editing of human germlines? Why or why not?

Notes

1   Sachedina, 8.
2   International Theological Commission.

Bibliography

Abdul-Mutakabbir, Jacinda C., Samuel Casey, Veatrice Jews, Andrea King, Kelvin Simmons, Michael D. Hogue, Juan Carlos Belliard, Ricardo Peverini, and Jennifer Veltman. "A Three-Tiered Approach to Address Barriers to COVID-19 Vaccine Delivery in the Black Community." *The Lancet Global Health* 9:6 (2021), e749–50.

Alimi, Toni, Elizabeth L. Antus, Alda Balthrop-Lewis, James F. Childress, Shannon Dunn, Ronald M. Green, Eric Gregory, et al. "COVID-19 and Religious Ethics." *Journal of Religious Ethics* 48:3 (2020), 349–87.

Beauchamp, Tom L., and James F. Childress. *Principles of Biomedical Ethics*. 8th ed. New York: Oxford University Press, 2019.

Bouhassira, E. (2015). "Buddhism," *Sage Encyclopedia of Stem Cell Research*, 160–62. https://www-doi-org.proxygw.wrlc.org/10.4135/9781483347660.n61.

Brockopp, Jonathan E. *Islamic Ethics of Life: Abortion, War, and Euthanasia*. Columbia: University of South Carolina Press, 2003.

Brockopp, Jonathan E. "Islam and Bioethics: Beyond Abortion and Euthanasia." *Journal of Religious Ethics* 36:1 (2008), 3–12.

Brockopp, Jonathan E., and Eich Thomas. *Muslim Medical Ethics: From Theory to Practice*. Columbia: University of South Carolina Press, 2008.

Cahill, Lisa Sowle. *Sex, Gender, and Christian Ethics*. Cambridge: Cambridge University Press, 1996.

Chuan, Voo Teck, and G. Own Schaefer. "Research in Research-Poor Countries," *Hastings Center Bioethics Briefings* (September 23, 2015) https://www.thehastingscenter.org/briefingbook/multinational-research/ (accessed 22 July 2021).

Crawford, S. Cromwell. *Hindu Bioethics for the Twenty-First Century*. Albany: State University of New York Press, 2003.

Doudna, Jennifer, Interview with Kara Swisher. "Sway." *New York Times*. https://www.nytimes.com/2020/10/22/opinion/sway-kara-swisher-jennifer-doudna.html?showTranscript=1.

Engelhardt, H. Tristram. *The Foundations of Christian Bioethics*. Lisse: Swets & Zeitlinger, 2000.

Fletcher, Joseph F. *Morals and Medicine: The Moral Problems of the Patient's Right to Know the Truth*. Princeton, NJ: Princeton University Press, 2015 (1954).

International Theological Commission, "Communion and Stewardship: Human Persons Created in the Image of God," https://www.vatican.va/roman_curia/congregations/cfaith/cti_documents/rc_con_cfaith_doc_20040723_communion-stewardship_en.html#_edn1.

Jakobovits, Immanuel. *Jewish Medical Ethics: A Comparative and Historical Study of the Jewish Religious Attitude to Medicine and Its Practice*. 2nd ed. New York: Bloch Publishing Co., 1975.

John Paul II. *Evangelium Vitae*. Washington, DC: United States Catholic Conference, 1995.

Jones, James H. *Bad Blood: The Tuskegee Syphilis Experiment*. London: Collier Macmillan Publishers, 1981.

Jotkowitz, Alan. "The Seminal Contribution of Rabbi Moshe Feinstein to the Development of Modern Jewish Medical Ethics." *Journal of Religious Ethics* 42:2 (2014), 285–309.

Keown, Damien. *Buddhism and Bioethics*. Basingstoke: Palgrave, 2001.

LaFleur, William R. *Liquid Life: Abortion and Buddhism in Japan*. Princeton, NJ: Princeton University Press, 1992.

Lander, Eric S., Françoise Baylis, Feng Zhang, Emmanuelle Charpentier, Paul Berg, Catherine Bourgain, Bärbel Friedrich, et al. "Adopt a Moratorium on Heritable Genome Editing." *Nature* 567:7747 (2019), 165–68.

Mackler, Aaron L. *Introduction to Jewish and Catholic Bioethics: A Comparative Analysis*. Washington, DC: Georgetown University Press, 2003.

Moaveni, Azadeh. "The Islamic Republic of Baby-Making." *Foreign Policy*, 204 (2014), 26–29.

Moazam, Farhat. *Bioethics and Organ Transplantation in a Muslim Society: A Study in Culture, Ethnography, and Religion*. Bloomington: Indiana University Press, 2006.

Ndugga, Nambi, Olivia Pham, et al., "Latest Data on COVID-19 Vaccinations by Race/Ethnicity," Kaiser Family Foundation (July 9, 2021) https://www.kff.org/coronavirus-covid-19/issue-brief/latest-data-on-covid-19-vaccinations-race-ethnicity/.

Messikomer, Carla M., Renée C. Fox, and Judith P. Swazey. "The Presence and Influence of Religion in American Bioethics." *Perspectives in Biology and Medicine* 44:4 (2001), 485–508.

Mustafa, Yassar. "Islam and the Four Principles of Medical Ethics." *Journal of Medical Ethics* 40:7 (2014), 479–83.

National Bioethics Advisory Commission (NBAC). *Cloning Human Beings: Report and Recommendations*. Rockville, MD: National Bioethics Advisory Commission, 1997.

National Bioethics Advisory Commission (NBAC). *Ethical Issues in Human Stem Cell Research: Report and Recommendations*. Rockville, MD: National Bioethics Advisory Commission, 1999.

Paul VI, and Marc Caligari. *Humanae Vitae: Encyclical Letter of His Holiness Pope Paul VI, On the Regulation of Births*. San Francisco, CA: Ignatius Press, 1983.

Pew Research Center. "Religious Groups' Views on End-of-Life Issues." November 21, 2013. https://www.pewforum.org/2013/11/21/religious-groups-views-on-end-of-life-issues/ (accessed June 28, 2022).

Prograis, Lawrence, and Edmund D. Pellegrino. *African American Bioethics: Culture, Race, and Identity.* Washington, DC: Georgetown University Press, 2007.

Religious Coalition for Reproductive Choice. https://rcrc.org/jewish/ (accessed July 20, 2021).

Sachedina, Abdulaziz. *Islamic Biomedical Ethics: Principles and Application.* Oxford: Oxford University Press, 2009.

Sen, Amartya. "More Than 100 Million Women are Missing." *New York Review of Books* 37:20 (1990), 61–66.

Taylor, Carol, and Roberto Dell'Oro. *Health and Human Flourishing: Religion, Medicine, and Moral Anthropology* Washington, DC: Georgetown University Press, 2006.

Whitehead, Andrew, and Samuel Perry. "How Culture Wars Delay Herd Immunity: Christian Nationalism and Anti-Vaccine Attitudes." *Socius: Sociological Research for a Dynamic World* 6 (2020). https://doi.org/10.1177/2378023120977727.

Wilson, Duncan. "What Can History Do for Bioethics?" *Bioethics* 27:4 (2013), 215–23.

Chapter 3

Climate Change and the Environment

I was already in college in the early 1990s when I received my first reusable water bottle. No one I knew owned an electric or even hybrid car. Growing up, our trash was not sorted into recyclables and non-recyclables. Today, even toddlers carry reusable water bottles to preschool. Many car buyers are seeking hybrid and electric vehicles. Many municipalities now require households to divide trash and recyclables, and a few also offer composting. When thinking through the impact of climate change with my undergraduate students, a generational divide clearly exists between the way those of my generation and members of Generation Z (those born in 1997 onward) approach the environment. Given the growing urgency of climate change over the last few decades, it is not surprising that this topic, which is literally existential in nature, has invoked religious reflection about humanity's responsibility for creation.

Every summer for the last few years, massive wildfires, record-setting heat waves, and deadly floods have made news headlines. Wildfires rage in California and Australia, hurricanes devastate Caribbean islands, and droughts plague India and South Africa. All reputable scientific data indicate that carbon emissions resulting from our burning of fossil fuels have created a global environmental crisis that will continue to worsen unless humanity takes drastic measures. Given the enormity of the problem, we cannot rely solely on scientific and manufacturing advances to stop the environmental crisis. In order to make the profound changes in both outlook and lifestyle to save our planet, we need to reconsider our ethical and religious understanding of humanity's relationship to the natural world. In re-framing our relationship to the environment, we commit ourselves to the protection of the environment not just for the sake of future human generations, but out of a sense of moral and religious obligation. In other words, we will need to understand natural resources as not merely for human exploitation, but as a part of our world that has moral standing. As such, their use demands careful consideration, even if it may be justifiable.

Currently, many of us do not feel a moral or religious imperative to make the kinds of changes necessary to reduce our impact on the environment.

DOI: 10.4324/9781003350637-4

A majority of us in the United States, for example, cannot imagine living without cars or eating meat, even though our dependence upon cars and the consumption of meat contribute significantly to carbon emissions. We are addicted to fossil fuels for the conveniences and comforts that they provide, to the acquisition of unnecessary material goods, and to the taste of beef, chicken, and pork. We enjoy driving and riding in comfortable vehicles that take us from place to place without having to wait for public transportation, if it even exists; we like our toasty homes in the cold winter and cool air-conditioning in the heat of summer; we enjoy the cheap thrill of "fast-fashion" with its on-trend, disposable clothes and accessories. These human pleasures, however, come at a cost that is all too easy to ignore. The price that we pay for these conveniences will come due with the next generation.

Arguably the greatest crisis facing humanity in the decades to come is climate change. Due to massive amounts of human-made carbon emissions in the atmosphere, global temperatures are rising. The elevation of global temperatures means that glaciers are melting at unprecedented rates, resulting in the elevation of sea temperatures and water levels. The rise in temperatures contributes to the intensification of hurricanes and typhoons, massive flooding, and the death of millions of animals and plants sensitive to these temperature fluctuations. Moreover, the changes in climate contribute to drought conditions and raging infernos. As Greta Thunberg, the young activist who has become the international face of climate change protest, implores, "our house is on fire!"

Although the news about climate change is undeniably bleak, glimmers of hope shine through. The activism of young people around the world has sparked a global movement that pressures government leaders and industry titans to take action. Some governments are taking serious measures to prevent reaching the 1.5°C average global temperature increase that the Intergovernmental Panel on Climate Change finds to be the tipping point for extreme temperature changes in many regions of the world. People are also more and more willing to adopt technologies that reduce our reliance upon fossil fuels and to take advantage of cleaner sources of energy such as the sun and wind. Along these lines, restaurants and food manufacturers are successfully selling plant-based sources of protein, which are making their way into mainstream markets. The motto of reduce-reuse-recycle is being taken seriously by many, especially children who have grown up with an ethos of environmentalism.

Perhaps most intriguing is how the environmental crisis has led to alliances between groups and communities that would not normally work together for political purposes. World religions all have something to say about our environment and the relationship that we humans have to other forms of life. Whether in scripture, practice, or tradition, Hinduism, Buddhism, Judaism, Christianity, and Islam have multiple resources to guide believers with regard to their attitudes toward and treatment of plants and animals. Jains advocate a way of living that prevents the suffering and death of all living beings. Native American and Indigenous religious traditions offer a wealth of knowledge for understanding how to sustain the natural environment. Because of our mutual concern over our shared home, people of different religious traditions find common ground when it comes to the environmental crisis. Unlike some other ethical issues, the future of our environment appears to be a shared interest among leaders of multiple religious traditions.

To be sure, there are some skeptics who deny the gravity of the environmental crisis or the role that humans have in it. Fewer than a third of American evangelical Christians believe that human activity is the cause of global warming and more than a third believe that there is no solid evidence of global warming, according to polls taken by the Pew Research Center. The scientific consensus, however, is clear. If humans do not drastically reduce their output of carbon emissions, then our planet will suffer severe consequences.

The role of the scholar of religious ethics is not to accept without question the claims of religious believers. We are not simply conduits of assertions made by followers of religious traditions. We are scholars who take seriously the quality of research and therefore distinguish between facts that have the backing of peer-reviews and subjective statements that are made to support ideological views. The scientific consensus is clear that humans have caused climate change and that the warming of the earth's atmosphere will lead to catastrophic events. In making normative claims about how religious believers might approach the environmental crisis, the scholar of religious ethics utilizes the most accurate facts about climate change that are available. Doing ethics responsibly requires distinguishing between facts and ideological views.

Given this, what resources do believers from different religious traditions have to understand and to act in the face of the environmental crisis? Although religious traditions differ with regard to how directly texts, traditions, and teachings address the human relationship to nature, they invariably discuss the proper attitudes we must have toward the environment and other living creatures. As one might expect, believers have interpreted these resources differently and, even within the same tradition, might differ dramatically with regard to these interpretations. In general, however, humans are to treat the natural world with respect and thoughtfulness. There is a sense that we are all in this together—whether because we are all part of God's creation or because we are connected by some force that transcends space and time—and therefore our actions ought to reflect this connectedness.

On the Moral Status of Nature and Non-Human Animals

Because the major religious traditions were established hundreds, if not thousands, of years before the era of global warming, the founding texts and teachings that address the environment do not directly discuss issues of climate change. Many religious believers therefore may not ascribe moral status to non-humans. The impact of climate change, however, lends an urgency to caring for the planet, if not for the animals and plants that inhabit it. There is moreover acknowledgment among some religious adherents that the natural world and non-human animals have some moral status, even if they do not stand as moral equals to human beings. This is important because if the natural world and non-human animals have moral status independent of human beings, then human beings have an obligation to care for the natural world and other living creatures for their own sake, rather than merely as objects for human use and exploitation. According to this perspective, humans may benefit from the natural world and from animals, but we are not to abuse or destroy them unnecessarily, to satisfy mere whims, or simply because we can. Religious teachings strongly suggest that might does not make right when it comes to human dominion over plants and animals.

When we consume meats from factory farms, drink water out of single-use plastic bottles, or buy clothing that we will only wear a few times before tossing, we are making choices that reflect our priorities. These choices suggest that too many of us are placing convenience over conscience. We may know intellectually that these choices have a negative impact upon animals and the environment, but our desires for consumption override scientifically informed and moral concerns. Perhaps this is why we find that religious believers acknowledge the value of the natural world, but nonetheless do not necessarily translate those beliefs into environmentally sound practices.

Indigenous Traditions

The term "Indigenous" attempts to unite nearly 400 million people across more than 70 countries under one umbrella category. Given this tremendous diversity, the Indigenous label fails to capture the variety of beliefs and practices found among these groups of people. Some Indigenous communities worship deities, while others are not at all religious or spiritual. Legal definitions of Indigenous further complicate matters because such definitions have changed over time and vary from country to country. In the United States, for example, there are over 570 legally recognized Indian tribes that have been given this designation through acts of Congress, federal petition, or a court decision. In other countries, Indigenous groups are so defined based upon factors such as genetic relations, historical evidence, or culture and lifestyle. Despite these differences, Indigenous communities generally agree that both genealogy and geography are important factors in determining membership to a particular Indigenous group. That is, membership is determined by kinship with a community that has historically inhabited a particular location.

Because Indigenous tribes understand their peoples as inextricably tied to the specific lands in which they reside, their traditions contain a wealth of knowledge about specific geographies, their climates, and native plants and animals. Often passed along through storytelling, knowledge about the natural world and non-human animals is handed down from one generation to the next through narratives about creation, animals, and natural phenomenon. In addition, elders may teach children skills such as sustainable methods of hunting and farming so that resources are available for future generations.

Imbued in Indigenous traditions is an understanding of the relationship between humans, animals, and the environment as familial. Trees, rivers, mountains, and animals, for example, may be likened to extended members of the family. Natural phenomenon may be anthropomorphized and thought of in terms that emphasize human qualities. In *Braiding Sweetgrass* (2013), Robin Wall Kimmerer, a biologist and member of the Citizen Potawatomi Nation, describes plants such as sweetgrass and wild strawberries not only with their scientific names, but through Indigenous creation stories. Stories featuring a figure called "Skywoman" and her daughter about the origins of sweetgrass and strawberries lend a human-like face to the natural world beyond their existence as mere plants. Likewise, Kimmerer's account of the "Three Sisters"—corn, beans, and squash—relays in anthropomorphic terms the symbiotic relationship among the three crops when planted together. Not only do the three plant foods grow more vigorously when planted next to each other rather than separately, but when planted together, nitrogen in the soil is replenished and ready for another season of growth.

In the United States, several Indigenous groups have been at the forefront of protests against developments that will alter sacred spaces, pose threats to the health of people, and destroy the natural environment. Native Hawaiians have been protesting the construction of a massive telescope on Mauna Kea, a dormant volcano on the island of Hawaii that is the most sacred mountain in the island chain. In the Dakotas, members of the Standing Rock Sioux tribe have been protesting the Dakota Access Pipeline, which would run under Lake Oahe, a reservoir of the Missouri River. Tribal members argue that the pipeline, which would transport oil from North Dakota, through South Dakota, and into Iowa and Illinois, disturbs scared burial grounds and poses an environmental hazard to their water supply. In Alaska, the Tlingit, Haida, and Tsimshian peoples successfully protested to keep the 2001 National Roadless Rule for the Tongass National Forest. The repeal of the Roadless Rule, which was proposed under the Trump administration, would have resulted in additional clear-cutting of old-growth trees to build logging roads. Indigenous tribes of the forest rely upon the Tongass National Forest for traditional hunting and fishing practices, which would be threatened by further development.

There is some controversy as to whether the adoption of Indigenous knowledge about the environment by non-Indigenous groups is appropriate, given the painful history of colonization during which Europeans destroyed Indigenous lands, cultures and traditions, and lives. On the one hand, given that all of humanity is bound together in the face of environmental catastrophe, knowledge that could save us—all of us, whether Indigenous or not—should be freely shared. On the other hand, Indigenous wisdom is often romanticized and not recognized as specific to particular geographic contexts and ways of life. As such, Indigenous wisdom may not be helpful unless the particularity of traditions is acknowledged.

Hinduism

Traditional Hindu thought does not directly address ecological problems. Hindu texts, however, are rife with imagery and teachings that suggest that Hindu concepts might be applied to advance ecological ethics.

As Christopher G. Framarin notes, most scholars of Hinduism find highly plausible the claim that plants and animals have moral standing.[1] Whether these scholars find the source of these claims in the *Bhagavad Gita*, concept of *brahman* (ultimate or supreme reality), the idea of *atman* (soul), or in the notion of reincarnation, the clear majority concludes that Hinduism advocates for the moral worth of the natural world independent of human beings.

We ought, however, not to confuse appreciation of the natural world in Hindu traditions with ecologically minded action. Indeed, there is scant evidence that beliefs about nature in Hinduism translate directly into environmental practice. Religious "reverence for nature does not always lead to the enactment of ecologically sound behaviors."[2] There is sometimes the temptation to romanticize Asian religious traditions as being at one with nature.

Buddhism

When looking at various important principles and practices in Buddhist traditions, concepts such as *ahimsa* (no harm) and the notion of interconnectedness appear to serve as potential sources of guidance for environmental ethics. The prominence of the concept of *ahimsa* in Buddhist thought, for example, may translate into a profound awareness of the health of the environment as necessary to sustaining life. Found also in Hinduism and Jainism, *ahimsa* may lead to action and behavior that protect not just human life, but also animal life and natural resources. The karmic consequences of harming life might further deter violence toward animals. The belief that all of nature is bound in *samsara* (cycles of reincarnation) imbues in the practitioner a sense of the equality of all beings. The concept of interconnectedness also helps to further environmental ethics because it encourages practitioners to consider the relationship between humankind and non-human life. If humans have an ethical responsibility to consider themselves as intrinsically related to other life, then the goal of reducing suffering ought to apply not just to oneself and other humans, but to any being. Other prominent ideas in Buddhism, such as compassion, might also suggest a nurturing attitude toward non-human beings. In Shinto traditions, found in Japan, animist influences would be helpful in constructing a world view that acknowledges the moral standing of non-humans.

Such ideas, while affirming, chronologically precede the concerns and values of contemporary environmentalists. Buddhist believers and practitioners adopt ideas from the past, but it would be incorrect to assume that the Buddha and notable monks from Buddhism's formative years were concerned about environmental degradation, climate change, or animal rights. While there are certain aspects to Buddhists' concerns that support an environmental ethic, in general such claims tend to be romanticized. The idea, for example, that Buddhists eschew eating meat out of concern for the suffering of animals slaughtered for human consumption ignores the fact that Theravada Buddhist monks do, in fact, consume meat given to them as alms so long as the animal consumed was not slaughtered for the sole purpose of feeding them. From the perspective of the monks, to refuse the food of alms-givers would be to deny the good karma acquired by the donation of food. The notion of reincarnation, which might encourage kindness toward animals, might also at the same time invite scorn because animals may be seen as souls that have moved further away from the goal of nirvana due to bad karma.

As with all religious traditions that claim large numbers of followers across geographical space and through time, the diversity within Buddhism means that in practice Buddhists today do not share uniform attitudes toward the environment.

Jainism

Because Jains believe that the soul (*jiva*) and matter (*ajiva*) are inextricably intertwined, bodies become the means by which humans are spiritually purified. Observant Jains, whether householders or ascetics, undertake some form of ascetic practice as part of their faith. Due to their worldly activities, householders are necessarily influenced by karma. Working, preparing food, and raising children are all activities that increase negative karma. However, householders can limit negative karma by adopting practices that are compatible with working and family life, such as fasting, maintaining a simple lifestyle, and refraining from excessive or luxurious activities.

Because the primary concept that drives religious practice among Jains is *ahimsa*, Jainism offers ways of thinking about environmental harm that are rooted in belief. Jains are well known for their concern for the lives of even the smallest of insects, which leads ascetics to brush the ground with a broom ahead of their footfall and to avoid even the boiling of water for cooking, which might result in the inadvertent death of microscopic forms of life. With this concern about non-human life—even that which the human eye cannot observe—Jainism lends itself to environmentally sensitive ethical actions and behaviors.

Judaism

The accounts of creation in Genesis, the first book the Torah, indicate that the natural world, plants, animals, and humans are all the product of God. Moreover, humans have been entrusted as stewards of creation. Genesis 1:26 states:

> Then God said, 'Let us make humankind in our image, according to our likeness; and let them have dominion over the fish of the sea, and over the birds of the air, and over the cattle, and over all the wild animals of the earth, and over every creeping thing that creeps upon the earth.'

God then instructs humankind to

> Be fruitful and multiply, and fill the earth and subdue it; and have dominion over the fish of the sea and over the birds of the air and over every living thing that moves upon the earth. . . . See, I have given you every plant yielding seed that is upon the face of all the earth, and every tree with seed in its fruit; you shall have them for food. And to every beast of the earth, and to every bird of the air, and to everything that creeps on the earth, everything that has the breath of life, I have given every green plant for food.
>
> Genesis 1:28–30

In this passage, God tells humankind, which is made in God's image, to have "dominion" over living things, animals and plants, and to use plants for food. This account of Genesis also suggests, according to one interpretation, that humans and animals were to eat only plants, and not flesh. This section of the Torah thus seems to offer resources that advocate for a plant-based, animal-friendly diet. After the flood, however, Genesis takes a different stance with regard to what is available for food: "Every moving thing that lives shall be food for you; and just as I gave you the green plants, I give you everything" (Genesis 9:3). Here, "moving thing" suggests that animals are available for human consumption along with "green plants."

Later in the Torah, in Leviticus, regulations with regard to land and animal use emerge. In what could be construed as a land ethic, the Torah regulates the use of land for crops and insists that land, like humans, be allowed to rest or lie fallow for a Sabbath year. Leviticus mandates that fruit-bearing trees be allowed to mature for three years before being harvested (19:23–25). These passages indicate an ethic by which humans are reminded that the land is God's creation and deserving of respect.

Generally, however, Jewish scripture indicates that meat-eating was assumed, and that the consumption of meats—and wine—was even considered celebratory. In fact, the avoidance of meat was a sign of mourning. Kosher dietary laws state that meat-eating is acceptable for Jews with the exception of certain types of animals, such as pigs and shellfish, but there is a sense that animals ought not to be taken for granted. Kosher laws dictate that animals to be consumed be raised and slaughtered in a humane way that minimizes their pain.

Leviticus and Deuteronomy require that Jews care for animals. Indeed, in Exodus, the Hebrews are told that the Sabbath day of rest applies not just to humans, but to animals as well. Animals that are used for labor should be adequately fed and newborn animals are not to be removed from their mothers. Maimonides (1138–1204), the most influential Jewish scholar of the medieval period, argues that the maternal-child bond exists in animals, just as it does in humans, and to kill an animal-child in front of its mother is unnecessarily cruel.

While recognizing God's creation as good, Judaism does permit humans to manipulate and use the environment to benefit humankind. In this sense, Judaism allows for the use of land, minerals, and animals if they can benefit humans. Natural resources, including trees, water, and fossil fuels, are therefore not necessarily immune from human over-use. Moreover, Jewish law permits the modification of genetic material, if this technology can be proven to benefit humanity. The genetic modification of plants, for example, to increase yield without generating harm to humans or to the environment, would likely be acceptable under Jewish law.

Christianity

Christians share with Jews the accounts of creation found in Genesis, and therefore believe that they have a responsibility to be faithful stewards of the earth. The world, as created by God, is good, and humans ought to recognize the imprint of the divine upon creation. The apostle Paul writes in his letter to the Romans that God intends for creation to be delivered from suffering:

> The universe itself is to be freed from the shackles of mortality and enter upon the liberty and splendor of the children of God. Up to the present, we know, the whole created universe groans in all its parts as if in the pangs of childbirth.
>
> Romans 8:21–22

In his influential 1967 essay, "The Historical Roots of our Ecological Crisis," historian Lynn White argues that Christianity is largely responsible for the destruction of our environment. In contrast to traditions that find spirits inhabiting natural formations, plants, and animals, the monotheistic God of Christianity exists separately outside of nature. The growth of Christianity meant the effective end of beliefs in which deities dwelled in plants, animals, mountains, and rivers. Christian thought, in other words, stopped equating the destruction of the natural world with the destruction of deities. Rather the tradition emphasizes the role of humans as having "dominion" and stewardship over plants and animals. Furthermore, the notion that Christians carry out "God's will" can be deployed as an excuse for the destruction of the natural world.

For White, the solution to the environmental crisis lies not in the elimination of Christianity altogether, but rather in the emphasis on ideas and figures within the tradition that promote an environmental ethic. In particular, White looks to St. Francis of Assisi (d. 1226), whose appreciation of animals and the natural world led to his sainthood. Lynn singles out the attitude of humility that St. Francis cultivates such that humans ought no longer to view themselves as superior to animals and the natural world. This humility before God's creation, Lynn argues, is an effective antidote to the attitude of entitled domination that has led to our ecological crisis. Until we can view animals, plants, and the natural world as existing on the same level as humans, rather than as mere objects for our exploitation, the environment will continue to suffer; and we will continue to suffer alongside it.

Islam

As with Judaism and Christianity, the notion of stewardship of plants and animals by humankind exists in Islamic thought. The title of "caliph," while normally designating a religious and political ruler, can be considered in a broader sense to mean a steward of God's creation. The Qur'an states: "He has made you inheritors of the earth" (Qur'an 35:39). The meaning of "Muslim," one who submits to God, applies not just to humans, but to all of creation. Although humans are distinct from animals and plants in that humans can choose how and whether to submit to God's will, Islam teaches that plants, non-human animals, and the cosmos all submit themselves to God, as evidenced through God's design.

The Qur'an reminds Muslims that other species that inhabit the earth are part of communities, like human ones. As such, humans are to treat other animals with the respect that is due to them, as communities created by God. The elimination of species, in other words, would go against God's teachings. Although the Qur'an sends a clear message that humans are not to exploit or irreparably harm the natural world, God does permit the use of natural resources to benefit humanity. The natural world is described by the Qur'an as containing "clean and pure" gifts from God to humankind for sustenance (Qur'an 7:32).

The Qur'an provides guidance for the cultivation of plants for food, as well as for the proper care of animals. God reminds Muslims that it is God who is ultimately responsible for the growth of fruits, vegetables, and grains. God therefore admonishes those who waste God's creation: "Waste not by excess: For God loves not the wasteful" (Qur'an 6:141). Similarly, God reminds Muslims that God has created "horses, mules, and donkeys" for the benefit of humankind, and therefore they ought to be treated with their creator in mind.

Sikhism

Although there is no creation story in Sikhism, there is an expectation that humans are responsible for maintaining the health of the planet. Explaining that because no human was present at the beginning of creation, there can be no certainty about how or why the cosmos was created. The focus should be on caring for what is present, including other humans, animals, plants, and the environment.

The Guru Granth Sahib states: "Air is the Guru, Water the Father, and the Earth is the Great Mother." This is interpreted by Sikhs as a command to respect the different aspects of the environment. Rather than view humans as stewards of the earth, Sikhs strive to live in harmony with the different elements of the planet.

Case Study: Vegetarianism in the Abrahamic Traditions

While Hinduism, Jainism, and Buddhism have strong traditions of vegetarianism, the Abrahamic traditions generally have not. Genesis, the first book of the Bible, alludes to a vegetarian-based diet, but the Abrahamic traditions have condoned the consumption of meat and have even made the sacrifice and consumption of animals a major part of their ritual traditions.

There are, of course, differences among the three traditions. Most notably, Judaism and Islam forbid the consumption of pork. Jewish dietary laws, also referred to as "kosher" food restrictions or kashrut, additionally forbid, among many other things, the eating of shellfish, animals without cloven hooves, and animals that do not chew their cud (i.e., non-ruminants). The Abrahamic traditions overall, however, tend to associate the consumption of meat with holidays and festivities. As noted previously, in the Jewish tradition, the avoidance of meat was typically equated with mourning, and the consumption of meat with celebration.

In Christianity, people often celebrate Easter with a special meal featuring lamb as a symbolic centerpiece. Jesus, referred to as the "lamb" in the Gospels, is sacrificed by God for the sins of humanity. Also called the Passover lamb, this references the lambs' blood that Jews painted around their doors while in bondage in Egypt so that God would spare their firstborn sons in the last of the plagues. In Islam, the end of Hajj, or pilgrimage to Mecca, is marked by the holiday Eid al-Adha, during which Muslims purchase animals for slaughter, sacrifice, and consumption. This ritual commemorates the story of Abraham's willingness to sacrifice his own son for God. In Jewish and Muslim traditions, special precautions are taken when raising and then butchering animals in order to minimize pain. Kosher and halal butchers are sought by believers to provide meats that have been raised, slaughtered, and prepared in ritually correct ways.

Although the Abrahamic traditions feature meat as a central and symbolic part of important rituals, many Jews, Christians, and Muslims find vegetarianism compatible with their religious beliefs. Virtues that are praised in the Abrahamic traditions, such as mercy and justice, apply not only to humans, but also to animals. Particularly given the conditions of modern "factory farms," in which animals suffer psychologically and physically, people might choose to avoid the consumption of these animals in order to avoid being complicit in their unwarranted suffering. Indeed, a number of religious believers find compelling the secular arguments of thinkers such as Jonathan Safran Foer, Michael Pollan, and Peter Singer. Foer makes the argument that if one is committed to an ethical life, then one must avoid the consumption of meat because of the ubiquity of factory farming as a source of meat products, particularly in the United States. Pollan concedes that the purchase of animals from farms that treat their animals humanely and slaughter them with a minimal amount of pain might provide an ethical way to consume meat without benefitting factory farms. Singer finds that because animals are sentient beings, and many are in fact quite intelligent, a vegetarian diet—if not a vegan diet, free of all animal products—is warranted in order to minimize suffering.

In addition to the problem of sentient creatures suffering to satiate an unnecessary desire for meat consumption, the pollution caused by factory farming and the enormous amount of water required to grow the crops used to feed animals place a tremendous strain on the environment. According to the United States Geological Survey, every pound of beef requires 450 gallons of water. An orange, on the other hand, takes 13 gallons of water to grow. Plants require fewer water resources than animals. Given the global water shortage, which is expected to worsen due to population growth and climate change, the reduction of factory farming and the increase of vegetarian diets can help to alleviate the problem of water scarcity.

Questions:

1   Should followers of the Abrahamic traditions—Judaism, Christianity, and Islam—follow vegetarian diets? Why or why not?
2   To what extent should Jews, Muslims, and Christians consider recent scientific findings concerning the sentience of animals and the degradation

of the environment in evaluating established religious rituals involving meat consumption?

3   Is there ever an ethical obligation to consume meat? Should vegetarians grant "exemptions" for meat consumption during religious rituals?

4   Michael Pollan has argued that consuming meat from small farms that treat animals well and then slaughter them humanely is less morally compromising than consuming meat from factory farms. Do you agree? Why or why not?

5   Although factory farms have been criticized for their treatment of animals and polluting effects, the mass production of eggs, milk, chicken, beef, and pork have enabled millions to consume high quality protein at affordable prices. How should the availability of affordable meat and dairy products fit into any moral advocacy in favor of vegetarian diets?

Notes

1   Framarin, "Hinduism," 81.
2   Drew, "Retreating Goddess," 32.

Bibliography

Aftandilian, Dave. "What Other Americans Can and Cannot Learn from Native American Environmental Ethics." *Worldviews* 15:3 (2011), 219–46. http://www.jstor.org/stable/43809445.

Chapple, Christopher Key, and Mary Evelyn. Tucker. *Hinduism and Ecology: The Intersection of Earth, Sky, and Water.* Cambridge, MA: Harvard University Press for the Center for the Study of World Religions, Harvard Divinity School, 2000.

Drew, Georgina. "A Retreating Goddess? Conflicting Perceptions of Ecological Change Near the Gangotri-Gaumukh Glacier." In *How the World's Religions Are Responding to Climate Change: Social Scientific Investigations,* edited by Robin G. Veldman, Andrew Saasz, and Randolph Haluza-DeLay, 23–36. New York: Routledge, 2014.

Foer, Jonathan Safran. *Eating Animals.* New York: Penguin, 2010.

Framarin, Christopher G. "Hinduism and Environmental Ethics: An Analysis and Defense of a Basic Assumption." *Asian Philosophy* 22:1 (March 2012), 75–91. https://doi.org/10.1080/09552367.2012.664884.

Gottlieb, Roger S. *This Sacred Earth: Religion, Nature, Environment.* 2nd ed. New York: Routledge, 2004.

Gupta, Lina. "Purity, Pollution and Hinduism." In *Ecofeminism and the Sacred,* edited by Carol J. Adams, 99–116. New York: Continuum, 1993.

IPCC. *Summary for Policymakers. In: Global Warming of 1.5°C. An IPCC Special Report on the impacts of global warming of 1.5°C above pre-industrial levels and related global greenhouse gas emission pathways, in the context of strengthening the global response to the threat of climate change, sustainable development, and efforts to eradicate poverty.* Edited by V. Masson-Delmotte, P. Zhai, H.-O. Pörtner, D. Roberts, J. Skea, P.R. Shukla, A. Pirani, et al. Geneva: World Meteorological Organization, 2018. https://www.ipcc.ch/sr15/chapter/spm/.

Intergovernmental Panel on Climate Change. *Climate Change and Land: Summary for Policy Makers* (August 7, 2019). https://www.ipcc.ch/site/assets/uploads/2019/08/4.-SPM_Approved_Microsite_FINAL.pdf.

Kidwell, Clara Sue, Homer Noley, and George E. Tinker. *A Native American Theology.* Maryknoll, NY: Orbis Books, 2001.

Kimmerer, Robin Wall. *Braiding Sweetgrass: Indigenous Wisdom, Scientific Knowledge and the Teachings of Plants.* First edition. Minneapolis, MN: Milkweed Editions, 2013.

Lal, Vinay. "Climate Change: Insights from Hinduism." *Journal of the American Academy of Religion* 83:2 (June 2015), 388–406. https://doi.org/10.1093/jaarel/lfv020.

Pew Research Center. "Religion and Views on Climate and Energy Issues." Last modified October 22, 2015. https://www.pewresearch.org/science/2015/10/22/religion-and-views-on-climate-and-energy-issues/.

Pollan, Michael. *The Omnivore's Dilemma: A Natural History of Four Meals.* New York: Penguin Books, 2007.

Ross-Bryant, Lynn. "Religion and the Environment." In *The Columbia Guide to Religion in American History,* edited by Paul Harvey and Edward J. Blum, 280–294. New York: Columbia University Press, 2012.

Singer, Peter. *Animal Liberation: The Definitive Classic of the Animal Movement.* 40th anniversary edition. New York: Open Road Integrated Media, 2015.

United Nations. *Report of the Secretary-General on the 2019 Climate Action Summit and The Way Forward in 2020.* https://www.un.org/en/climatechange/assets/pdf/cas_report_11_dec.pdf.

Veldman, Robin G., Andrew Szasz, and Randolph Laluza-DeLay, eds. *How the World's Religions Are Responding to Climate Change: Social Scientific Investigations.* New York: Routledge, 2014.

Chapter 4

Poverty and Wealth Disparity

When college students from all around the country and the world arrive in Washington, DC, they are excited about living in the capital of the United States. They marvel at being able to walk to the White House, mere blocks away from the center of campus. They take the Metro a few short stops to visit the Capitol, the Supreme Court of the United States, and the Library of Congress. These are the images we conjure when we think of Washington, DC, a city rife with institutions of power. The city, however, is a city of contrasts. Encompassing fewer than 70 square miles, these hallowed structures are within walking distance to some of the poorest neighborhoods in the nation's capital. In Washington, the wealth gap is especially pronounced and follows racial demographics. The Black and Hispanic populations in DC are more than twice as likely to live below the poverty line than Whites, less likely to own their own home or business, and have much smaller household net worth.

In the United States, the rise of poverty and the growing wealth gap has become an increasingly urgent issue, exacerbated by the COVID-19 pandemic. According to the Federal Reserve, the wealthiest one percent of Americans possesses over $40 trillion in assets, whereas the bottom 50% of the American population *collectively* possesses just over $2.5 trillion. The United Nations Department of Social and Economic Affairs reports that the United States is not alone in the growing wealth gap. Over 70% of the world's population lives in countries where wealth inequality has grown since 1990. Around the globe, the wealthiest one percent saw an increase in income share, whereas the bottom 40% earned less than a quarter of the share of income. The unequal distribution of wealth both within and across nations means that very large amounts of wealth are held by a miniscule percentage of the world's populations, while much of the world's population lives at or below poverty levels.

Poverty and wealth gaps matter because poverty is linked to worse health outcomes, lower educational attainment, particularly for girls, and greater political disenfranchisement, among other measures. Large wealth gaps correlate to higher rates of political instability, reduction in economic mobility,

DOI: 10.4324/9781003350637-5

and generational poverty. Although the completely equal distribution of wealth is neither likely nor desired, many agree that extreme disparities in wealth are, at minimum, not conducive to stable democracies. Assuming that we desire better health, political stability, and economic opportunity for all, we need to minimize poverty and reduce massive wealth disparities. Religious traditions offer rich resources for thinking about wealth and poverty and how to value properly the various goods, both material and non-material, in life.

Several major religious traditions consider *voluntary* poverty praise-worthy. Indeed, ascetic and monastic traditions found in Hinduism, Buddhism, Jainism, Christianity, and Islam suggest that the absence of material comforts may well be necessary to achieve the highest stages of the religious life. The Buddha and Jesus are well known for having denounced wealth and power and declaring them to be impediments to morality. For the vast majority of religious believers, however, the complete rejection of wealth and power appears both unlikely and unreasonable. Having adequate housing, food, and clothing, at minimum, typically requires that participation in the workforce to earn money, and engagement with local and global markets. The pressure to acquire wealth is undoubtedly even greater for those who have children or elderly family members dependent upon them. In other words, monastic or ascetic lifestyles in which one renounces material comforts are neither likely nor practical for most followers of religious traditions.

Given that most believers of various religions are unlikely to follow ascetic or monastic paths, traditions provide some guidance with regard to the place of wealth in one's life. Although some religious traditions advocate a frugal approach to wealth, other traditions place few restrictions on the accumulation of wealth. Indeed, some religious communities even encourage a life-style marked by extravagance and view wealth as a reward bestowed by God unto the faithful. Approaches to wealth vary widely both among and within specific religious traditions.

In foundational religious texts, the word "poor" describes people whom today we might describe as living in poverty or below the poverty line. Poverty, a relatively recent sociological framework for assessing persons and communities, describes a number of different circumstances and not simply the absence of money. In addition to a person or family's lack of wealth, poverty also may describe the lack of adequate housing, food insecurity, or inadequate access to education or healthcare. Poverty involves a complex set of circumstances that affects people and societies in multiple ways. The United Nations' comprehensive definition of poverty reads:

> It means lack of basic capacity to participate effectively in society. It means not having enough to feed and clothe a family, not having a school or clinic to go to, not having the land on which to grow one's food or a job to earn one's living, not having access to credit. It means insecurity,

powerlessness and exclusion of individuals, households and communities. It means susceptibility to violence, and it often implies living in marginal or fragile environments, without access to clean water or sanitation.

Poverty, as defined by the United Nations, does not distinguish between voluntary and involuntary poverty, but the assumption is that people generally do not choose a lifestyle for themselves or their families that fails to meet basic needs. Indeed, in order for poverty to be described as "voluntary," as it is within some religious traditions, believers would first need to have a lifestyle such that they are able to make the choice to relinquish certain material comforts.

Religious traditions offer insights into both voluntary and involuntary poverty. While none of the world's major traditions advocates involuntary poverty, their pronouncements on voluntary poverty are tremendously varied. Leaders of several religious traditions have taken firm stands against involuntary poverty and its causes. Most notably, the liberation theology movement within the Roman Catholic tradition denounces involuntary poverty as a violation of Jesus's teachings, particularly given the wealth and power of church leadership.

In this chapter, we will explore the various teachings, both implied and explicit, of religious traditions about the place of money and wealth in an ethical life. Because access to wealth is so critical to obtaining healthcare, shelter, education, and other facets of living a healthy and well-rounded life, insights into wealth and its distribution have implications for social institutions and communities. In other words, discussions of wealth and money are not simply about wealth and money; they are also commentaries about what we value and prioritize, and whom we value and prioritize. What do religious traditions tell us about the place of money and wealth in an ethical life?

Hinduism

Ethics in Hinduism may best be described as "situational," that is, the rightness or wrongness of actions depend upon a number of relevant factors. One's age, gender, and caste play a role in determining the appropriateness of particular behaviors. The fact of caste, in which wealth generally increases as one moves up the caste, presents challenges to policies that call for the eradication of poverty. Although involuntary poverty, that would lead, for example, to starvation, is not condoned by the religious tradition, large disparities in wealth are both acceptable and expected as a result of traditional Hindu beliefs about karma and caste. Economist Vani Borooah has found that income and wealth disparities between the upper castes and the lowest caste members of India can be attributed to unequal treatment of the latter group.[1]

The *Rig Veda*, considered one of the foundational texts in Hinduism, metaphorically describes the caste system as the different parts of the human body.

If the body represents society as a whole, then the Brahmins (priests and intellectuals) are the head; the Kshatriyas (political rulers and military) are arms; the Vaishyas (merchants and farmers) are legs; and the Shudras (servants and laborers) are the feet. The Dalits, formerly referred to as "untouchables," are not considered part of the caste system and are literally "out-castes." Dalits often serve as sanitation workers or find employment in poorly paid, unsafe, and otherwise low-status work.

The *Rig Veda* furthermore asserts in the *Purusha Sukta* that the caste system functions as a normative way to structure society. When the British colonized India, they drew parallels between caste and a class system and thereby reinforced social and economic hierarchies. Although the Indian government has over the last several decades attempted to improve access to educational and professional opportunities for Dalits and lower castes, caste remains culturally relevant. Caste status is hereditary, meaning that one is born into the same caste as one's parents, and inter-caste marriage, while increasingly popular, is nonetheless relatively uncommon. Because people tend to marry within their own castes, wealth does not transfer from the upper castes to the lower castes. Moreover, government efforts to improve the economic standing of Dalits and lower castes have had only measured success. Policies that target disenfranchised Hindu groups, for example, may not benefit the numerous Dalits and Shudras who had converted to Christianity.

Karma, the notion that actions have moral consequences across reincarnated lives, manifests through wealth or the lack thereof. Involuntary poverty and low caste status suggest that in a previous life, one had accrued negative karma; wealth and high caste status suggest that in a previous life, one had accrued positive karma. Thus, economic status and corresponding caste are viewed as cosmological outcomes consistent with Hindu world views. To be a poor Shudra or a wealthy Brahmin follows karmic logic. At the same time, should a wealthy member of the lower castes acquire significant wealth, or a member of the upper castes become destitute, such rises or falls in fortune might signal karmic repercussions from previous or even current lives. Such discrepancies in the social and economic order, however, are just as likely to rouse suspicion. The ancient Laws of Manu (*Manu Smriti*) state that "a shudra who acquires wealth gives pains to Brahmins" (10.129).

For the upper castes, the acquisition of wealth is appropriate and encouraged when men become husbands and fathers. *Ashramas*, the progressive stages in life recommended for men of the upper castes, dictate that when a man establishes a household as a married man and father, the acquisition of wealth and power is entirely proper. The pursuit of *artha* (prosperity and power) and the provision of material comforts for one's wife, children, and extended family are fitting for these particular circumstances. So long as wealth is acquired morally and does not blind one to other pursuits in life, the householder is encouraged to accumulate wealth and is understood to play an important role in the economy. The householder not only supports a family, but also pays servants and merchants, in addition to offering alms to priests. As a man enters the last stages of his life, however, he gradually ceases the pursuit of *artha* and transitions to a more contemplative lifestyle as a "forest dweller." Eventually, he is expected to renounce the worldly pleasures of the householder and become an ascetic.

Buddhism

The story of the Buddha explains that Siddhartha Gautama grew up as a wealthy prince whose family sheltered him from suffering. Upon seeing for the first time the suffering of a sick man, a dying man, and a corpse, Siddhartha decides to venture beyond the palace gates to become a holy man and seeks to understand why suffering occurs. Along his journey, Siddhartha explores various methods to enlightenment. One of these methods, the way of the ascetic, nearly proves to be the death of him. When he is nursed back to health by a companion, Siddhartha denounces extreme renunciation of material comforts and commits to a more moderate lifestyle that lies in between the extraordinary privilege of royalty and the complete rejection of physical and psychological comforts. Referred to as the Middle Way, the Eight-fold Path prescribes the life between extremes necessary for achieving enlightenment.

Because Buddhist teachings find that attachment is the root of suffering, Buddhist practice aims to minimize and then eliminate attachment to wealth and material goods. With this comes the recognition that if people are starving and lacking adequate shelter and clothing, the possibility of detachment is psychologically impossible. If one is starving, for example, then one becomes obsessed with food. The desperation to eat interferes with the spiritual practice of detachment. Similarly, if one lacks adequate clothing and shelter, then one becomes desirous of clothing and shelter and is unable to detach oneself from these desires. Basic human needs must first be met in order to pursue the middle way.

The voluntary vows of poverty undertaken by Buddhist monks and nuns differ significantly from the involuntary poverty that results from unjust economic relations and political corruption. A number of texts from the Pali Canon encourage voluntary poverty among members of religious orders so as to emulate the voluntary sacrifice of wealth by the Buddha, Siddhartha Gautama. In the poetic *Dhaniya-sutta*, a shepherd who grieves the loss of his home in a storm realizes, upon meeting the Buddha, that his suffering emerges from attachment. Not having a home, like the Buddha, and therefore not having to suffer when one loses it, represents progress on the path toward enlightenment. In the *Dhammapada*, a collection of Buddhist teachings, enlightened humans have no attachment to material comforts, including homes. The *Sāmaññaphala sutta* describes the contentment of the homeless Buddhist monk who needs only his robes for cover and alms for food. For those emulating the way of the Buddha, such as monks and nuns, homelessness is viewed as mastery over attachment and a sign of enlightenment.

Buddhist thought, however, offers multiple perspectives on wealth and material comfort. Although homelessness might be considered praiseworthy for monks and nuns, inadequate shelter for a young family would be considered a form of suffering and morally negligent. The acquisition of wealth, from Buddhist perspectives, is not necessarily problematic for householders. Unlike monks and nuns, who take vows of poverty, householders are expected to earn and possess sufficient wealth to support themselves and their families. How one spends one's wealth, assuming that it was rightly and honestly acquired, ought to follow the Middle Way. One may use wealth to support one's family and friends, to pay for basic needs, and to support worthy causes, particularly the sangha, the Buddhist community. Householders should share their wealth with monks and nuns through gifts of food and financial support. Indeed, the sangha would likely not survive if Buddhist householders were unable to provide financial assistance to monasteries. Holding onto money for the sake of simply acquiring more wealth or spending money lavishly are both discouraged. For householders, the primary ethical concern with the acquisition of wealth is not whether one has wealth, but the means by which one acquires it. One step of the Eightfold Path is "right livelihood," which discourages occupations that bring undue harm and suffering to other living beings.

In some texts, Buddhist thinkers associate poverty and wealth with the karmic outcome of previous lives. Poverty results from the negative karma accumulated in previous lives, and wealth accrues due to positive karma. This stands in contrast to texts, such as the *Dhaniya-sutta*, that associate poverty with enlightenment. The *Culakammavibhanga sutta* and the *Vimānavatthu*, parts of the Pali Canon that contain early Theravadin Buddhist texts, claim that people who donated gifts to monks and the sangha in previous lives are likely to have wealth in future lives, whereas those who failed to give are likely to experience poverty in future lives.

Another text from the Pali Canon, the *Cakkavatti Sīhanāda Sutta* further describes a just kingdom as one that prospers. Known as the "Discourse of the Lion's Roar on the Wheel-Turning King," the treatise advises rulers to give money to poor subjects so as to deter crimes of desperation. In this story, generations of rulers follow this advice, give money to the poor, and reign over flourishing kingdoms, but one king decides not to follow this custom only to see poverty rise. With the rise in poverty, comes a rise in thefts. In addition to the association the text makes between poverty and thievery, it also implicates poverty and theft with an increase in weapons, a loss of beauty, and significantly shortened human life spans. This ruler's failure to provide assistance to the poor therefore leads not only to poverty, but to a whole host of crimes and the worsening of living standards for the entire society. The lesson here is that leaders who have mastered *dharma*, or the teachings of the

Buddha, comprehend not just superficial correlations between the variables of society, but understand a profound web of causality. Such rulers recognize that the alleviation of poverty is tied to well-being and social stability.

In contemporary Buddhist thought, extreme wealth inequality that leads to poverty exacerbates suffering. Drawing from basic Buddhist principles such as compassion, dependent origination, and interconnectedness, thinkers from within the tradition, including figures such as the Dalai Lama, argue for the necessity of basic goods and services required for human flourishing. Involuntary poverty that results from unjust distribution of wealth and power requires correction. Moreover, conditions such as climate change disproportionately affect the poor and disenfranchised. In their analyses, Buddhist leaders acknowledge that individually acquired karma is a factor in poverty, but that the impact of individually acquired karma is insufficient for eliminating the suffering caused by social and economic structures that give rise to involuntary poverty and wealth inequality. Correcting these larger societal ills requires compassionate government policies, the work of non-governmental organizations, and the assistance of charitable organizations. Moreover, the solution to widespread poverty and unjust wealth distribution requires the ability to see the connections between the multiple and complex factors that give rise to these forms of suffering. Like the wise ruler who has mastered *dharma* in the *Cakkavatti Sīhanāda Sutta*, government and community leaders today need to have a firm grasp of the consequences of actions and policies.

Jainism

Asceticism, the voluntary rejection of material comforts, plays a major role in Jainism. Asceticism is viewed as an important means of escaping cycles of karmic rebirth. Jain literature contains numerous examples of kings and princes who gave up all their riches—and left behind their wives and children—in order to follow an ascetic lifestyle. Jain monks and nuns take a vow of non-possession, *aparigraha vrata*. As in Buddhism, we find in Jainism an approach to living that emphasizes non-attachment as the primary means to end suffering.

At the same time, Jains believe that poverty, though the result of karmic influence, can be eradicated. Moral individuals, moral families, and moral societies together can eliminate the bad karma that accumulates over time. Poverty, which is viewed as evidence of negative karma in previous lives, would eventually cease to exist. In the meantime, Jains encourage charitable giving to help the poor alleviate their suffering. The *Tattvartha Sutra*, an early Jain text, explains that *dana*, or charitable giving, benefits not only the recipient, but also the giver. The giver acquires karmic merit, and the outflowing of compassion leads to peace, happiness, and well-being for all.

For householders in the Jain tradition and for those who choose not to embrace asceticism, the acquisition of necessary wealth through labor is permissible. There are, however, constraints in the type of work that one pursues; certain trades generate negative karma and should be avoided. *Karmadana* refers to the Jain guidance on forbidding some businesses and types of employment because of the harm they produce. These range from operating a brothel to the slaughter of animals and are strongly discouraged because they violate the concept of *ahimsa* (no harm). Trading and banking, however, as means of earning a living adhere to the principles of *ahimsa* and have become relatively popular occupations among Jains. In determining the suitability of work based upon *ahimsa*, the Jains reject the dominant Hindu use of caste. Rather than assign work based upon caste distinctions, Jains categorically reject certain types of work based upon their negative karmic qualities.

Householders, while not held to the same level of asceticism adopted by monks and nuns, are nonetheless asked to limit their possessions in the following categories: land, silver and gold, money and grain, servants and working animals, and household goods. Although householders need possessions to survive, they are nonetheless encouraged to limit their belongings to achieve non-attachment.

Today, Jains are a relatively wealthy religious minority in India. Due to their long-established businesses in trade, high levels of education, and insular patterns of marriage, wealth has remained within this tight knit community. Because of the expectation to limit possessions, practices of charitable giving and donation of items to the needy are common.

Judaism

Jewish teachings do not prohibit the accumulation of wealth, but offer guidance as to its purpose. Because Jews have long lived in exile and were, in many places, prohibited from owning property, poverty was not idealized. Historically, Jews have lived under economic structures and policies often not of their own creation. Nonetheless, Judaism offers insights into the alleviation of poverty and moral uses of wealth.

As a tradition that does not focus on the rewards of an after-life or on future re-incarnated lives, justice is expected to be carried out in the present time. This means that Jews have a moral imperative to correct gross inequalities in wealth and to eliminate dire poverty. The ability to provide for oneself and for others is assumed as a form of justice. The tradition encourages those within the community with financial means to assist the poor with a tenth of their wealth. The term for charity in Hebrew, *tzedaka*, translates also into justice, suggesting that to provide material aid to those in need constitutes an act of righteousness.

Biblical sources assume that humans need to labor for their livelihood. Whether it be tending to crops, raising livestock, or engaging in trade, Jewish texts view work as central to human and communal identity. The profits earned from honest work, as well as wealth that could be passed onto future generations, were considered blessings. Wealth was condemned only if acquired or used dishonestly and unjustly.

The Hebrew Scriptures contain numerous verses concerning wealth, the poor, and giving. The world and its products are considered to be the creation of God, and seen therefore as good. Material life should not be shunned, but rather appreciated as divine gift to humankind. One could read the narrative about the Garden of Eden as a theological understanding of the economically dependent nature of humanity on God. God provides food to eat for the first humans, and when they are banished from the Garden of Eden, the Talmud teaches that God taught Adam how to create fire to keep warm. Fire, a gift from God, symbolizes the light and warmth of God that allowed Adam and Eve to survive outside the Garden.

Deuteronomy, the last of the five books of the Torah, includes a series of *mitzvot* or divine commands, that the Israelites are to follow in obedience to a monotheistic God. In addition to laws concerning religious practice and the conduct of officials, Deuteronomy also contains a series of civil laws. These laws command that debt be forgiven every seven years (Deut. 15:1–11), usury be limited (Deut. 23:19–20), workers be paid fairly (Deut. 24:14–15), and aid be given to the needy (Deut. 24:17–18). Individuals are expected to follow these rules, and communities to enforce them.

Rabbi Akiva, the leading Jewish thinker of late first and early second centuries CE, argued that differences in wealth were not reflections of moral standing; rather that wealth and poverty were the result of a number of factors, including luck, effort, and talent. Both the rich and the poor are made in the image of God, and the factors that determine a person's economic standing are determined by God as well. This does not mean, however, that the wealthy have no need to absolve themselves of moral responsibilities toward the less well off. Rabbi Akiva suggests that God gives wealthy people the opportunity to practice their philanthropy and to provide generously for the poor.

The twelfth century Jewish philosopher Maimonides categorized charity into eight levels. The lowest type of charity is that given begrudgingly, whereas the highest level of charity is a virtuous act that teaches recipients to become self-sufficient through dignified trades. Because recipients of charity may feel humiliated by the need to accept donations, the gift of a skill not only ameliorates economic hardship, but also preserves human dignity. According to Maimonides, to give generously in this way constitutes a form of justice, and the charitable person is synonymous with the righteous person.

Christianity

As Christianity evolved, diverse views about the proper place of wealth for its believers emerged. In its earliest years, Christianity was not aligned with political or economic power. As a small Jewish movement comprised of outsiders and marginalized members of society, Christianity began as a community that was likely poor and powerless. Jesus himself is depicted in the Bible as having been born of humble means. With a trade in carpentry, Jesus as an adult likely was not wealthy, and as a rabbi often spoke out on behalf of the poor while criticizing the wealthy. In the Gospel of Mark, Jesus advises a wealthy young man, "Go, sell all you have and give to the poor" (Mark 10:21). Jesus also famously preaches, "It is easier for a camel to pass through the eye of a needle than for a rich man to enter the Kingdom of God" (Mark 10:25). In the Gospel of Luke, Jesus warns, "You cannot serve God and Money" (Luke 16:13). In perhaps the most well-known of Jesus' sayings, the Beatitudes, he forcefully proclaims, "Blessed are you who are poor, for yours shall be the kingdom of God" (Luke 6:20). These early documents suggest that the first Christians eschewed the lifestyles of the wealthy and adhered to an ethos that was deeply sympathetic to the poor.

As Christianity grew in numbers, and then was funded and promoted in the fourth century CE by the Roman emperor Constantine, Christianity could no longer accurately be described as a tradition that aligned itself with the poor and marginalized. Indeed, perhaps as early as the late first century, we find middle- and upper-class Christians struggling with the morality of wealth. The second century author, Clement of Alexandria, in his *Discourse Concerning the Salvation of Rich Men*, argues that wealth is morally neutral, which stands in contradiction to Jesus' admonitions against wealth. Clement proclaims that Christians should view material comforts with dispassion, neither as things to be eschewed nor as things to be worshiped. By 380 CE, Christianity became the official religion of the Roman Empire and with that recognition, the religion of the poor and the meek also became the religion of the rich and powerful.

The development of ascetic monastic communities rose in parallel with the increasing wealth of the church. The third and fourth century desert fathers were Christian ascetics who led lives of austerity in the deserts of Egypt. In imitation of Jesus, they eschewed wealth and became models for future monastics. Some well-known Christian saints, such as thirteenth century Saint Francis of Assisi, voluntarily gave up a life of privilege to follow Jesus' teachings and relinquished his possessions to the poor. There remains a well-established tradition within Christianity that adopts voluntary poverty as a moral ideal, and often engages in service activities as part of its mission. Along similar lines, many Christian sects have robust charitable programs that provide education, food, and medical care to communities in dire poverty around the world.

Although concern for the poor has remained in theory a constant moral imperative throughout the history of Christianity, the church in practice has regularly struggled to embody that ideal. The poverty of the peasant class and the urban poor stood in stark contrast to the riches of the papal hierarchy and the grandeur of magnificent churches and cathedrals. When in 1517, the German priest and theologian, Martin Luther, posted "95 Theses" and sparked the Protestant Reformation, he gave voice to protests against the unjust practice of demanding indulgences from the poor by the Roman Catholic Church. Indulgences were abused by agents of the church, who frightened the poor into making payments to commute punishment for sinful acts, even for deceased loved ones in purgatory. The scandal and controversy eventually lead to a massive schism within the Roman Catholic Church and the development of Protestant branches of Christianity.

Nearly four centuries later, German sociologist Max Weber would theorize in *The Protestant Ethic and the Spirit of Capitalism* (1905) that the Protestant Reformation, in dignifying the common laborer, would fuel the rise of capitalism. Mundane work became meaningful before God; and with the development of the Calvinist concept of predestination, the fruits of one's labors became proof of one's worthiness of salvation. Weber argued that the accumulation of wealth from work, combined with a disdain for frivolous adornment, would result in the investments necessary for the growth of the capitalist economy. Wealth under this framework was not necessarily viewed as the root of all evil, but rather as proof of one's saved soul.

More recently, the liberation theology movement, which began in Central and South America by Catholic activists in the 1960s, was a protest against the complicity of the Roman Catholic Church in political and economic structures that marginalized the concerns of the poor. Proclaiming God's "preferential option for the poor," theologians such as Gustavo Gutiérrez and Oscar Romero argued for an understanding of the Bible and of the Christian message that alleviated the suffering of the poor. They believed that Jesus spoke to the poor and that church had a moral responsibility to improve the material conditions of those who lived in abject poverty.

Under the very large umbrella of Christianity, some adherents take vows of voluntary poverty, others commit to helping the poor, and yet others believe that their faith will bring them riches. The prosperity gospel, also known as the "health and wealth" gospel, claims that true believers will be rewarded with money and good health. Drawing from verses in the Bible such as the Parable of the Talents, in which a servant who invests wisely is rewarded, the prosperity gospel offers followers a narrative in which the faithful live in luxury. Although the prosperity gospel has its roots in the philanthropy of late nineteenth century American industrial titans, the prosperity gospel today has grown massively in popularity through televangelism and social media.

Islam

Muhammad, the founding prophet of Islam, was a respected merchant when he first began receiving messages from God. As a member of the Quraysh tribe, which exercised considerable economic influence in Mecca, Muhammad did not denounce material comforts unless they were attained through immoral or illicit means. Indeed, in the larger culture in which

Muhammad was raised, the ability to provide both for one's own family and for others was lauded, and the generous host was praised for showering guests with abundant food and comfortable beds. Muhammad's first wife, also the first convert to Islam, Khadijah, was a successful businesswoman who managed a number of trading caravans. Not surprisingly, Islam with few exceptions did not develop traditions in which wealth was repudiated in favor of a life of voluntary poverty.

Orphaned at a young age, Muhammad championed the care of the weakest members of society. Although people who were capable of working were expected to contribute to society, members of the *umma*, the Muslim community, had a moral obligation to provide for those who were unable to work or to support themselves. *Zakat*, one of the five pillars of Islam, asks Muslims to donate a portion of their wealth to help those in need. In giving away a percentage of their monies, Muslims "purify" their wealth. In addition to helping the needy, *zakat* is also used to support recent converts to Islam and to provide aid to stranded travelers. Devout Muslims consider *zakat* to be mandatory and maintain that governments may collect a portion of their citizens' wealth to pay for these charitable causes. The Qur'an implores, "perform the prayer, and pay the alms (*zakat*); whatever good you shall forward to your souls' account, you shall find it with God; assuredly God sees the things you do" (Qur'an 2:110).

At the end of the holy month of Ramadan, Muslim heads of families offer a special *zakat al-fitr* to the poor. This donation caps a month of fasting, during which observant Muslims experience the hunger of those without food. The sunset breaking of the fast, which usually consists of the sharing sweets such as dates and special pastries, is a ritual celebration in which members of the community share food with those in need. During the *hajj*, the ritual pilgrimage to Mecca that Muslims are instructed to make at least once in their lives, Muslims are to donate food and money to the poor. The meat from ritually slaughtered animals during the *hajj* is to be distributed to the needy.

If *zakat* is considered a mandatory form of charitable giving, *sadaqah* would be considered voluntary giving. *Sadaqah* ranges from the sharing of sweets to the establishment of monetary trusts meant to aid the poor in a significant way. Major donations, referred to as *waqf*, would include endowments that establish schools and hospitals. Meant to support those in need into perpetuity, *waqf* are mentioned in Islamic law as early as the ninth century CE as a means of charitable giving even after death. *Waqf* are considered irrevocable, and should a *waqf* become obsolete, it may be sold under the condition that the assets from the sale used to create another *waqf*.

In keeping with the belief that those in need should be supported by the *umma*, Islamic tradition forbids the charging of interest (*riba*) to those who need to borrow money. *Riba*, while generally translated as interest, also extends to any form of unfair financial practice that takes advantage of the poor or ignorant. Islamic practice dictates that Muslims ought not to profit from those who find themselves under financial duress. In other words, underlying Islamic banking principles are notions of social justice and moral conduct. In addition to the prohibition against usury, Islamic banks are also to avoid complicity with *haram* or forbidden businesses, such as alcoholic beverage manufacturers, casinos, and publishers of pornographic material.

The Qur'an and Islamic law encourage trade and business so long as the content of trade is morally acceptable and money is not used for the sole purpose of earning more money. The Qur'an warns,

> Those who consume interest will stand on Judgment Day like those driven to madness by Satan's touch. That is because they say, "Trade is no different than interest." But Allah has permitted trading and forbidden interest. Whoever refrains—after having received warning from their Lord—may keep their previous gains, and their case is left to Allah. As for those who persist, it is they who will be the residents of the Fire. They will be there forever.
>
> Qur'an 2:275

Notably, in this verse, the Qur'an approves of trading as a legitimate means of acquiring wealth, but clearly forbids the charging of interest. In other verses, the Qur'an reaffirms the sin of profiting from the lending of money.

At present, banks in Muslim-majority countries often adhere to *shariah* principles and do not charge interest. In order to stay solvent, lenders instead engage in a form of profit and loss sharing, such that lenders and borrowers become financial partners and share in both profits and losses. Lenders may also charge a nominal fee, akin to a consulting or administrative fee, to help offset any losses. A number of micro-lending financial institutions in Muslim-majority countries have found that by structuring banking practices to align with *shariah*, and by receiving a *fatwa* from an imam, Muslim women feel more confident taking out loans to start their own businesses. These businesses often lead to greater economic independence, investment in girls' education, and greater gender equality within families and in the larger community.

Although today there are a number of extremely wealthy, typically oil-rich Muslim nations, there are also many under-developed Muslim-majority countries, particularly in South Asia and in sub-Saharan Africa. Muslim countries have relatively low rates of development compared to non-Muslim nations. The United Nations Development Program uses the measure of "human development" to assess not only per capita wealth as a measure of well-being, but also the application of wealth to create environments in which people have the ability and choice to pursue educational and work opportunities. Poverty, economic inequality, and corruption suppress the ability of governments to implement human development programs. Certainly, recent warfare and violence in Muslim-majority nations have profoundly affected the ability of governments to respond effectively to poverty.

Sikhism

Although differences in wealth are considered to be permanent features of society, Guru Nanak, the founder of the tradition, eschewed caste. "Nanak seeks the company of those who are lowest of the low caste. He has no desire to compete with the rich and the powerful" (GGS, 15). Guru Nanak rejected his high caste birth in favor of the low castes and blamed the caste system for creating unjust inequities in society. Along these lines, Guru Nanak advocated for the poor, and criticized the attitudes of the wealthy. The *Guru Granth Sahib*, the main scripture of Sikhism, states:

> No one respects the poor. No matter how hard the poor man tries, the rich ignore him. When the poor man goes to the rich man, the latter turns his back on him. When the rich man goes to the poor man, the latter welcomes him warmly and offers him a seat with respect.
>
> *Guru Granth Sahib*, 1159

In addition to rejecting the Hindu caste system, Sikh tradition also deemphasizes the final ascetic stage found in traditional Hindu notions of *ashrama*, the appropriate stages of life for the upper caste male. Instead, great emphasis is placed upon the responsibilities of the householder, who is fully engaged in the world. Living up to the ideal of *dharmsal*, or just living, the householder has economic responsibilities to his family and to his community. The acquisition of wealth is encouraged so long as one acquires wealth through just means, and ideally through one's own labor. The *Guru Granth Sahib*, the primary scripture in Sikhism, states, "He who eats what he earns through honest work and shares with others, he alone O Nanak recognizes the true path in life" (GGS, 1245).

The ritual of the *langar*, or feeding the community, emphasizes the rejection of caste and gender hierarchy. The gurdwara, or Sikh house of worship, feeds free of charge those who come for a meal. Supported by a tithe (*daswandh*), members of the Sikh community contribute a portion of their income to supporting the *langar* and other community services. Gurdwaras have recently been featured in news stories for their charitable work. During the COVID pandemic, gurdwaras provided meals to front-line workers and to the needy. Given their experience and large kitchens for the *langar* meal, gurdwaras were particularly well-suited to provide emergency meals en masse. During massive wildfires in California and along the west coast of the United States, Sikh communities are lauded for providing food and shelter for neighbors who lose their homes.

Case Study: Anti-Poverty Measures in Hindu India

The Indian government has over the last several decades pursed an aggressive agenda to reduce poverty. Poverty in India has traditionally fallen along caste lines, with the highest castes generally owning the most wealth, and the lowest castes and the *Dalits*, living in poverty. Indigenous groups, who claim to be original inhabitants of the subcontinent and referred to as *Adivasis*, comprise the poorest strata of Indian society. Together, the *Dalits* and the *Adivasis* make up the segment of society previously referred to as "untouchables." The United Nations Multi-dimensional Poverty Index finds that approximately half of *Adivasis* and a third of *Dalits* live in poverty, compared to just over a quarter for the remainder of the Indian population.

In 1932, Bhimrao Ramji Ambedkar, representing *Dalits*, and Mohandas Gandhi, representing the Indian independence movement, signed the Poona Pact, which signaled a commitment to end "untouchability" in a new Indian national state. The Poona Pact assured that *Dalits* would be guaranteed meaningful political representation within a Hindu electorate. The Constitution of India, adopted in 1950 to replace the British Government of India Act, abolishes "untouchability" (Article 17) and assures that "reservations" are set aside for representation of marginalized groups in parliament (Articles 15 and 16).

Referred to as "scheduled castes" (SCs) and "scheduled tribes" (STs) the *Dalits* and *Adivasis* were assured a percentage of seats in government, public sector jobs, and public schools proportional to their presence in the larger population. As many as half of certain public sector jobs may be reserved for SC and ST candidates. The types of jobs available are varied, ranging from school teachers to postal carriers to bank clerks. These civil service jobs are assumed to be held for life and are therefore extremely important in guaranteeing consistent wages. A number of these positions remain unfilled, however, and rates of local civil service employment seem to parallel the lack of *Dalit* and *Adivasi* political representation in regional governments. Given this, a National Commission for Scheduled Castes and Scheduled Tribes was created to improve implementation of various laws and policies, but this commission is relatively weak and does not possess the power to enforce laws meant to protect SCs and STs.

Although India has taken significant measures to eradicate poverty based on caste discrimination, these measures have not proven effective. Poverty rates still closely follow caste lines. According to the

World Bank, *Dalits* and *Adivasis* continue to lag behind higher castes with regard to education, salaried jobs, and professional social networks. Although the Indian economy has radically transformed in the last decade, historically marginalized groups are not benefitting from the improved economy as quickly as high caste groups. Caste may not be immutable, but the advances in education and in the labor force in India have benefited upper caste society in far greater numbers and more quickly than members of the *Dalit* and *Adivasi* communities.

Questions:

1 What do the failed efforts of the Indian government to alleviate caste discrimination tell us about the intractability of certain religious beliefs? Why does the practice of caste discrimination continue to persist?
2 If focusing on caste is ineffective in reducing poverty, what might be some alternative approaches to ending poverty in India?
3 Do non-Hindu organizations, including Christian and Buddhist aid groups, have a role in alleviating poverty in India? What about charitable organizations based outside of India?

Note

1 Boorah, Vani. "Caste, Inequality and Poverty in India." *Review of Development Economics* 9:3 (August 2005), 399–434.

Bibliography

Beit-Hallahmi, Benjamin, Waleed Chellan, Logan Cochrane, Divya Kannan, Alvin Lim, Atara Moscovich, Sabine Muller, and Jeremiah Unterman. *Religion and Poverty*. Portland: Neofelis Verlag UG (haftungsbeschrankt), 2015. Accessed November 12, 2020. ProQuest Ebook Central.

Borooah, Vani K., Dilip Diwakar, Vinod Kumar Mishra, Ajaya Kumar Naik, and Nidhi S. Sabharwal. "Caste, Inequality, and Poverty in India: A Re-Assessment." *Development Studies Research* 1:1 (2014), 279–94.

Brackney, William H., and Rupen Das, eds. *Poverty and the Poor in the World's Religious Traditions: Religious Responses to the Problem of Poverty*. Santa Barbara, CA: ABC-CLIO, LLC, 2018. Accessed October 29, 2020. ProQuest Ebook Central.

Clapp, Jennifer, and Rorden Wilkinson. *Global Governance, Poverty, and Inequality*. New York: Routledge, 2010.

Das, Maitreyi Bordia and Soumya Kapoor Mehta. *Poverty and Social Exclusion in India: Dalits*. Washington, DC: World Bank. 2012. https://openknowledge.worldbank.org/handle/10986/26336 License: CC BY 3.0 IGO.

Gille, Véronique. "Applying for Social Programs in India: Roles of Local Politics and Caste Networks in Affirmative Action." *Journal of Comparative Economics* 46:2 (2018), 436–56.

Greenspoon, Leonard J., and Leonard J. Greenspoon. *Wealth and Poverty in Jewish Tradition*, Volume 26. West Lafayette, IN: Purdue University Press, 2015.

Kettell, Brian. *Introduction to Islamic Banking and Finance.* Chichester: Wiley, 2011.

Thorat, Amit. "Ethnicity, Caste and Religion: Implications for Poverty Outcomes." *Economic and Political Weekly* 45:51 (2010), 47–53. http://www.jstor.org/stable/25764242 (accessed 9 February 2021).

Thorat, Amit, Reeve Vanneman, Sonalde Desai, and Amaresh Dubey. "Escaping and Falling into Poverty in India Today." *World Development* 93 (2017), 413–26.

United Nations, Department of Economic and Social Affairs, "World Social Report 2020: Inequality in a Rapidly Changing World." https://www.un.org/development/desa/dspd/wp-content/uploads/sites/22/2020/02/World-Social-Report2020-ExecutiveSummary.pdf.

Chapter 5

War and Violence

College students in Washington, DC, tend to be very interested in peace and conflict. Not surprisingly, the reason why so many of my students come to the US capital for college is because they want to learn more about politics and the kinds of decision-making that go on at high levels of government. Indeed, some of the most pressing and urgent issues of our lifetime deal with violent conflict on the world stage. Violence, however, is not a phenomenon that is monopolized by international actors. We also deal with violence on individual, domestic, and community levels. We must account for violence not just on a global scale, as in the case of war, but also in the home.

The common thread that binds violence on a large scale and violence on a smaller one, is the capacity for human beings to harm and kill with intent. When it comes to the issue of violence and war, much attention has been paid to people who perpetuate violence, or those who are responsible for it. However, if we want a full accounting of violence, we must also learn about the victims of violence, as well as the witnesses and bystanders to violence.

How should we define violence? Definitions are important in ethical thinking because they help to define the boundaries of the discussion. How should we think about violence? Specifically, how should we think about violence in the context of religion? What do religions have to say about violence? What do we think about religious views regarding violence? When is violence justified—if ever—and when is it not? Have our own views toward violence changed over time?

While religions generally have discouraged or tried to limit violence, there are some glaring exceptions. Most often, when religious institutions are complicit or gain to benefit from violence, religions have remained silent about violence. Some well-known commandments against violence are found in the Bible—the Ten Commandments state that "thou shall not kill"—and religions like Buddhism and Hinduism share concepts like *ahimsa* or "non-violence," a central tenet of their beliefs. Jains take *ahimsa* as a responsibility to prevent even the unintentional killing of insects when walking. As we have seen, several religions encourage vegetarian diets in order to prevent unnecessary harm to and killing of animals. There is no question that religions have much to say

DOI: 10.4324/9781003350637-6

about preventing the unnecessary loss of life. Many religious assert that people who take lives unnecessarily ought to be punished.

For most religious traditions, however, restrictions against killing are not absolute. Even a cursory sweep of history reveals the serious inconsistencies with regard to religious stances on violence. While murder might not be sanctioned, killing other soldiers in war is permissible. Widely held impressions of Buddhism as a peaceful religion do not seem to comport with the fact that Buddhist countries invest in their own standing armies, wage war, and commit human rights atrocities. The Catholic Church, among other Christian denominations, condemns abortion, but permits killing in war. Moreover, when we widen the scope of killing to include not just humans, but also non-human animals, we can see that many religious traditions even encourage the killing of animals for the purpose of ritual sacrifice.

One can think of various ways in which religions are seemingly inconsistent with regard to their views toward violence. If we expand our definition of violence to include structural violence, we find religious institutions and leaders complicit in the death of millions. Structural violence refers to harms that are not the result of direct action, but of the political, social, and economic policies and norms that lead to the early death of groups of people. Between the failure of religions as moral authorities to challenge corrupt political regimes and their historic complicity, if not approval, of slavery and colonization, religions seem to hold contradictory, arguably hypocritical, positions on violence.

Sometimes religious authorities and believers are blind to violence that is widely accepted due to cultural norms. Domestic violence, for example, has only recently been accepted as a crime punishable by the state. Physical violence against children and partners was not only considered to be a private matter, but even encouraged in some communities. To this day, some parents believe that violence against children, particularly in the form of spanking and other types of corporal punishment, is beneficial for children's moral development. Research in child psychology teaches us, to the contrary, that such views are deeply misguided. Studies on the brain in young children show that children who are exposed to violence in the home suffer from adverse neurological changes and even early death compared to children in households without violence. Violence in childhood accomplishes no good that can be brought about through non-violent means; violence, even if it does not result in long-term physical damage, may very well result in psychological harm that persists well into adulthood.[1] Sadly, the appalling accounts that have recently come to light about the sexual abuse of children in the Catholic Church, which protected adult male priests instead of the young victims of their crimes, demonstrates the Church's failure to shield children from violence at their own hands.

Domestic violence has been implicitly sanctioned by predominantly male leaders across virtually all religious traditions. Marriage, particularly heterosexual marriage, is nearly universally supported as an institution by religions and cultures, even in instances when girls and women have no desire to be married. Married women have long been subject to their husbands in sexist hierarchies sanctioned by patriarchal religions, and violence against women has only recently been addressed by leaders. Religious rules and cultural pressure to remain married even when there is evidence of domestic abuse disregard the plight of millions of victims.

The target of violence also affects how we perceive the act. As the Black Lives Matter movement has painfully revealed, unwarranted deaths of Black Americans in the United States at the hands of law enforcement officers all too often have escaped the attention of the media and the courts. News sources pay less attention when poor, Black people die than when wealthy, White people die.

Historically, the media, the government, and major institutions have tended to value White communities more than others. Indeed, entire categories of human beings were deemed inferior, which enabled authorities to colonize peoples, enslave them, and treat them as property. Because entire groups of people were considered less intelligent, less developed, and less God-like, they were not only denied basic rights—such as the right to vote or to own property—but were also considered less valuable. They could be sold, forced into labor, and killed without consequence to the perpetrators of violence. Although we would now recognize slavery and colonialism as violent institutions, they were not considered immoral or violent at the time by most of their White perpetrators.

Carrying out random acts of violence is generally considered immoral, but many religious and philosophical thinkers have argued that violence under specific circumstances is justifiable, and perhaps even required. Rules of just war derived from Christian and Western European thought—including basic principles about when it is morally acceptable for states to enter into war (*jus ad bellum*) and the rules that govern behavior once in war (*jus in bello*)— have allowed for exceptions to presumptive stances against violence. In multiple religious traditions, rules of war have tended to limit the authority to declare war, justifications for war, and the scope of war. Similarly, guidelines that apply to behavior in war tend to curb when and on whom violence is inflicted. Several scholars of just war theory have proclaimed that there has never been a just war fought. Even so, many would agree that some causes are morally sound (e.g., protecting Jews from Nazi Germany).

Most of our sympathies with regard to violence tend to lie with victims of violence. We are, however, becoming increasingly aware of the harmful psychological effects of violence on the perpetrator. Perpetrators of violence may not suffer outwardly visible trauma, but there is a growing body of research showing that perpetrators of violence suffer from stress and mental illness as a result of participation in violence. Especially when coerced into committing acts of violence, whereby the actor knows what the ramifications of the acts of violence will be, the perpetrators are both victims and agents. When we consider cases like child soldiers, the responsibility of such situations simply cannot be placed on those who are not old enough give consent. Even adult soldiers who enter into war, voluntarily or otherwise, often do not fully anticipate the psychological trauma of participating in violent acts and living under conditions of extreme stress. The impact of those experiences frequently leads to post-traumatic stress disorder, drug abuse, and suicide. The concept of "moral injury" or harms that result from the violation of moral norms is gaining increasing recognition.

What counts as violence depends upon the status of target of violence. Violence also depends somewhat upon the intention of the perpetrator. When we think of someone committing an act of violence, we differentiate between a deliberate intent to harm and perhaps a similar act without intent. For example, someone driving a car who runs over a pedestrian with the intent to harm or kill would be considered a violent person. However, a driver who suffers a heart attack at the wheel and unintentionally runs over a pedestrian would not be considered to have committed a violent act, and the incident would be likely described as tragic, rather than violent.

There are multiple ways to think about violence, and it is helpful to consider this broad topic in terms of categories that organize this complex issue. We can, for example, think about (1) victims of violence; (2) perpetrators of violence; (3) violence committed by groups; (4) violence committed by individuals; (5) intentions of the perpetrator of violence; (6) justifications for violence; (7) views on violence in historical context; (8) violence filtered through the lenses of race, ethnicity, gender, socio-economic class, and age. There are, moreover, multiple ways to "count" violence. If we are discussing the law, violence is fairly specific. There are differences, legally, between assault and battery, homicide and manslaughter, and even among degrees of these crimes.

When discussing religious ethics and violence, we also need to consider factors such as moral agency. By this, we mean who decides whether or not violence is morally justified and who carries out the violence. Violence on a large scale, such as that found in war, may be authorized by a person or small group of persons in power; individual acts of violence, however, may be carried out by individual soldiers, who typically do not have the authority to declare war. Soldiers do, nonetheless, have moral responsibilities within war; they are not to engage in conduct that violates commonly accepted rules of warfare. The principles of *jus in bello* prescribe acceptable conduct of soldiers in war, including using proportional force and avoiding attacks on civilians. Often, the power to decide issues of moral importance, including issues that involve violence, rests with religious authorities. This has significant implications, especially if religious authorities do not recognize victims of violence or if religious authorities themselves are complicit in violence. In the latter case, religious authorities have at times dismissed accounts of violence that implicate them in what would be generally understood as immoral behavior. In states in which religious figures hold significant political influence, we have seen the denial of the complicity by the religion for state abuse. For example, the liberation theology movement, which emerged as a critique of the Roman Catholic Church in Latin America in the 1960s, named the Church as a perpetrator of the economic injustices in the region. In 2022, the Russian Orthodox Church has been complicit in sanctioning the invasion of Ukraine. Patriarch Kirill of Moscow defended the invasion as a spiritual battle against the West and its "gay pride" parades.

In defining the severity of the violence, religious authorities again have significant influence in determining whether some kinds of violence are morally more egregious than others. To determine the magnitude of violence, victims must be allowed to provide testimony of the impact of violence upon their lives and communities. This contributes to a fuller account of the potential impact and scope of violence. A rich account of violence would describe both the immediate impact and the long-term repercussions of violence. Additionally, religious authorities might take a position on structural violence, which does not necessarily have a single perpetrator or clear agent. Discussions of violence might also consider whether, indeed, an act of violence needs to have a human victim in order for it to have moral significance. Here, accounts of suffering of non-human animals and the destruction of the natural environment would be vital to broadening accounts of violence.

Still other accounts of violence might point to beliefs about human nature. Some religious accounts of humanity paint humans as innately sinful, prideful, and prone to violence. Yet others posit that humans are innately good and that violence results from environmental factors. If, as some scientists have suggested, humans are "hard-wired" with violent tendencies, the question arises as to whether violence can therefore be morally excused. Today, we might ask whether hormones, drugs, alcohol, or a history of abuse might have been contributing factors to acts of violence. If so, intent or motivation becomes difficult to determine.

Defining and assessing violence with its many facets and dimensions help to determine whether we have a moral obligation to limit or to end violence. In determining the appropriate response to violence, there are once again a number of relevant details to consider. Some of these details might include information about the victims of violence, the perpetrators, and the extent and scope of the violence. In ending violence, details about the agent who acts to stop violence are also highly relevant. The people who act to end violence as a moral obligation would need to comprehend the risks of such intervention, which could bring harm to oneself. Asking very young children, for example, to intervene would be morally irresponsible because they are not mature enough to comprehend fully the gravity of the situation. As children grow older, however, they become more competent to provide informed consent.

Given the unfortunate ubiquity of violence, we might also ask how to prioritize our interventions, if any. In the Judeo-Christian religious traditions, believers might frame the question as one of determining one's "neighbor." If adherents to these traditions believe that they ought to love our neighbors as themselves, then they may be obligated to protect neighbors from violence just as we would protect themselves. The term, neighbor, however, may encompass many persons. Neighbors may include the persons who literally live in the dwelling adjacent to us, or members of a national state with a shared border, an ally on another continent, or any person or community in need of help from persecution.

Are we ever morally justified to do nothing in the face of extreme violence, such as genocide? If we put ourselves at harm—at significant harm—perhaps not. If we are not properly equipped to stop it, or if our actions will make things worse, perhaps not. Acting against violent dictators without a carefully considered plan can lead to worse violence in the long run. The concept of *jus post bellum* ("justice after war"), which follows the principles found in *jus ad bellum* and *jus in bello*, asks whether the capacity for a society to rebuild after violence exists. If justifications for entering into war and wartime behavior meet just war guidelines, but the destruction of war will be so extensive that a society cannot resume with a sense of normalcy within a reasonable amount of time, then the war may, in fact, not be justified. *Jus post bellum* principles are often raised in discussions about the invasion of Iraq following 9/11.

This chapter on violence and war will discuss several of the relevant major ideas and themes in religious traditions. While the traditions differ in terms of their approaches to war and violence—indeed, we find significant variations *within* these traditions themselves—in general, there appears to be a presumption against violence. If there are exceptions made for violence, as in the case of war, the exceptions are circumscribed.

Hinduism

In Hinduism, we find the concept of *ahimsa* appears in multiple sources. At the same time, the caste system accounts for a "warrior" class that obviously exists to fight. This seeming contradiction points to the understanding that although *ahimsa* is an ideal toward which we ought to strive, karmic imbalances require at times violent intervention.

The *Mahabharata* (12.254.29) states that *ahimsa* constitutes the highest *dharma*, or moral obligation. The phrase *ahimsa paramo dharma* conveys the sense that *ahimsa* is the supreme duty for Hindus. At the same time, violence that is undertaken as a moral obligation is also highly praiseworthy. War waged, for example, to protect the innocent or to destroy an evil enemy would be justified, if not praised as a moral obligation especially when one has the means to do so. Killing in self-defense, also, is not considered a violation of *dharma*, as one has the duty to preserve one's own life. Although the *Mahabharata* insists upon the significance of *ahimsa*, we also find the protagonist, Arjuna, counseled that upholding *dharma* may very well require him to fight members of his own family.

The *Mahabharata* advises that states should use diplomacy to avoid violent conflict. Diplomatic efforts should be exhausted before deciding to engage in war, which should always be the last resort. In the case of armed conflict between disproportionally weak states and powerful states, weaker states ought to surrender rather than hope for a Pyrrhic victory. The *Arthashāstra*, an early treatise on statecraft, offers guidelines for warfare so as to minimize unnecessary fighting. Such guidelines include limiting the time and location for armed conflict, avoiding civilian casualties, and humane treatment of prisoners. The *Arthashāstra* also advises consideration of the long-term goals of warfare. Because one's enemy in war may become one's subjects upon victory, care ought to be taken not to humiliate the defeated in order to facilitate post-bellum integration. Enemies treated well in conflict are less likely to foment internal rebellion, and goodwill to subjects who were former enemies must be extended. Proportional use of force, minimizing necessary use of force, and acceptance of surrender are tactics that should be employed in conflict to minimize post-conflict strife.

Buddhism

Buddhism's central tenets oppose violence and warfare. Buddhist teachings that elevate the concept of *ahimsa* and the elimination of suffering clash with the realities of armed conflict and other struggles that invariably bring both suffering and harm to individuals and their communities. The Noble Eightfold Path, which offers guidance to followers on how to end suffering, advises against speech, actions, and livelihoods that would potentially bring pain to others. Asoka, who reigned in India during the third-century BCE and is regarded among Buddhists as among the most enlightened of rulers, purportedly converted to Buddhism after having witnessed the horrors of war. At least in theory, the tradition takes a clear stand against war and violence.

The reality, of course, is that Buddhist nations, rulers, and peoples have regularly engaged in violent conflict. Moreover, variations among Buddhist traditions mean that Buddhists have held differing positions concerning the ethics of violence. Buddhists adhering to strict Theravada teachings may hold, for example, that violence even in self-defense is not morally permissible, whereas Buddhists in Mahayana traditions may interpret violence in self-defense or to protect the innocent as morally permissible.

Although there is no Buddhist "just war" tradition, Buddhists have participated in violent conflict throughout their history. In the second century BCE, King Dutthagāmani who ruled Sri Lanka reportedly enlisted Buddhist monks to join the army in war against Hindu Tamils. The *Mahāvamsa*, a fifth century history of Sri Lanka, chronicles this story, which has been used to justify fighting against foreign invaders, specifically Hindu Tamils. Nationalism and Buddhism, in other words, are inextricably intertwined aspects of Sri Lankan identity.

In the twentieth century, events such as the atomic bombings of Hiroshima and Nagasaki, as well as the Vietnam War, led to the rise of prominent Buddhist anti-war movements. Nichidatsu Fujii (1885–1985), founder of the Nipponzan-Myōhōji Buddhist order, led the construction of dozens of Peace Pagodas following death of nearly 150,000 Japanese civilians in Hiroshima and Nagasaki. The Peace Pagodas today serve to unite people from around the world in a shared quest for peace.

The Engaged Buddhism movement, a term coined by the Vietnamese Zen monk Thich Nhat Hanh (1926–2022), grows out of his experiences protesting the Vietnam War. Drawing from Gandhi, B.R. Ambedkar (1891–1956), and Martin Luther King Jr., among others, Engaged Buddhism embraces Buddhist concepts such as compassion and inter-dependence as reasons for political and social activism. Engaged Buddhism is meant to follow the example of the Buddha and bodhisattvas in helping others to eliminate suffering. The causes taken up by Engaged Buddhists include the Chinese occupation of Tibet, military dictatorship in Burma, and past genocide in Cambodia under the Khmer Rouge and Pol Pot.

Judaism

Jewish tradition holds conflicting views with regard to peace and violence. On the one hand, God is intimately associated with peace. The *kaddish*, a prayer offered in praise of God that is frequently recited during ritual ceremonies, describes God as the one who brings peace to humanity. The prophet Isaiah proclaims a messianic vision in which God "shall judge between the nations, and shall arbitrate for many peoples; shall beat their swords into plowshares, and their spears into pruning hooks; nation shall not lift up sword against nation, neither shall they learn war any more" (Isaiah 2:4). Hillel, the first century religious leader, urged his followers to seek and pursue peace.

Even in times of warfare, Hebrew scripture suggests that unnecessary violence ought to be avoided. Indeed, throughout Jewish history, leaders and rabbis have invoked peace as an ideal that is sanctioned by God and revealed in scripture. Deuteronomy, one of the five books of the Torah, lays down the principles of *bal tashchit* ("do not destroy") as a guide during warfare. With few exceptions, armies ought to attempt to preserve life during battle and enable the continuation of life following battle. Deuteronomy advises that when deciding to attack a town, Israelites ought first to offer conditions for peace before engaging in violent conflict: "When you draw near to a town to fight against it, offer it terms of peace" (Deuteronomy 20:10). Later rabbinic commentary even advises that members of besieged towns be allowed to escape prior to the start of conflict. Prisoners of war are not to be killed, but are taken as slaves.

(Women, children, and livestock are considered property and taken as booty.) Soldiers may be exempt from fighting if they are newlyweds or have recently built a home. The opportunity to prevent the loss of life through warfare ought to be extended, and waging war ought to be a last resort.

Other rules in Deuteronomy also detail ways in which the Israelites can minimize the repercussions of violent conflict. During long sieges, for example, armies ought to preserve fruit trees, and must avoid chopping down fruit-bearing trees for lumber when building forts:

> If you besiege a town for a long time, making war against it in order to take it, you must not destroy its trees by wielding an ax against them. Although you may take food from them, you must not cut them down. ... You may destroy only the trees that you know do not produce food; you may cut them down for use in building siegeworks against the town that makes war with you, until it falls.
>
> Deuteronomy 20:19–20

In preserving food-producing plants, armies avoid starving populations after a conflict ends. So-called "scorched earth" policies, such as those in which soil is salted and wells poisoned so that people can no longer survive on those lands, are discouraged.

On the other hand, elements within the Hebrew Scriptures justify violence and warfare under certain conditions. Deuteronomy 20:16–17, for example, makes clear that

> as for the towns of these peoples that the Lord your God is giving you as an inheritance, you must not let anything that breathes remain alive. You shall annihilate them—the Hittites and the Amorites, the Canaanites and the Perizzites, the Hivites and the Jebusites—just as the Lord your God has commanded.

The rationale that is provided for this seeming contradiction to the previous verses explains that by annihilating these communities, "they may not teach you to do all the abhorrent things that they do for their gods, and you thus sin against the Lord your God" (Deuteronomy 20:18). Today, scholars of religion consider this part of Deuteronomy as historically circumscribed and specifically commanded by God, and no longer relevant to most discussions about just war in Jewish traditions. The use of violence is nonetheless ethically permissible if defending one's own life. Indeed, God even commands the use of force as necessary for self-preservation.

The Holocaust, during which six million Jews were murdered by Nazis, and the long history of Jewish statelessness intensify arguments for the necessity of violence for the preservation of life. The creation of Israel in 1948 provided a homeland for Jews in that spirit. Soon after the creation of the

Jewish nation state, however, religious laws about war and violence based in ancient texts would need to be applied to a contemporary setting in which international law and advanced weapons, including weapons of mass destruction, played a major role in thinking about the ethics of warfare. Today, we find a wide variety of interpretations of Jewish law and scripture regarding the ethics of violence and war, ranging from pacifist views to positions that assert the necessity of wars of aggression.

Christianity

The diversity of thought within Christian traditions with regard to violence and war ranges from the pacifist views of historic "peace churches" to Christian-identified militias. As such, identifying a singular shared Christian worldview is impossible. There are, however, a number of texts and traditions that have widely informed Christian views about the ethics of violence and war, even if some of those views are ultimately in tension with each other.

Certainly, the stories of Israelites fighting to possess lands they believe to be divinely endowed to them establish a strong connection between religious belief and justification for war. Christian scriptures add a layer of complexity to Jewish texts about war. In the Beatitudes, Jesus proclaims, "Blessed are the peacemakers, for they will be called children of God" (Matthew 5:9). Jesus also teaches,

> You have heard that it was said, 'An eye for an eye and a tooth for a tooth.' But I say to you, do not resist an evildoer. But if anyone strikes you on the right cheek, turn the other also.
>
> Matthew 5:38–39

Although these and other texts emphasize the non-violent teachings of Jesus, his horrific death by crucifixion presents a view of violence that arguably sanctions harm and suffering, particularly if seen as sacrifice for a greater good. The centrality of suffering for the sins of humanity raises profound questions about the presumption of violence in Christian teachings.

The corpus of materials that eventually constitutes just war theory in Christianity draws from biblical narratives, interpretations of Christian doctrine, and the analyses of prominent scholars such as Ambrose (339–397), Augustine (354–430), and Aquinas (1225–1274). In addition, the development of international law by thinkers such as Francisco de Vitoria (1483–1546) and Hugo Grotius (1583–1645) would solidify important just war criteria. Concepts that became incorporated into just war thinking eventually included principles such as: declaration of war by proper authorities; clarification of just causes; appropriate intent; probability of success; and proportionality both with regard to the rationale for entering into war and to the means of combat. These criteria served as a guide to systematically analyzing the reasons for entering into a conflict.

Because war almost invariably results in the loss of life and inflicts tremendous suffering, just war criteria set a high bar. Even though violence may be permissible under these just war criteria, the general understanding is that war ought never to be entered into lightly. Given these stringent criteria, some scholars have argued that there has never been a just war fought, although some are more just than others, including the decision by the United States to enter into the Second World War in response to both the attack on Pearl Harbor by Japan and to German aggression. The decisions to send American citizens of Japanese descent to internment camps and to use atomic weapons, however, compromise the integrity of fighting a just war.

In the twentieth century, the invention and use of weapons of mass destruction, as well as the increasing frequency of guerrilla wars, have resulted in a re-thinking of classical just war theory. Nuclear weapons, as well as chemical and biological agents, pose a substantially greater threat to civilians and have longer lasting detrimental effects on the environment compared to conventional weapons. As such, some have argued that the imminent threat of their use may justify pre-eminent attack, which presents a reversal of the traditional understanding that just wars are defensive wars. Guerilla warfare, too, presents challenges to classical notions of just war. In traditional just war theory, civilians and combatants ought to be distinguished from each other by markers such as distinctive uniforms for soldiers. Guerilla warfare, however, blurs the distinction between civilians and combatants by eschewing military uniforms and fighting in areas dominated by civilian activities. Guerilla warfare complicates the just war principle of avoiding harm to civilians and frequently reduces the probability of success.

Given the undeniable harms and suffering that even the most "just" of wars incur, a number of Christian communities embrace pacifist views and eschew violence. Often associated with historic peace churches, such as the Church of the Brethren, the Religious Society of Friends ("Quakers"), Mennonites, and the Amish, these Christians believe that Jesus teaches nonviolence. Many peace church followers will take a position of non-violent resistance, rather than fighting in self-defense. During large scale conflicts, some members of historic peace churches may participate as a civic duty to one's nation, but will typically not bear arms and serve in non-combatant roles, such as medics. Organizations affiliated with historic peace churches, such as the American Friends Service Committee, often offer humanitarian aid during conflict regardless of the political loyalty of the beneficiary.

Islam

The reputation that Islam has acquired since the 9/11 attacks is one of violent extremism and intolerance. Violent extremist groups such as the Taliban, al-Qaeda, and ISIS (ISIL) have dominated the media with their relentless campaigns to establish political and military dominance in Muslim-majority areas. Although these groups justify their violence and oppression through their particular interpretations of Islam, the vast majority of Muslims disapprove of these groups and their tactics. The leadership of important Muslim institutions has formally denounced these organizations. The Grand Imam of al-Azhar, considered the leading center of Islamic and Arabic study in the world, formally denounced such acts as crimes and expressed grave concerns about the damage they have done to the reputation of Islam. He and other leaders have uniformly condemned their slaughter of innocents in the name of Islam.

Discussion about violence in Islamic traditions in North America and Western Europe typically concern either violence against women or *jihad*, sometimes translated as "Islamic holy war." The misogynistic laws and abusive treatment of women in Afghanistan under Taliban rule, for example, have attracted global concern and have been denounced by both Muslims and non-Muslims alike. The abuse of women under the Taliban was well documented and ranged from extreme isolation to murder. Women were kept in *purdah*, or hidden from public view unless absolutely necessary, and required to wear the *burka*, a gown that covers the female body from head to toe with a small opening for the eyes, when they needed to leave their homes. Girls were restricted from formal education; and schools that enrolled girls were destroyed by the Taliban. Although the Taliban represent an extreme form of Islam, they have had an enormous influence in shaping the perception of Islam in Europe and North America as a profoundly misogynistic religion. Not surprisingly, laws banning female Muslim clothing would soon follow in countries with Muslim minority populations for the ostensible purpose of removing "oppressive" female symbols from public view.

Much attention has been drawn to the term *jihad*, which is often translated as a type of Muslim holy war. Islamic law provides strong parallels to the Christian just war tradition with regard to the morality of conflict. As in the Christian just war tradition, in Islamic law we find guidance indicating the need for proper authority to wage war. Islamic scholars have also discussed legitimate causes for entering into war, including defending one's people. Additionally, right intent appears as a significant concern within the Islamic discourse on war. The primary purpose of entering into war should be to establish or maintain justice, and even then only if one has a reasonable chance of success. Proportionality, in other words, is an important concern and any benefit gained through victory must be great enough to justify the loss of human life. As with the Christian just war tradition, *jus in bello* criteria for Muslim warriors require the distinction between combatants and civilians and proportionate use of force.

Since 9/11, extremist groups such as al-Qaeda and ISIS have attempted to alter the traditional understanding of just war criteria in the Islamic tradition. These two groups have, in particular, challenged traditional understandings of proper authority, proportionality, and non-combatant immunity. With regard to non-combatant immunity, ISIS has controversially killed Muslims who have disagreed with their extremist ideology.

Case Study: Judaism, Israel, and Nuclear Weapons

The possession of nuclear weapons by the state of Israel has long stirred controversy among Jews. On the one hand, historical threats by neighboring countries have prompted Israel to amass nuclear weapons as a deterrence to war. On the other hand, Jewish law and ethical teachings take a strong stance, even during times of war, against the kind of mass destruction that nuclear weapons would wreak. Although Israel is unlikely to relinquish its nuclear arsenal, many Jews have argued for the reduction of its stockpile.

Informed by WWII and the Holocaust, Jews have mixed responses to the development, possession, and use of nuclear weapons. Prominent Jewish scientists, including Leo Szilard and Joseph Rotblat, worked on the Manhattan Project to help the United States develop an atomic bomb. While these scientists believed that the creation of such a weapon could deter future warfare, the decision to deploy them led to profound ambivalence about atomic weapons. Szilard, for example, petitioned for the destructive capacity of atomic weapons to be demonstrated first to enemies, rather than have them deployed in Hiroshima and Nagasaki. Rotblat, who initially signed onto the Manhattan Project so that the United States could develop an atomic bomb before the Nazis, resigned in 1944 when he learned that Germany had abandoned its atomic plans. Both Rotblat and Szilard became political activists following WWII and protested the use of the atomic weapons they had been so instrumental in developing.

Much of the debate surrounding nuclear weapons centers on their ability to deter war rather than their deployment. While the deterrence of war would be preferable to the mass death and destruction caused by nuclear weapons, the fear that nuclear weapons could be deployed cannot be dismissed. Prominent Jewish Orthodox thinkers, Maurice Lamm, Immanuel Jakobovits, and Michael Wyschogrod argued in a series of debates during the Cold War as to whether or not the use of nuclear weapons could be justified. While Lamm claimed that their use could be construed as a form of martyrdom, Jakobovits and Wyschogrod disagreed. Martyrdom applies only when one sacrifices oneself, not others, which is the outcome in a nuclear war; moreover, the idea of nuclear war as "defensive" is illogical if nuclear war results in the elimination of entire populations.

Assuming nuclear weapons are never to be used, but held merely as a deterrent, then Jewish law seems to permit their possession. Using analogous reasoning, scholars have argued that the possession of a nuclear arsenal is the equivalent to a threat or a lie necessary to preserve life. As such, Israel is ethically justified in amassing these and other weapons of mass destruction with the knowledge that the state does not actually intend to carry out the threat of detonating atomic bombs on enemies. If the threat is sufficient to deter the enemy from attacking Israel, then the threat is permissible. By this logic, reducing the nuclear arsenal would be the equivalent of weakening the will to survive and, as such, Israel should not pursue disarmament. Acknowledging the terrible capacity of atomic weapons for mass destruction, Israeli Jews may argue that being a nuclear state is the lesser of two evils. If Israel chose not to maintain nuclear weapons, then its alternative would be to open itself to destruction by hostile neighbors.

After Hiroshima and Nagasaki, no nation has used nuclear weapons in war. The depth of their destruction changed the calculus of the ethics of war. Not only the existence of atomic bombs, but also their subsequent proliferation, has resulted in an international arms race that strives for peace at the risk of the elimination of humanity. The position of Israel with regard to its own nuclear arsenal captures this tension. While Israel's status as a nuclear nation helps to ensure its security, it also ironically jeopardizes its own survival along with that of its neighbors.

Questions:

1   How should ancient religious texts, which have no mention of nuclear weapons, be interpreted to apply to contemporary situations?
2   What are some historical arguments in favor of Israel becoming a nuclear state?
3   Why should Israel consider reducing its nuclear capacity?
4   How might Jews from different sects interpret the ethics of nuclear weapons?
5   Do nuclear weapons pose a different ethical dilemma for Jews compared to other weapons of mass destruction? Why or why not?

Note

1   There comes a point in moral argumentation when one is pushed up against science. It is virtually impossible to argue against people who refuse to accept scientific medical evidence. While scientific and medical data are not without flaws, not all such data is so biased as to be considered unreliable. Indeed, we cannot be paralyzed by the belief that all data is politically tainted. When we talk about the violent effects of American football on players' brains, for example, the brain damage caused by years of playing football is irrefutable. There is a difference between acknowledging the facts of the matter and the opinions one develops based on those facts. One can argue that football should be continued to

be played as a sport because players are willing to play while fully acknowledging the risks of the sport. One can also argue that so long as players are willing to put their brains at risk, we should be allowed to watch, indeed even enjoy, the sport. One cannot, however, argue cogently that football players do not suffer brain damage and therefore spectators can support football without moral consideration. Given this, at what point are spectators complicit in players' willingness to suffer permanent brain damage?

References

Hammer, Juliane. *Peaceful Families: American Muslim Efforts against Domestic Violence.* Princeton, NJ: Princeton University Press, 2019.

Harris, Elizabeth J. "Buddhism in War: A Study of Cause and Effect from Sri Lanka." *Culture and Religion* 2:2 (2001), 197–222.

Jayasuriya, Laksiri. "Just War Tradition and Buddhism." *International Studies* 46:4 (October 2009), 423–38. https://doi.org/10.1177/002088171004600403.

Kelsay, John. *Arguing the Just War in Islam.* Cambridge, MA: Harvard University Press, 2007.

Maurice Lamm, Immanuel Jakobovits, and Michael Wyschogrod. "'Red or Dead?': An Attempt at Formulating a Jewish Attitude." *Tradition* 4:2 (1962), 165–209.

Rodin, David, and Richard Sorabji, eds. *The Ethics of War: Shared Problems in Different Traditions.* Aldershot: Ashgate, 2006.

Walzer, Michael. "The Ethics of Warfare in the Jewish Tradition." *Philosophia* 40 (2012), 633–41. https://doi.org/10.1007/s11406-012-9390-5.

Walzer, Michael. *Just and Unjust War: A Moral Argument with Historical Illustrations.* 5th edition. New York: Basic Books, 2015.

Chapter 6

Feminism, Sex, and Gender

For some of my students, sexism and gender discrimination in their own religious traditions have proven the most difficult of all the ethical issues to confront. The patriarchal histories of virtually all long-established religious traditions stand in stark contrast to the egalitarian beliefs and practices familiar to students today. The recognition, moreover, of the lingering remnants of discrimination—even when given theological justification—in a number of religious denominations invokes powerful responses among my students ranging from anger to disbelief. Over the course of the semester, the vast majority of students eventually reconcile these histories and practices with their loyalty to the religious traditions in which they grew up. I have had a small handful of students, almost all women from religious backgrounds, who struggled beyond the semester with the information encountered in their studies of sex and gender in religious ethics. These students felt they had to choose between defending their faith and acknowledging their equal worth as women. The knowledge that religious sects and denominations often accommodate believers with a variety of perspectives, and that religious teachings and practices evolve over time, provided them little comfort.

Women's experiences as followers of the world's religions are profoundly varied. Both within religious traditions and among them, women's religious lives can differ dramatically as a result of diverse cultural, political, and economic factors. Even within a particular religious tradition, the experiences of women shift through history and across geographies. A woman's life, whether as a Buddhist or Jew, as a Hindu or Christian, depends on many factors in addition to the religious tradition to which she might belong. Women of similar economic class and educational levels living in the same geographic region, but who identify with different religious traditions, for example, may very well have more in common with each other than women of the same religious tradition who live in geographically disparate regions with differing levels of economic security and educational attainment. While acknowledging these differences and the variety of women's experiences, we can nonetheless attempt to draw some similarities across religions that have affected and continue to affect many women because of their female sex or feminine gender.

DOI: 10.4324/9781003350637-7

The world's major religious traditions tend to have patriarchal histories. Although exceptions exist, religious traditions have typically privileged men over women. Men, far more often than women, have been credited as founders, leaders, and authorities of religions. Moses, Jesus, Mohammad, and Siddhartha Gautama were men. The Pope, the Dalai Lama, and the Ayatollah have always been men. Women's rights and feminist movements have certainly had an impact in improving gender and sex equity in the policies and practices of many religious institutions, but full equality is rare. Moreover, for some religious believers, full gender equality is not necessarily desired, either. Rather, in more traditional religious communities, men and women ideally take on complementary roles based on sex. Women in these communities often assume primary responsibility for domestic chores and childcare, while men work outside the home and provide financially for their families. Men, also, are assumed to be heads of households and to take on leadership positions in religious congregations and in public office.

Sex (which refers to one's biological sex) and gender (which refers cultural notions of masculinity and femininity) are categories that are woven into discussions of power, economic status, and tradition. Although the two terms are used interchangeably in colloquial discussions, sex in academic discourse typically refers to biological sex, while gender is understood as performative and culturally determined. To be sure, the performativity of gender, though ostensibly freely exercised, can be in practice highly restrained due to strong cultural norms and expectations. With regard to religious practice and discourse, sex and gender are obvious and important topics of inquiry. The significance of sex and gender in the teachings of religious traditions cannot be underestimated.

Until very recently, cis-gendered heterosexuality was considered normative, even though gay, lesbian, bi-sexual, and transgendered persons have always existed as members of religious communities. From the cradle to the grave, whether one is born female, male, or intersex, has had tremendous implications for how one can and will live one's life. Educational opportunities, expectations of behavior, marriage, childbirth and child-rearing, occupation, and economic security—all of these aspects of one's life are important to religious ethics and have often been described in gendered terms.

Within religious traditions, positions of authority have typically been granted to men. The vast majority of leaders of religious communities, congregations, and groups in all of the major world traditions have been men. On local, national, and international levels, religious institutions typically grant authority to men to lead religious rituals; to oversee churches, mosques, and temples; and to represent the religious institutions to the wider public. Women, of course, have played an important role in religious traditions, but their roles have often been relegated to lower status positions with little or no authority. While men might hold positions as priests, for example, women cannot hold that title even if they manage religious events and organizations.

Women are recognized, at times, as the mothers, wives, sisters, and daughters of important religious figures. Their status, however, results primarily from their relationship to men, rather than their own accomplishments.

Ethical issues arise for women, as well as for men, not merely in reference to institutional positions of authority, but rather in everyday life. Although most religious traditions make claims about the value and worth of every human being, the reality for many women is that they are less powerful economically, politically, and culturally compared to men. The adoration of and respect for women and mothers reflected in scripture and teachings may reflect an ideal that obscures gender-based discrimination found in women's actual experiences. In other words, we find a gap between the religious ideal and lived reality.

Economically, women around the world are poorer than men; women own less capital, lead fewer businesses, and may even be considered the property of their fathers, husbands, or sons. Politically, far fewer women than men hold government offices on local, national, and international levels. Culturally, far fewer women than men are celebrated as creators of great literature, music, and art. Women are less likely to pursue careers and become recognized as important contributors to culture. Religions, as much as they are shaping forces, are also reflective of the larger cultures in which they exist and so much of the sexism that we find within and perpetuated by them reflect the ideas of the surrounding society.

As much as religious institutions have enforced a gender hierarchy, religious traditions have also inspired movements for gender equality. The suffrage movement in the United States, for example, grew out of the Christian temperance movement. In an attempt to prohibit excessive alcohol consumption that was destroying families, Christian wives and mothers mobilized to influence political policy. A large part of their political strategy was to give women the right to vote. If women, they argued, were expected to uphold morality in the family and in the community, they should also be entrusted with the right to help select moral leaders.

Feminism, which in its most basic form seeks equality between the sexes, has had a significant impact not just upon the treatment of women within religious traditions, but also upon the study of religious traditions. The two developments often progressed in tandem. The scholarly pursuit of feminist interpretations of biblical scripture, for example, has been utilized to advance arguments in favor of women's leadership in religious institutions, including churches, synagogues, and mosques. Feminist scholars have also questioned patriarchal assumptions found in theological accounts of human nature, sin, and virtue.

Although early feminist movements focused largely on the concerns of White, middle class, Christian women, subsequent "waves" of feminism critiqued the movement's narrow focus and considered the experiences of women of color, poor women, lesbians, women in post-colonial contexts, and women in religious traditions other than Christianity. Because women draw from different sources of strength and face different challenges depending upon their unique contexts, the inclusion of post-colonial critiques and non-Christian religious views has been vitally important for expanding the feminist movement. Moreover, scholarship about religious women who embrace traditional, ostensibly anti-feminist values, has both enriched and challenged the liberal assumptions that undergird feminism. Most recently, the feminist movement has grown to encompass the voices of transgendered and transsexual persons, who face discrimination, persecution, and violence in many communities, including religious ones. Acknowledging the tremendous diversity of women's experiences—even when perspectives are at odds with each other—is necessary for acquiring an accurate understanding of the complex religious lives and ethical values of women.

In each of the global religions, women's experiences may or may not reflect institutional norms regarding sex and gender. However, women's participation in these traditions reflects commonly accepted customs and norms, and women's efforts to perpetuate or to challenge these traditions demonstrate that religions are human institutions. None of these traditions has remained static with regard to sex and gender, and these traditions will surely evolve in the years to come.

Hinduism

Hinduism presents conflicting views toward gender that are complicated by the influence of British colonialism. On the one hand, there is a long and rich history of ancient foundational texts that expound upon the power and beauty of the feminine. Women scholars contributed to the Vedas, and the *Upanishads* refer to women and mothers as teachers. There is also a pre-Vedic tradition of goddess worship that indicates a historic reverence for the potential creative and destructive powers wielded by women. On the other hand, historical practices suggest that Hindu women in reality were subject to patriarchal norms. Rituals, such sati, and the suicide of Hindu widows more generally, were practiced for several centuries in various parts of the Indian subcontinent even though they are not condoned in the Vedic texts. The custom of child marriage, in which pre-pubescent girls were betrothed to much older men, severely limited their educational and economic opportunities. However, these practices, historically viewed through the lens of British colonialists, painted Hindu women as oppressed in order to provide a moral excuse for controlling the subcontinent. In other words, the British justified their political and economic control of India with arguments that the Hindus were morally stunted, and evidence such as sati and child brides bolstered their cause.

India today is regarded as one of the worst countries for women as measured by statistics such as "boy preference" (e.g., the percentage of female fetuses aborted compared to male fetuses, or rates of female infanticide) and girls' access to education. There are, however, notable regional differences with regard to the status of women. Women in southern and northeastern regions of India, for example, tend to have high rates of literacy, marry later, bear fewer children, work independently, and live longer than women in northern and northwestern regions. In contemporary India, national policies have been put into place that aim to increase women's access to education and wealth.

For much of the history of Hinduism, women have not had the same opportunities and freedoms as men. *Ashramas*, or stages of life that upper-caste Hindu men traditionally followed, did not apply to women. Typically, an upper-caste boy would become a student; marry, have children, and become a householder; retire to become a "forest dweller"; and in his final years, live the life of ascetic. Upper-caste girls, on the other hand, experienced child-hood under the protection of their parents; once married, they would follow their husbands. Members of the lower-castes and *shudras*, regardless of sex or gender, typically did not receive lengthy educations as children and did not retire as forest dwellers or ascetics.

For Hindu women, purity in the form of sexual chastity was very impor-tant for maintaining social standing. In the Hindu epic the *Ramayana*, Sita is praised for remaining loyal to her husband, Prince Rama, while she was held captive by the villain, Ravana. In subsequent stories to the *Ramayana*, Sita's sexual purity during her captivity is questioned by villagers, and so Rama banishes Sita, pregnant with twins, into exile to raise their children alone. Although Sita remains a paragon of virtue despite the accusations against her, she attains this elevated status not for her bravery, but because of her sexual purity—even while she was kidnapped and imprisoned against her will—and her sexual loyalty to Rama during her long captivity.

Like Sita, women today are expected to be sexually inexperienced at mar-riage and to remain faithful to their husbands. Hindu boys are expected, also, to remain sexually pure until marriage, but if they are not, they do not suffer the social stigma that sexually experienced Hindu girls do. These existing cultural norms stressing the importance of a girl's sexual purity were further reinforced by colonial-era Christian missionaries from Great Britain.

Many Hindus have found inspiration in goddess traditions. Also referred to as *Shaktism*, goddess traditions center around the vitality and power of the creative forces of female goddesses. Divine figures associated with *Shakti* include goddesses such as Kali, who symbolizes death and destruction; Uma, the gentle consort of Shiva; and the powerful Durga, who represents protec-tion and strength. Brahman, the great unifying force sometimes depicted as a god, is considered genderless.

In contemporary India, Hinduism has a complicated relationship with pol-itics and the enactment of laws and policies that would improve the lives of women and the LGBTQIA+ community. On the one hand, Hindus are advocating to grant rights and opportunities to marginalized groups and see no incompatibility between traditional Hindu values and progressive politics. On the other hand, conservative Hindu-nationalist political groups are becoming increasingly popular and resisting change that would extend rights to LGBTQIA+ citizens. Hindus are, for example, increasingly celebrating same-sex marriages officiated by vedic priests, but their marriages are not yet recognized by Indian law. In 2018, the Indian Supreme Court struck down a ban on gay sex, although it has not recognized the legality of same-sex marriages. With regard to transgendered persons, India in 2014 recognized transgendered persons as a "third" gender, but regulations passed in 2019 that require transgendered persons to register as male or female have been contested as regressive.

Buddhism

The possibility of enlightenment for Buddhist men in the tradition's 2500 years of existence rarely, if ever, hinged on the question of their sex. Buddhist literature makes the assumption that men, through proper training, commitment, and circumstances, could attain enlightenment. For women, however, the possibility of enlightenment has varied throughout the tradition's history and across geographies. Sometimes it was thought that women, if reincarnated as men, could eventually attain enlightenment. According to this way of thinking, men were viewed as morally superior in the cycles of reincarnation, and so rebirth as a man would indicate that one was closer to the goal of nirvana. At other times, Buddhist teachings have claimed that women themselves could attain enlightenment and so nunneries were established where women could dedicate their lives to reaching that goal. More frequently, however, women have been encouraged and praised for carrying out their duties as devout laypersons who support male monks by providing food and alms.

According to popular hagiography, Siddhartha Gautama himself was a husband and father before he set out to seek enlightenment. In his journey to attain *nirvana*, Siddhartha renounced his home and his family, and thus demonstrated his detachment from worldly concerns. Some narratives explain that Siddhartha's wife, Yasodhara, gave him permission to leave their home and family in order to lead an ascetic life, and that Yasodhara, too, overcame her attachment to her husband and her son, and became a nun later in life. Other accounts portray a grieving Yasodhara, who was either pregnant or had just recently given birth to their son, when Siddhartha left to seek enlightenment. The variations of Yasodhara's story suggest that Buddhists have often debated not only if women are capable of renouncing home and family, but also whether women ought to renounce home and family. Those in favor of nunneries and women's enlightenment pointed to Yasodhara, as well as the aunt who cared for the Buddha in childhood, as exemplars who were surely deserving at least the same opportunities as men. When

Mahapajapati, Siddhartha's aunt, asked the Buddha to allow her to become a nun, he initially refused. Only after the monk Ananda, one of the Buddha's trusted companions, intervened on Mahapajapati's behalf, was she permitted to become a nun. Although the early texts provide no rationale for the Buddha's initial refusal, he may have had concerns about women eschewing marriage and children. Nonetheless, the Buddha's ultimate decision to establish nunneries was predicated upon the belief that the *dharma* applied to all, not just to men, and that women could choose to live a life dedicated to the pursuit of enlightenment. Today, Buddhist nunneries continue to exist, but nuns number far fewer than monks.

The concept of *anatman*, or "no-self," which is found in both Theravada and Mahayana traditions, implies that one's gender ultimately bears no relevance when seeking enlightenment, and that attachment to one's gender may in fact present obstacles in the path to nirvana. In the *Soma Sutta*, the nun Soma, who was one of the earliest followers of the Buddha, vanquishes the evil Māra by refusing to succumb to his sexist taunts. Māra derides Soma for possessing low intelligence because she is a woman, but Soma causes Māra to flee when she asserts that understanding the dharma does not rely upon one's sex, and, moreover, that the assertion of one's sex in pursuit of dharma is a sign of evil. Although the narrative of Soma and the example of Mahapajapati present arguments in favor of women's equal status to men, for many women, the goal of reincarnation was—as noted above—rebirth as men. This held true even though women, particularly as mothers, were, in theory, worthy of great respect.

Theravada and Mahayana traditions include texts, rituals, and customs that express a range of attitudes toward women. Although some women turned to the Mahayana *sangha* for full ordination, which was denied to them in Theravada communities, women in Mahayana Buddhism nonetheless faced discrimination. The path to becoming a *bodhisattva*—one who postponed enlightenment and eventual Buddhahood in order to help others to attain enlightenment—is limited for women according to some Mahayana traditions. Women could only attain a certain level of *bodhisattvahood* and must first become men in order to advance to the highest levels of *bodhisattvahood*. Other Mahayana narratives describe women who are *bodhisattvas* of the highest order, including Tara and Quan-Yin, both of whom have generations of large followings.

Today, largely in response to women's concerns about discrimination, the Sakyadhita International Association of Buddhist Women has attempted to re-establish lost communities of nuns. Established in 1987, Sakyadhita has been especially active in Theravada countries and regularly hosts conferences to promote gender equity in Buddhism. Although some have criticized Sakyadhita as unduly influenced by the agenda of "Western" feminists, there does appear to be movement within Buddhism to promote gender equality. More recently, the 14th Dalai Lama has stated that the next incarnation of the Dalai Lama could be a woman.

With regard to homosexuality, Buddhists have mixed views that tend to reflect larger cultural norms. Historically, Buddhist teachings forbade homosexual relations. Early commentaries mention the immorality of non-vaginal sex and assert that sexual relationships should take place within marriage. Monasteries, in theory, rejected gay men and intersex persons. Today, however, attitudes about gays and lesbians are changing. Buddhists are generally open to advances in scientific knowledge about homosexuality, which has shown that sexual orientation is not a choice, but rather biologically and genetically determined. As such, many Buddhists have been reluctant to condemn homosexuality and have acknowledged that right action and right attitude are often historically determined. Whereas homosexuality may have been condemned in the past, today it is accepted in many—although not all—parts of the world where Buddhists live.

Jainism

As with Hindus and Buddhists, Jains aim to attain a state of enlightenment and release from cycles of reincarnation. The role of women in Jainism is distinctive, however, in that nuns and female ascetics (*sadhvis*) have been a part of the tradition since its earliest days, and that the number of nuns outnumbers the number of monks in major sects of the tradition. Within Jainism, however, there are differences that have emerged regarding whether one could attain enlightenment directly as a woman.

One of the two major sects of Jainism, the Svetambara ("white-robed" or "white-clad") believed that one could enter into a state of nirvana as a woman. The other main sect, the Digambara ("sky-clad") insisted that only men could attain nirvana; women had to first be reincarnated as men in order to achieve enlightenment. For the Svetambara, recognized by the white gauze robes worn by both nuns and monks, gender and sex ought not to matter in the pursuit of enlightenment. Rather, the Svetambara focus on internal measures, such as mastery of the three gems of "right faith, right knowledge, and right behavior," as the primary vehicles toward enlightenment. In practice, however, nuns within the Svetambara sect are subordinate to monks. Although nuns have historically outnumbered monks, men nevertheless assume positions of authority above nuns.

For the Digambara, nuns are incapable of attaining enlightenment within their lifetimes. Whereas monks are permitted to eschew clothing in a pious display of *aparigraha*, or detachment from objects, nuns are required to cover their bodies. The sect prevents women from displaying this level of commitment to *aparigraha* ostensibly out of concerns about sexual harassment and assault. Moreover, the Digambara hold that because women's bodies contain microbes unique to the female sex, women are biologically impure and cannot attain enlightenment.

For lay Jains, women play an important role because of the intensive cooking methods traditional to their cuisine. Jains' strict observance of *ahimsa* requires careful cooking so as to prevent the accidental death and consumption of insects and micro-organisms believed to contain *jivas*, or souls. Even though the Jain diet is generally vegetarian, devout Jains will also eschew garlic and onions, root vegetables, certain fruits and vegetables (such as eggplant), and even honey, among other things. Water, too, should be strained and boiled before being drunk or used for food preparation, in consideration of possible *jivas*. Jain lay women typically take responsibility for preparing meals and providing food to monks and nuns. This requires knowledge of which types of plants are appropriate for consumption, the proper preparation of these foods, and the correct means of food presentation. Although Jain women today still tend to adhere to traditionally domestic roles, they have the highest literacy rate, at 90%, of any religious group in the subcontinent.

Although Jainism has not escaped the hierarchy of gender common to many subcontinental traditions, Jain ideas concerning non-binary genders are distinctive and relatively extensive. Jain teachings include, for example, discussions about a "third sex" *napumsaka* (biological males who present as women) and a "fourth sex" *purusa napumsaka* (biological females who present as men). References to the third sex are found in classical Hindu texts, and transgender and intersex *hijras* ("third gender" persons) have long been part of Hindu ritual tradition, but Jain writings on gender are detailed in part because of early debates about the possibility of women attaining enlightenment. The question of what counts as male or female during these discussions gave rise to scholarly speculation about the nature of gender.

Judaism

While Jews believe that all humans are equal before God, Jews disagree as to the proper roles of women and men as dictated by interpretations of this religious tradition. Views toward women, gender, and homosexuality exist on a continuum, with the most traditional views held by Orthodox sects and the most progressive views held by Reform, Reconstructionist, and secular Jews. These differences among the sects of Judaism can be attributed to their various approaches to scripture, law, and tradition.

In Orthodox communities, men and women typically shoulder different responsibilities and perform different tasks and rituals based on their sex. In Reform and Reconstructionist communities, women and men may perform the same rituals and assume the same roles. Conservative Jews hold a position in between Orthodox and Reform and Reconstructionist Jews. Secular Jews, who identify with Judaism predominantly as cultural practice, typically maintain progressive views toward sex and gender.

In Orthodox Judaism, men and women assume different roles in the home and in the synagogue based upon their sex. In the home, women take primary responsibility for domestic duties and childcare. Because Orthodox homes observe kosher dietary laws, women are expected to know the rules that govern food preparation and eating. Preparing for weekly Shabbat, numerous holiday meals, and keeping a kosher kitchen fall under the category of women's work. Women are also expected to have children and care for them, especially while they are young. Responsibility for home life, however, does not preclude Orthodox women from working outside the home. Following the image of the "capable wife" described in Proverbs 31:10–31, a number of Orthodox wives and mothers pursue work and career opportunities in addition to maintaining the home. Orthodox Jewish men, while encouraged to participate actively in domestic rituals and home life, preside over the synagogue and in public leadership roles. Only men are permitted to become rabbis, hold positions of religious authority, and lead services outside the home.

In Conservative and Reform communities, women take on more public roles and assume positions of religious authority. Not only do women serve as rabbis, but many Conservative and Reform sects also allow for gay and lesbian rabbis. Since 2006, Conservative synagogues and temples have authorized commitment ceremonies for gay and lesbian couples, and since 2012 they have permitted same-sex marriages. Reform Judaism has been among the most progressive of religious sects with regard to homosexuality and, more recently, transgender and transsexual rights. In 1965, the group Women of Reform Judaism advocated for the decriminalization of homosexuality; in 1977, the Union for Reform Judaism demanded human rights for gays and lesbians. Since then, various arms of Reform Judaism have called for expanding the rights and privileges of LBGTQIA+ persons. More recently, the Reform community has released guidelines for inclusivity of transgender, transsexual, and gender non-conforming synagogue members. In Orthodox communities, heterosexuality is considered the norm, and non-conforming members of the community tend to remain closeted or ostracized. Although Jewish scripture affirms the equality of each human, *halakha* and Orthodox rulings condemn homosexual relations and do not permit gay marriage. In recent years, particularly with the growing acceptance of LBGTQIA+ persons and increased scientific awareness of the biological and genetic aspects of gender, a number of Orthodox communities have moved to include LBGTQIA+ individuals.

Christianity

In both practice and doctrine, Christian communities display a wide variety of approaches toward issues of gender, gay marriage, and LBGTQIA+ rights. Given the long history, global reach, and popularity of the tradition, it is not surprising that Christian sects and denominations hold varying views on these topics. These differences are apparent even within individual Christian communities. Issues such as women in the ministry, abortion, and gay marriage have been hot button topics within many Christian groups. As with other religious traditions, Christian beliefs may reflect the norms of their surrounding cultures, which accounts for some of the variation in views toward sex and gender in Christianity as a whole.

Even within the first century, the Jesus movement that would eventually develop into the religion of Christianity manifested differences with regard to the role of women. Accounts of Jesus in the New Testament indicate that he welcomed women into his community, including women who would have been considered of low social status. Jesus ate alongside these women, did not consider women to be property of men, and helped to alleviate the suffering of women. Mary Magdalene, although not an apostle, served as an important witness to the death and resurrection of Jesus. Since the earliest services were held in private homes, women sometimes took on leadership roles. The letters of Paul, the apostle and first century missionary, indicate that women played a significant role in the early development of the church. However, in epistles attributed to but likely not written by Paul, we find theological statements asserting the dominance of men over women that have ramifications to this day. Statements such as "the man is the head of the woman, as Christ is the head of the Church" (Ephesians 5:21) and "I do not permit a woman to be a teacher, nor must woman domineer over man; she should be quiet" (1 Timothy 2:12) mark a departure from the relatively egalitarian practices of Jesus and the earliest Church.

With the spread of Christianity throughout the Mediterranean, restrictions against female leadership increased, primarily because the movement began to reflect the norms of the surrounding society. Cultural and philosophical arguments that associated men with virtue and strength and women with evil and weakness reinforced claims about the lower status of the female sex. The subsequent growth of the church beyond the domestic sphere into public spaces, where men would normally have presided, contributed to the dominance of male authority in early Christianity. By the time that the Church became the official state religion of the Roman Empire in 380 CE, the restrictions against women were firmly in place.

Despite the relatively low status of women in much of Christendom, a number of women found opportunities to escape the larger society by entering into ascetic communities. Here, women did not have to marry or bear children, pursued educational opportunities denied to them in the larger world, and held positions of authority. Women such as Syncletica of Alexandria (ca. 270–350), Hildegaard of Bingen (1098–1179), Catherine of Sienna (1347–80), and Teresa of Avila (1515–82) were part of the Christian mystical tradition, which emphasized a direct, deeply emotional connection to God. Mysticism afforded women a place for religious contemplation, independent of traditional, male structures of authority.

With the Protestant Reformation, which stressed an understanding of Christianity through scripture, faith, and God's grace, opportunities for women changed accordingly. After monasteries and nunneries were abolished in Protestant countries, ministers and priests were allowed to marry. Former nuns, however, were forbidden from holding positions of authority and were expected to marry. Although girls and women were now educated, as the ability to read the Bible was important for Protestant Christians, that same text reinforced the notion that women should remain silent and subordinate to their husbands.

The evolution of women's positions of authority in the church, particularly in Protestant denominations, often tracked their political gains outside of the church. In the United States, for example, Christian women developed political skills to advocate for women's suffrage through church-based abolitionist and temperance movements. Over the following decades, women in Protestant denominations would gradually achieve the right to earn seminary degrees, become ordained as ministers, and hold powerful positions within their churches. In 1863, Anna Brown (1835–1926) became the first American woman to be ordained with the consent of her denomination, the Universalist Church. Soon after, the Methodist Church ordained Anna Howard Shaw (1847–1919). Black women fought parallel battles, advocating for their right to preach in the African Methodist Episcopal (AME) Church.

The theological claims of women of color in Christianity, however, were often overlooked in the otherwise ground-breaking work of White, twentieth century Christian feminists. Particularly with the incorporation of feminist thought into Christian thought and practice, Black women—and women who did not share the middle class, White experiences of many early Christian feminists—sought to develop a way of thinking about Christianity that honored their distinct histories and stark realities. Womanist theology, which developed out of the experiences and histories of Black American women, demonstrates both a kinship to and difference from feminist theology. Mujerista theology, developed by Cuban American theologian Ada María Isasi-Días, highlights the experiences of Latina women in the United States and incorporates insights taken from liberation theology, feminist, and womanist thought. The recent rise of Asian American Christian feminist theologies features the unique experiences of Asian and Asian American women, particularly in post-colonial contexts. In each of these visions of feminist theologies, we find a shared struggle in patriarchal and racist societies, as well as a recognition of the different struggles of various racial and ethnic communities.

Women in the Roman Catholic Church, Orthodox Christian churches, and more conservative Protestant denominations, such as the Southern Baptist Convention (SBC), have somewhat expanded women's roles within their organizations. While women are, with very few exceptions, not in positions of higher authority, they are now holding positions of power that had previously been denied to them. These communities believe that men and women, although equally valued by God, have complementary roles to play based upon their sex. Like Martha and Mary, who were not apostles but nonetheless important witnesses to Jesus, women are to serve in supporting roles to male leadership. This argument has been applied to the pulpit and in positions of authority with claims that because Jesus was male, heads of churches ought also to be male.

The SBC, the largest Protestant denomination in the United States, resolved in 1984 that women were not allowed to be ordained so as "to preserve a submission God requires because man was first in creation and woman was first in the Edenic fall." Despite this resolution, individual churches have defied the SBC. Most notably, the highly influential Saddleback Church ordained three women in May 2021 in defiance of the SBC's teachings. These efforts, however, were insufficient to counter the growing criticisms about the misogynistic culture of the SBC. Just prior to Saddleback Church's announcement, the popular Bible study teacher, Beth Moore, declared that she was no longer Southern Baptist. Her disillusionment with the SBC's support of Donald Trump, who had openly acknowledged sexually assaulting women, resulted in her decision to leave the SBC. In May 2022, the SBC released a 288-page independent report that detailed nearly two decades of sexual abuse by hundreds of clergymen, the cover-up of their crimes, and their denigration of victims.

Although women still cannot become ministers in these and similarly conservative congregations, there has been a gradual increase of women's visible participation. In the Roman Catholic Church, a movement to ordain "womenpriests" has resulted in approximately 250 women holding the title of priest at various churches across the globe. Although not officially sanctioned by the Church, womenpriests have been embraced by their congregations and entrusted with the care and ministration of their communities. Like their male counterparts, womenpriests perform sacraments and are ordained in apostolic succession, in which bishops ordain deacons, priests, and other bishops. Although the Roman Catholic hierarchy has not embraced the idea of womenpriests, nevertheless, in 2021, Pope Francis expanded liturgical roles of women during mass, and he also appointed Sister Nathalie Becquart as one of the two undersecretaries for the Vatican's Synod of Bishops. In Orthodox Christianity, women have not been allowed to become priests or to hold office, but arguments against the ordination of women have moved from claims of women's incompetence to claims about preserving tradition.

With regard to issues such as abortion, gay marriage, and inclusion of transgendered and transsexual persons, churches generally fall along a continuum that corresponds to attitudes toward female leadership. For the churches that have expanded church leadership to include women, not only are the requirements based upon male sex and masculine gender deemed irrelevant compared to other attributes of a person, but women are also understood as having equal moral agency as men. When the question of abortion is framed as an issue of women's moral and physical autonomy—in addition to questions about the moral status of the fetus—churches are more likely to accept abortion as morally permissible. When women are not in significant positions of authority in a religious denomination, as in the Roman Catholic Church or conservative evangelical churches, abortion is typically viewed as a wholly immoral act.

Importantly, the official positions of Christian sects differ from the ways in which Christians actually behave and what they believe. The National Survey for Family Growth, conducted by the Centers for Disease Control, has found that women have very similar patterns of contraceptive use regardless of religious identity. While the Roman Catholic Church, for example, forbids birth control, the majority of Roman Catholic women use birth control regularly. With regard to pre-marital sex, co-habitation, divorce, and remarriage, we also find that Catholics disregard Church teachings.

With regard to gay marriage, the acceptance of scientific knowledge about the biological drivers of homosexuality has contributed to the willingness of less conservative Christian churches to perform marriage ceremonies for gay and lesbian couples. A number of such churches began performing commitment ceremonies or blessing same-sex unions, and then allowed church-sanctioned marriages, regardless of the sex of the couple. Orthodox and Roman Catholic Churches do not affirm same-sex unions. Recently, however, several Roman Catholic priests in Germany have openly blessed same-sex unions in defiance of and as protest against official Church teachings.

Islam

In post-9/11 America and Western Europe, the topic of Muslim women invites a tremendous amount of controversy. In the American and Western European imagination, Muslim women have been fetishized objects of orientalist imagery. On the one hand, Muslim women were depicted in European art as seductive concubines, scantily clad and sensual inhabitants of the luxurious harem; on the other hand, we read in the news media about Muslim women horrifically oppressed and even killed for failing to behave modestly. The hijab and demure dress of observant Muslim women supposedly symbolize oppression imposed by patriarchal, Muslim-majority cultures. Muslim women, according to local French laws, needed literally to be stripped in order to demonstrate their allegiance to the values of their adopted country. For Americans, the perceived oppression of women in Muslim majority-countries abroad served, at least in part, to legitimize military intervention in those countries. Although women's basic rights are indeed violated in some Muslim communities, the perception that Muslim women need "saving" from their own religion has been vociferously challenged by Muslim women themselves.[1] Given that many Muslim-majority countries struggle with poverty, political corruption, and poor infrastructure, the suffering of women—and men—in those countries may be attributable to any number of sources beyond religion and culture.

With the 1500-year history of the tradition and its global reach, diversity among Muslims is a given. As with adherents of other popular religions, Muslims represent a very wide range of attitudes, practices, and beliefs toward sex and gender. Within the tradition itself, variation among the sects of Islam, localized cultural practices, economic class, educational levels, and age also often correlate to diversity in attitudes toward sex and gender. Religion is one of many factors to be considered when analyzing Muslim views with regard to the status of women, homosexuality, and LBGTQIA+ rights.

The Qur'an, which for Muslims is the word of God, is subject to multiple interpretations that lead to different conclusions about the status of persons based on their biological sex. Although mullahs, sheiks, and other religious figures may cite the Qur'an in determining proper attitudes toward sex and gender, the way in which practicing Muslims actually choose to live their lives may diverge considerably from these authoritative sources. It is also important to note that historically the various legal schools within Islam have vigorously debated many points of law, and, moreover, accepted each other's varying interpretations as legitimate. When the Qur'an is used to justify certain positions with regard to women and sexuality, these mediating factors ought to be taken into consideration.

According to Sura 49:13 ("the Dwellings"), God "created you male and female, and appointed you races and tribes, that you may know one another. Surely the noblest among you in the sight of God is the most god-fearing of you." This verse suggests that although God created two different sexes, the most important attribute for a human to have is to be "god-fearing." Much of Muslim ethical thinking about men and women is based on the notion of sex complementarity, or the idea that men and women are not to be considered the same in terms of their roles with regard to one another, but rather to "complement" each other. Traditionally, this has meant that women care for young children and the home, while men maintain economic resources for the family and hold positions of authority.

Much has been said about the revolutionary aspects of Islam, which forbade practices of female infanticide and established women's right to inheritance. Also noteworthy is the example of Mohammad's first wife, Khadijah, who not only proposed marriage to Mohammad, but was a well-respected businesswoman in her own right. These seemingly progressive aspects of the tradition are contrasted with the acceptance of polygamy, albeit limited to four wives, each of whom must be treated equally (4:129). Perhaps the most controversial verse of the Qur'an with regard to women, verse 4:34, describes men as the "managers" of women, labels righteous women as "obedient," and allows men to "beat" rebellious wives. The way in which this verse has been interpreted, whether to reaffirm the hierarchy of husbands over wives or to place this behavior in the historical context of seventh century Arabia, reflects the values and motives of the interpreter. These controversial verses may also be viewed in the context of other parts of the Qur'an that describe marriage as a source of tranquility, love, and mercy (30:21).

For non-Muslims, two issues related to Islam and women seem to dominate the news media: honor killings and the hijab. These issues, while not limited to Muslim communities, are strongly associated with Islam because of their association with Muslim immigrant communities in Europe. However, honor killings have taken place not just among Muslims, but also among Hindus, Sikhs, and Christians; and the practice of wearing (or not wearing) the hijab is tremendously varied among Muslim women.

Honor killings, so called because the perpetrators of the crime tend to be fathers, brothers, and other relatives who claim that the murders of their daughters/wives are necessary to defend the family's honor, are not bound by geography, belief system, or socio-economic class. Rather, honor killings are a form of gender-based violence that take place within patriarchal communities that prioritize tribal or familial identity and loyalty. In these communities, maintaining familial honor is of the utmost importance, even more so than protecting individual life. According to the United Nations, approximately 5,000 honor killings take place annually, although accurate statistics are difficult to collect due to their high rates of under-reporting, particularly in rural areas. Moreover, in some regions, the murder of wives by husbands might be more typically classified as "crimes of passion," rather than as honor killings.

Honor killings are tied to highly patriarchal cultural notions of women and girls as commodities that are given economic value, whether in the form of bride price, dowries, or as prostitutes. Sexual purity, chastity, and monogamy are closely aligned with girls' and women's worth in patriarchal communities. When girls and women engage in sexual relations before or outside of marriage, threaten divorce, or attempt to leave the community, they jeopardize their families' reputation, thus potentially disrupting the stability of their families in the larger community. Male relatives accuse these girls and women of bringing shame upon their families, and they justify such murders as defense of family honor. Men who engage in homosexual activity are also targets of honor killings, presumably because they bring shame upon the family by defying masculine, heteronormative standards.

Imperialist countries had often imposed legal codes, such as the Napoleonic Code and British colonial law, on their colonies that actually facilitated honor killings by granting leniency toward perpetrators. Today, a number of nations penalize or outlaw honor killings. Furthermore, muftis, imams, and clerics have uniformly declared that Islam does not condone honor killings or domestic violence.

The sensationalism of honor killings, which simplifies a complex history and context, parallels the quick condemnation of the hijab as a symbol of the oppression of Muslim women. The reality, of course, is that Muslim, as well as non-Muslim, women wear a wide variety of head coverings for a wide variety of reasons. The most conservative forms of covering drape the entire body from head to toe, such as the chador in Iran or abaya in Saudi Arabia, while more progressive styles of head coverings may consist of a colorful scarf knotted under the chin or at the nape of the neck. In Iran and in Saudi Arabia, where modest dress is mandatory by law and the chador and abaya are the default covering, the vast majority of women will cover their hair and wear loose clothing that covers the body. In other countries, particularly in the United States, some Muslim women choose to wear, in addition to their normal dress, the hijab as a form of religious expression or as a symbol of Muslim pride. Muslim women may don the hijab for certain occasions or when visiting the mosque, but not as part of their everyday wear. In many Muslim communities, men wear modest dress in accordance with religious and cultural norms. Men will often wear long pants, rather than shorts, and loose-fitting shirts, rather than tight shirts or tank tops.

In France, the hijab has symbolized conflict between Muslim immigrant communities and French nationalist identity. It is also a highly gendered conflict, in that Muslim women's bodies, but not Muslim men's, are the site of political contestation. The height of the controversy over the hijab occurred following a terrorist attack in Nice in 2016. Shortly after a Tunisian immigrant killed 86 people celebrating Bastille Day on a beach promenade, the mayors of several towns along the French Riviera, including Nice and Cannes, declared bans on "burkinis" out of fear that they would incite further violence. Burkinis, which are coined from the terms burka and bikini, are made of swimwear material, but cover the arms and legs, and are often worn by observant Muslim women so that they can enjoy the beach while maintaining modesty. Women who wore burkinis were forced to remove their burkinis; accused of violating the French rules regarding secularism, laïcité; and faced financial penalties. Although the highest court of France, the Conseil d'État, eventually found these unconstitutional, the majority of French support banning burkinis. In other countries, particularly in the United States and Great Britain, the French reaction to the burkini was met with surprise and disagreement.

Although the topics of honor killings and the hijab have roused global reactions, for many Muslims the less sensational but pressing issues of homosexuality and gay marriage are a source of intra-community conflict. Muslim clerics across the globe assert that homosexuality presents a deviation from the divine order that creates men and women as complementary binaries. Among Shi'ite clerics in Iran, being transsexual presents less of an ethical problem than homosexuality. Indeed, sex change operations are permissible and even funded by the Iranian government partially because a heterosexual couple, even if one person was born with a different sex, is more acceptable than a homosexual couple. Recent polls have shown that many Muslims in countries where gay marriage is legal believe that same-sex marriage should be accepted. A 2014 Pew Research poll, for example, found that 81% of American Muslims "strongly" favored the view that homosexuality should be accepted.[2] Within the Muslim scholarly community, as well, we find arguments for the acceptance of various forms of masculinities, expressions of love, and acceptance of relationships that encourage human flourishing.

Sikhism

God, according to Sikh traditions, is genderless. Although Guru Gobind Singh refers to different parts of God as "father" and as "mother," God is described in Sikh scripture in genderless terms, such as creator, the one, and the all-pervasive spirit. Guru Nanak famously credits women as necessary, and acknowledges that without women, no great men would exist. From the founding of the tradition, male Sikh leaders upheld women as spiritual equals to men. All ten Gurus who are considered founders of the tradition, however, are men. There are no female Gurus in the tradition despite the genderless understanding of God and theoretical equality between the sexes. Moreover, many cultural practices such as female infanticide were historically as common in Sikh communities as in Hindu ones. Thus, while in theory Sikhism introduced innovations that promoted gender equality, the reality was much more complicated.

Although there is a minor ascetic tradition within Sikhism that is dominated by men, Sikhs understand family life, headed by a mother and father, as an important vehicle toward enlightenment. This marks a departure from other Indian religious traditions, in which family life is considered to be a distraction from the attainment of enlightenment, and detachment from one's family is considered necessary to obtaining nirvana. Like the Buddha, this model has typically meant that husbands and fathers leave mothers and children behind to seek enlightenment. Wives and mothers leaving behind husbands and children, of course, would have been unfathomable. For Sikhs, however, the responsibilities of maintaining a household and rearing children count as devotional practice toward enlightenment for both men and women. The Guru Har Gobind was married and, when asked why, responded that his wife was "his conscience." For women, as wives and mothers, to have their domestic labor considered religious practice allowed them access to enlightenment as women.

While some of these practices in Sikhism appear to elevate the status of women relative to other religious traditions in the area, these innovations also served the purpose of distinguishing Sikhs from Hindus, Buddhists, and Muslims. Sikh women were discouraged from wearing head-coverings, which would have been the norm for Muslim and Hindu women. Other practices, such as *purdah*, or keeping women cloistered from public view, and *sati* were discouraged by Sikhs. Sikh women were, however, expected as was the general custom to dress modestly, behave deferentially, and to adopt gender-specific domestic roles. Sikh women, like the vast majority of women in the region, also assumed primary responsibility for domestic duties, including childcare and cooking.

More recently, the acceptance of homosexuality and gay marriage has revealed rifts in the Sikh community. The early teachings of the tradition and the Guru Granth Sahib do not expound on homosexuality because the heterosexual norm was simply assumed. The Guru Granth Sahib describes marriage between a man and a woman, maintaining a household, and raising children as a path to liberation. The lack of commentary about homosexuality leaves open the possibility for interpretations ranging from the condemnation of homosexuality to acceptance of homosexuality and gay marriage. The issue came to a head when in 2005 the Canadian government sought Sikh opinions about passing legislation to legalize gay marriage. Sikh members of parliament expressed that the tradition does not permit homosexuality, much less gay marriage. As homosexuality and gay marriage have become more acceptable in the larger society however, many Sikhs disagree with more traditional views and assert that in the Sikh tradition, all humans are children of God and should not be discriminated against because of their sexual orientation.

Case Study: Women as Religious Leaders in Islam

On a Friday afternoon in March 2005, Dr. Amina Wadud, a Black American scholar of Islam and activist, led a group of over 100 Muslim men and women in communal prayer in New York City. Following the call to prayer, which was sounded by a woman who did not wear a hijab, Wadud began the ritual prayer at the Synod House of the Cathedral of St. John the Divine, an Episcopal church. No mosque would accommodate the group, and an art gallery that had been willing to accommodate the group rescinded their offer after receiving a bomb threat.

Protesters near and far condemned the event. A prominent Islamic thinker from Qatar, Sheik Yousef al-Qaradawi, claimed that scholars

> agree that women do not lead men in (performing) religious duties . . . one wishes our sisters who are enthusiastic about women's rights would revive the practice of women leading women in prayers, instead of coming up with the heresy of women leading men in prayers.

Other scholars explained that Wadud violated the tradition of separating the sexes during prayer, where the women typically pray in a section behind the men, off to the side, or on a separate floor, so as not to distract the men with their movements and prostrations. Notably, many Muslim women, in addition to men, were disturbed by Wadud's performance. Although women are permitted to lead other women or immediate members of their household in prayer, women generally do not stand before unknown men for communal prayers. In China, the establishment of women's mosques has provided women the opportunity to serve as imams, albeit to single-sex congregations. Women, while prohibited from leading men in prayer, are allowed to teach, preach to, and otherwise guide Muslims of both sexes if they are qualified to do so.

For Wadud, the patriarchal aspects of Islam, including assumptions about the responsibility of women to control the sexual appetites of men during prayer, are not supported by the religion. She insists that the sexist parts of the Qur'an exist because they enabled the religion to flourish in the cultural environment of seventh century Arabia. The Qur'an, in fact, neither describes how Muslims should pray nor dictates that only men should lead prayers. Conservative Muslims cite sections of the Qur'an and hadith about men's guardianship over women to defend men's leadership in prayer: "Men are the protectors and maintainers of women, because Allah has given the one more (strength) than the other, and because they support them from their means. Therefore, the righteous women are devoutly obedient" (Qur'an 4:34). Progressive Muslims assert that these and similar parts of the Qur'an are not directly relevant to women's equality and need to be placed in their proper historical context. These verses no longer apply to the moral, financial, or political standards of the twenty-first century.

Progressive Muslims often point to examples of women as leaders in early Islamic history as a way to refute conservative arguments. Khadijah, Muhammad's first wife, successfully ran her own trading business and was the first convert to Islam. Aisha, who was married to Muhammad following the death of Khadijah, was highly regarded as a repository of knowledge concerning religious teachings and practices and even led troops during the Battle of the Camel. Fatimah, the daughter of Khadijah and Muhammad, is praised by both Sunni and Shi'ite Muslims for her eloquence. Her Fadak sermon, defending her ownership of inherited land, was performed at the Masjid al-Nawabi, which was built by Muhammad and considered one of the holiest sites in Islam. A hadith about Umm Waraqa, a contemporary of Muhammad's who had committed the entirety of the Qur'an to memory, is often cited to support arguments in favor of women leading prayer. According to the hadith, Muhammad instructed Umm Waraqa to lead prayer because she was considered to be the most knowledgeable about Islam in her community. Whether the community consisted only of members of her household or included men outside of her household is debated.

Since Wadud, a number of other Muslim women in countries around the world have led mixed congregations in Friday prayer. They have been met with variety of responses.

Questions:

1   If women in Islam are allowed to teach and preach to men, why should they not be allowed to lead men in prayer? What might praying be considered qualitatively different than teaching and preaching?

2   How should Muslims evaluate sections of the Qur'an, hadith, and sunna that no longer seem relevant to the present day?

3   Do arguments about religious leadership based upon sex differ from arguments about religious leadership based upon race? Why or why not?

4   How might Wadud's identity as a Black American woman affect the way in which Muslims from other parts of the world view her work?

5   Conservative and Reform Judaism, as well as a number of Christian denominations, have in recent decades permitted women to serve as rabbis, ministers, and priests. What are some of the similarities and differences among the Abrahamic traditions with regard to women as religious leaders?

Notes

1   Abu-Lughod, Lila. *Do Muslim Women Need Saving?* Cambridge, MA: Harvard University Press, 2013.

2   https://www.pewforum.org/religious-landscape-study/compare/views-about-same-sex-marriage/by/views-about-homosexuality/among/religious-tradition/muslim/.

Bibliography

Abdo, Geneive. "When Islam Clashes with Women's Rights." *The Boston Globe.* 9 April 2005. http://archive.boston.com/news/globe/editorial_opinion/oped/articles/2005/04/09/when_islam_clashes_with_womens_rights/ (accessed 25 August 2021).

Abu-Lughod, Lila. *Do Muslim Women Need Saving?* Cambridge, MA: Harvard University Press, 2013.

Ali, Kecia. *Sexual Ethics and Islam: Feminist Reflections on Qur'an, Hadith, and Jurisprudence.* Oxford: Oneworld, 2006.

Bano, Masooda, and Hilary Kalmbach. *Women, Leadership and Mosques Changes in Contemporary Islamic Authority.* Leiden: Brill, 2012.

Cabezón, José Ignacio. *Sexuality in Classical South Asian Buddhism.* Somerville, MA: Wisdom Publications, 2017.

Deonandan, Raywat. "Thoughts on the Ethics of Gestational Surrogacy: Perspectives from Religions, Western Liberalism, and Comparisons with Adoption." *Journal of Assisted Reproduction and Genetics* 37:2 (2020), 269–79.

Elewa, Ahmed, and Laury Silvers. "'I Am One of the People': A Survey and Analysis of Legal Arguments on Woman-Led Prayer in Islam." *Journal of Law and Religion* 26:1 (2010), 141–71.

Fildis, Ayse Tekdal. "The Historical Roots and Occurrence of Honour-Related Violence in Non-Muslim and Muslim Societies." *HAWWA: Journal of Women of the Middle East and the Islamic World* 11:1 (2013), 1–15. https://doi.org/10.1163/15692086-12341240.

Fuchs, Esther. *Jewish Feminism: Framed and Reframed.* Lanham, MD: Lexington Books, 2018.

Greenberg, Blu. *On Women and Judaism: A View from Tradition.* Philadelphia, PA: Jewish Publication Society of America, 1985.

Gross, Rita M. *Buddhism Beyond Gender: Liberation from Attachment to Identity.* Boulder, CO: Shambala Publications, 2018.

Haddad, Yvonne Yazbeck, and John L. Esposito. *Islam, Gender & Social Change.* New York: Oxford University Press, 1998.

Hammer, Juliane. "Queer Love, Abrahamic Morality, and (the Limits of) American Muslim Marriage." *Theology & Sexuality* 27:1 (January 2021), 20–43. doi:10.1080/13558358.2020.1830700.

Harvard University Pluralism Project Archive, "Amina Wadud." https://hwpi.harvard.edu/pluralismarchive/amina-wadud-2005#fn6 (accessed 25 August 2021).

Hogan, Linda. *From Women's Experience to Feminist Theology.* London: Bloomsbury, 2016.

Instruction on Respect for Human Life in Its Origin and On the Dignity of Procreation (Donum Vitae). Rome: Congregation for the Doctrine of the Faith, 1987.

Kashani-Sabet, Firoozeh, and Beth S. Wenger. *Gender in Judaism and Islam: Common Lives, Uncommon Heritage.* New York: New York University Press, 2015.

Kirk-Duggan, Cheryl A., and Karen Jo Torjesen. *Women and Christianity.* Santa Barbara, CA: Praeger/ABC-CLIO, 2010.

Kugle, Scott Alan. *Homosexuality in Islam: Critical Reflection on Gay, Lesbian, and Transgender Muslims.* Oxford: Oneworld, 2010.

Mahmood, Saba. *Politics of Piety: The Islamic Revival and the Feminist Subject.* Princeton: Princeton University Press, 2011.

Patton, L. Laurie, ed. *Jewels of Authority: Women and Textual Tradition in Hindu India.* Delhi: Oxford University Press, 2002.

Peterfeso, Jill. *Womanpriest: Tradition and Transgression in the Contemporary Roman Catholic Church.* New York: Fordham University Press, 2020. doi:10.1353/book.75860.

Pew Research Center. "Views about Same-sex Marriage among Muslims By views about Homosexuality," (May 12, 2015). https://www.pewresearch.org/religion/religious-landscape-study/compare/views-about-same-sex-marriage/by/views-about-homosexuality/among/religious-tradition/muslim/.

Pintchman, Tracy. *The Rise of the Goddess in the Hindu Tradition.* Albany, NY: SUNY Press, 1994.

Roman Catholic Womenpriests—USA., Inc. "A New Way to be Catholic with Women Priests." Roman Catholic Women Priests, 2022. https://www.romancatholicwomenpriests.org (accessed 24 May 2022).

Ross, Tamar. *Expanding the Palace of Torah: Orthodoxy and Feminism.* Hanover: Brandeis University Press, 2004.

United Nations. "In-depth Study on all Forms of Violence against Women, Report of the Secretary-General," A/61/122/Add.1, 2006.

Wadud, Amina. *Qur'an and Woman Rereading the Sacred Text from a Woman's Perspective,* 2nd ed. New York: Oxford University Press, 1999.

Zwilling, Leonard, and Michael J. Sweet. "'Like a City Ablaze': The Third Sex and the Creation of Sexuality in Jain Religious Literature." *Journal of the History of Sexuality* 6:3 (1996), 359–84. http://www.jstor.org/stable/4629615 (accessed 9 June 2021).

Chapter 7

Race, Racism, and Christianity

I am writing the introduction to this chapter on June 19 or "Juneteenth." Juneteenth celebrates the summer day in 1865 when Black American slaves in Galveston, Texas, finally received the news that they were now free—a full two-and-a-half years after President Abraham Lincoln's Emancipation Proclamation officially took effect. Juneteenth was the subject of numerous news stories shortly after the protests demanding justice for George Floyd, a Black American man murdered by Minneapolis police officers. The holiday was in the news also because then-President Donald Trump had planned to hold a massive political rally on that day in Tulsa, Oklahoma, the city where in 1921, White mobs massacred hundreds of Black Americans. The forceful and widespread criticism of Trump's insensitivity in planning this rally resulted in his moving the rally to the following day. Although he attempted to claim ignorance, Trump's decision to hold his first major rally—political gatherings had been postponed due to the COVID-19 pandemic—on Juneteenth in a city where hundreds of Black Americans were massacred by White mobs simply seemed to reinforce his approval of White supremacy.

When Trump won the Presidential election in 2016, he did so with the support of White evangelical Christians. The Pew Research Center, one of the foremost non-partisan think tanks in the United States focused on public opinion, social policy, and demographic trends, closely examined "the relationship between religion and politics, including perceptions about President Donald Trump among White evangelical Protestants, a key part of his electoral base." They found that "White evangelicals largely see Trump as fighting for their beliefs and advancing their interests, and they feel their side generally has been winning recently on political matters important to them."[1] The intersection of both religion and race here is key. As sociologist Penny Edgell observes, the Trump Presidency cannot be explained through the lens of religion, specifically evangelical Christianity, alone. Rather, we must take an *intersectional* look at his supporters—that is, we should examine categories of identification such as race, sex, gender, religion, and class not as separate and discrete categories, but as identities that converge in individuals.

DOI: 10.4324/9781003350637-8

The observation that a significant majority of White evangelical Christians, as well as White Catholics, voted for Trump points to the racialized character of American Christian culture. All of Trump's "core constituencies are White" and "all share a preference for cultural Christianity, understanding Christian traditions as grounding our civic life and fostering national identity."[2] Indeed, even though Black and Hispanic Christians are similarly concerned about issues such as abortion, only White evangelicals voted for Trump in significant numbers.[3] Edgell further explains that the "appeal to evangelical voters went hand in hand with an appeal to those who favor traditional gender roles, xenophobic restrictions on immigration, disenfranchisement of voters of color, and distrust of economic and political elites."[4]

Racism and Christianity

Racism extends beyond the mere dislike of people because of the color of their skin; rather, racism involves the systematic oppression of a group of persons based on perceived racial differences by communities, states, and their institutions. Race is a cultural construct; it does not have a basis in biology. The attributes that people equate with particular races—such as athleticism, intelligence, and morality—formed as the result of decades, if not centuries, of cultural, social, economic, and political forces that created conditions by which racial groups became associated with specific stereotypes. Religious institutions and leaders, as well as practitioners, have long used their beliefs and their texts to explain the phenomenon of race and to justify—or denounce— racism. Perhaps the most significant of the religious groups involved in the development of racism is Christianity. Christianity played a major role in the perpetuation and intensification of racism in the early modern period through its complicity in colonialism and slavery. We cannot understand the development of racism unless we understand how Christianity made possible the oppression of entire groups of peoples through its dictates, financial support, and institutions.

Although racism is found in different parts of the world, this chapter will focus primarily on racism and Christianity in the United States. Racism in the United States is notable both for its severity and its complex relationship with Christianity. As the religion of White slave owners and Black slaves, White supremacists and Black American civil rights leaders, Christianity is deeply interwoven into the historical narrative of race in the United States.

The origins of racism in the United States can be traced to European Christian colonialism. Indeed, the very idea of religion as a distinct category of the human experience and as a label to be placed on persons and cultures likely arose in tandem with the notion of racial hierarchy. As Nelson Maldonado-Torres explains, "the emerging concept of religion" during the period of early colonization "is intimately linked with the modern concept of race, and … both race and religion play a key role in the formation of modernity/coloniality."[5] Maldonado-Torres and Sylvia Wynter argue that Christian European colonizers created hierarchical categories of religions and race in order to make sense of and to justify the conquests of foreign people and lands. Of course, being White and Christian—and male—placed one at the very top of this ontological hierarchy.

Even prior to Columbus's encounter with the "New World," the Portuguese, with the explicit approval of the Pope, began to enslave Africans under the pretense of theologically justified war. In 1455 King Alphonso of Portugal received permission from Pope Nicholas V to seize non-Christian lands and to conquer, purchase, and reduce their peoples to a lifetime of servitude and slavery. By the time Columbus arrived in the New World, it would not have been uncommon to find enslaved Africans in the Iberian Peninsula. When Columbus encountered brown-skinned Indigenous peoples, he viewed them as idolators, that is, as neither Christian nor monotheists. Mistakenly believing that he had reached India, Columbus labeled the Native Americans he encountered as *Indians* and assessed that these Indigenous populations did not have any religion at all, but could eventually—like the Africans enslaved by the Portuguese—be converted to Christianity and used as servants to White Europeans. In fact, Europeans preferred the enslavement of "pagans" over the enslavement of Jews, Christians, or Muslims because pagans who were enslaved prior to their conversion to Christianity could still, according to the Pope, remain a slave. As non-Christians, non-monotheists, and non-Whites, Indigenous peoples and dark-skinned Africans fell under a category of lesser beings that did not deserve the full dignities and freedoms allotted to fair-skinned Christian Europeans. The trade, slaughter, enslavement, and conversion of Indigenous peoples and Africans on a mass scale carried little moral consequence for White European Christians.

White Christians created religious justifications to establish and maintain slavery in the United States. Slave owners and politicians quoted the Bible to enforce racist practices and policies well beyond the Civil War and the end of slavery. White Christians would continue to use religious reasons to deny Black Americans (and other non-White groups) the right to vote and to justify Jim Crow laws that segregated Black Americans from White Americans in virtually all sectors of public life. Christians also used theological arguments about race to outlaw what they called miscegenation, that is, marriage between people of different races. Claims about the superiority of Whites over Black peoples drew from religious interpretations about the order of creation established by God.

To be sure, although some Christians turned to religion to justify racism, other Christians used religion to argue against racism. The abolitionist movement to end slavery, as well as the civil rights movement of the 1960s had Christian roots. Moreover, enslaved Africans who converted to Christianity gave rise over the generations to a vibrant Black church tradition. Today, we find many Christians continuing to work for racial equality in the form of efforts to end the death penalty, to alleviate poverty, and to support the Black Lives Matter movement.

The range of views with regard to racism that we find in the history of American Christianity persists to the present day. Just as many churches are working to end racism, many are ambivalent about or indifferent toward the race protests of 2020, and a few are actively racist. Some students ask, when confronted with the fact of blatantly racist Christian churches, whether or not such persons affiliated with such groups are actually Christians.

The tremendous diversity within Christianity means that Christian identity is often self-proclaimed. Unlike, for example, state citizenship which is conferred by a nation with administrative offices that keep track of its citizenry, there is no such centralized office for Christianity that determines who is a Christian and who is not. Furthermore, the idea that Christian identity depends upon one's moral values is neither borne out historically nor congruent with Christian notions of sin and redemption. There are, to put it in the simplest of terms, Christian racists even though racism is no longer morally acceptable to the larger society.

In this chapter, I will review the ways in which Christians have employed religious reasoning with regard to racism in the United States. Focusing on key historical moments, this chapter will illuminate how religion has worked to shape the moral course of a nation. The case study found at the end of this chapter asks whether, and if so, to what extent, religious institutions ought to pay reparations to the descendants of slaves.

The Trans-Atlantic Slave Trade

The trans-Atlantic slave trade involved the brutal transport of 12.5 million Africans aboard 35,000 ships across the Atlantic Ocean to the Americas from the sixteenth through the nineteenth centuries. Anywhere between a third to half of captured Africans died along marches toward ports in Africa even prior to boarding trading vessels. The notorious Middle Passage from the west coast of Africa to the Americas resulted in the deaths of up to a third of the enslaved aboard a ship. Up to a quarter of enslaved Africans forced aboard ships were children. Once aboard, European crews crammed shackled Africans into cargo-holds below deck without access to fresh air, water, food, or even movement. The enslaved were separated from their family members with no knowledge of what happened to their spouses, fathers, mothers, siblings, or children. Malnutrition, disease, dysentery, and suicide were rampant. When food and water ran low, crews would throw Africans overboard in order to preserve rations. After this horror, Africans were then auctioned off to spend their entire lives working on plantations.

The Middle Passage constituted the second of three legs of trans-Atlantic trade. The first of the three legs led from Europe to Africa, where goods such as textiles, wine, and weapons were sold to Africans. The third leg of the passage took crops, such as sugar and coffee, that were grown and harvested by enslaved Africans in the Americas to be sold to Europeans. The Middle Passage was the lynchpin that held colonial commerce together. Europeans relied upon imported slave labor from Africa to work on plantations in North America, Brazil, Cuba, and several Caribbean islands because they themselves unwilling to suffer the back-breaking labor required to grow such crops. Also, notably, Europeans' earlier forays into these areas wiped out through disease and warfare significant Indigenous populations, who would have otherwise supplied plantation labor.

White, Christian Europeans often relied upon a particular understanding of God and creation in order to justify the gruesome Middle Passage. From their perspective, the enslavement of Africans "violated neither divine nor natural law."[6] Using the Bible as their guide, many European imperialists performed feats of scriptural interpretation to convince themselves that the enslavement of Africans was ordained by God. Moreover, many slave sellers, slave buyers, and plantation owners claimed that God had given them the responsibility to correct the "deficiencies" found in Africans, and therefore argued that the violence wielded unto Black bodies to assert discipline was divinely sanctioned.

As David Goldberg observes, the "Bible makes no mention of a curse of blackness; it knows only a curse of slavery."[7] However, the fusion of various interpretations of the "Curse of Ham" eventually found its way as a popular justification for Black slavery. The Curse of Ham derives from Genesis 9:20–27, in which Noah curses his grandson Canaan, the son of Ham, into slavery after Ham sees his father Noah's nakedness. This section of the Bible is unfortunately replete with obfuscation. It is unclear, for example, why Canaan rather than Ham was cursed, or why the punishment for seeing nakedness was so severe, or why the slavery would endure for more than one generation. Regardless, Christians arguing for the slave trade relied upon this interpretation of the Bible to argue that Africans were the progeny of Ham, and therefore were biblically mandated to become slaves.

In addition to the Curse of Ham, Biblical narratives about the Cush, the descendants of Ham and associated with north Africans from the Nile region, reinforced for slavers the notion that dark-skinned Africans were cursed with slavery. Some slave traders pointed to trade winds that blew in a westerly direction from the coast of Africa to the Americas as divine proof that Africans were meant to be sent to the Americas. God, they claimed, would not have created winds to blow in that particular direction unless God had so ordained the movement.

Finally, the claim that the enslavement of great numbers of Africans would result in greater numbers of Christian converts undergirded all aspects of the slave trade. This argument, often reinforced by fifteenth century popes, played into the notion that increasing numbers of Christians in Africa and the New World would lead to the imminent return of Christ. The fact that

Christianity in north Africa was already well established and had, in fact, existed there since at least the second century CE, was largely ignored by the slave industry. Origen, Tertullian, and Augustine were all highly influential Christians from north Africa who shaped Christian theology and the development of the church. Christian communities for more than a millennium had made their homes in Egypt and spread from the Nile region south toward Ethiopia. Fifteenth century European Christians generally disregarded the Christianity already extant in Africa, despite the proselytization and conversion that the African churches themselves undertook. The slave economy offered a lucrative reason for European missionizing that rationalized unprecedented brutality on the African continent in the name of Christianity.

Slavery in the United States

The first African slaves were brought to the United States in 1619, arriving in Jamestown, Virginia, aboard a Dutch ship. For the next two and half centuries, until 1862 with President Abraham Lincoln's signing of the Emancipation Proclamation, some 300,000 African slaves would arrive in the United States. (The vast majority of African slaves were sent to Brazil and the West Indies.) In the United States, slaves lived throughout the colonies, both north and south, although the largest concentration of slaves was found in southern plantations. Up to a quarter of Boston's population at the time of the American Revolution were slaves, and slaves made up a sizeable portion of the population in New York and Philadelphia. In South Carolina and Virginia, slaves would make up about half of the population. In the northern cities, slaves tended to work as urban laborers—as domestics, tailors, shoemakers, and longshoremen. In the South, slaves worked on plantations to grow and harvest crops such as tobacco and cotton. Whether in the North or the South, slaves were considered property—not human employees—and purchased, insured, and sold accordingly.

The decades leading up to the American Revolution proved to be a major turning point for slavery in the United States. If colonists were fighting for their own emancipation from Britain, and rallying against the injustice of having to send Britain a portion of their wages without their consent, then White colonists could not also in good conscience continue with the practice of not paying wages to enslaved Africans. With American independence, many northern states abolished slavery, while the southern states did not. Because the economy of southern states relied almost entirely on slave labor, they were far more reluctant to give up what South Carolina politician John Calhoun referred to as "the peculiar institution." Indeed, it would take a long and bloody Civil War for southern states to be forced to give up the institution of slavery.

Believing that Africans were divinely cursed to serve as slaves—and that Whites were divinely elevated to an ontological status above Africans—enabled those who benefited from the slave trade to make peace with the torturous reality of slave life. This allowed slave traders and plantation owners, and the Whites of southern society, to claim that Africans were not entitled to any of the rights and wages to which other laborers were entitled. Treated like chattel, the enslaved were relegated to a sub-human status theologically reinforced by arguments about racial identity.

Southerners, as historian Eugene Genovese explains, "grounded the pro-slavery argument in an appeal to Scripture and denounced abolitionists as infidels who were abandoning the plain words of the Bible."[8] This appeal to Scripture included arguments about the existence of slavery in the Bible and observations about Jesus's acceptance of slavery. Debates about slavery in the South focused less on whether or not God sanctioned slavery, than on whether or not the conditions of slavery met Christian norms. Given the fact that slaves, too, were ostensibly Christian, just like their masters, they ought to be treated according to "standards of humanity described as scriptural or Abrahamic or Christian."[9]

In the widely read debates between the Baptist Reverend Richard Fuller, one of the founders of the Southern Baptist movement, and Reverend Francis Wayland, the fourth president of Brown University, Fuller denies the inherent sinfulness of slavery, even while expressing misgivings about its existence and denying its ability to continue into perpetuity. The Southern Baptist Convention, which split with its northern counterpart over the issue of slavery, would ultimately attempt to make a case for the humane, "biblical" treatment of slaves, rather than the abolition of slavery altogether.

Viewing themselves as proponents in favor of the "stewardship" of slaves, Southern religious leaders proclaimed Confederate victories during the Civil War as a sign of God's approval. Other Southern ministers tempered their zeal with warnings that assumptions about God's favor could well go awry. When the Civil War ended and the Union prevailed, a variety of opinions emerged regarding the future of slaves. Some proclaimed that the South had done its Christian duty and helped to transition slaves to emancipation. Others insisted that those of African origin would always remain intellectually, culturally, and morally inferior to Whites. In the North, racism grounded in biological differences gained popularity, which theorized that Whites and Blacks evolved from different origins and were essentially separate species. Throughout the nation, many Whites held the belief that even if slavery was no longer biblically mandated, White supremacy and Black subordination were necessary for a well-functioning society. With slavery outlawed, Blacks were nonetheless to spend their lives in servitude to Whites.

Reconstruction and Jim Crow

The promise of Reconstruction—i.e., the dozen years following the Civil War during which the United States attempted to bring southern secessionist states back into the Union and affirm rights for newly freed slaves—was followed by nearly a century of Jim Crow laws in the South and in border states. During Reconstruction, the federal government passed the 13th (1865), 14th (1868), and 15th (1870) Amendments to the Constitution, which abolished slavery and granted Black Americans the right to citizenship, equal protection under the law, and the vote. With the 1876 election of President Rutherford B. Hayes, however, much of the racial progress achieved during Reconstruction was dialed back. Southern states protested federal efforts to fully integrate Black Americans into society, and so imposed a number of state and local laws to segregate Black Americans from White ones.

Jim Crow laws ostensibly kept Black Americans "separate, but equal." In truth, Jim Crow laws reinforced White supremacy and Black subordination. Named after a fictitious slave who was caricatured by a White minstrel performer in blackface, Jim Crow laws, like their eponymous character, were meant to humiliate Black Americans into submission. Examples of Jim Crow laws included requiring Blacks to drink at separate water fountains, to enter and leave buildings through separate (typically inconvenient) entrances, to avoid swimming pools (reserved for Whites only), to be educated at separate schools from Whites, to ride in separate train cars or only in the back of buses, and to be buried in separate cemeteries. The Supreme Court case *Plessy v. Ferguson* (1896) maintained that Jim Crow laws did not violate the 14th amendment. In practice, Jim Crow laws meant that Black Americans were prevented from ever attaining full equality with Whites. The fact that Jim Crow made barriers to voting lawful—in the form of poll taxes, civics exams, and targeted misinformation—ensured that Black Americans would continue to face an uphill struggle for equality.

Although Jim Crow typically refers to laws and statues, Jim Crow referred also to etiquette and social norms that dictated how Blacks were to defer to Whites. Blacks could never talk or behave in a way that assumed equality with Whites; to do so would mean that Blacks were behaving in an "uppity" fashion, and could therefore be punished for their transgression. Black boys and men, in particular, were to avoid interacting with White girls and women in any way that could be interpreted as a sexual advance. The chastity of White girls and women was to be protected, and if necessary, vindicated with violence by angry White mobs. Over 3,000 Black Americans were murdered by lynch mobs during the Jim Crow era. White police forces and the White newspapers typically collaborated with the White perpetrators. No true justice would be served for the victims of lynching.

Throughout the era of Jim Crow, prominent Christian denominations failed to advance the promises of racial equality set by Reconstruction. Indeed, by the beginning of the twentieth century, both the Methodist and the Roman Catholic Churches adopted segregationist positions, even though they had at previous points expressed hopes of racial integration. For the Methodist and the Roman Catholic Churches—two of the largest potentially integrated Christian denominations in the United States—to settle on segregation confirmed the pervasiveness of racism in American culture. While it is true that during Reconstruction, Black Americans formed their own Christian sects so as to be able to worship freely without Whites, the fact that the White leadership of formerly integrated Methodist and Roman Catholic Churches chose to segregate indicated their unwillingness to embrace Black Americans as equals before God.

> Perhaps aware of the inconsistencies, whites avoided religious language when they used churches to advance their segregationist agenda. White church members defended segregation in light of institutional rather than theological concerns. But segregation became a religious issue when it entered churches, white protests to the contrary.[10]

For Black Christians, segregation was never merely an issue of institutional concern, but also a religious one. While Biblical and theological arguments were commonly deployed by Whites to force their submission, Black Christians also used biblical texts and religious reasoning to demand better treatment and to strive for equality. The use of religion by Black Christians to critique injustice was to be critical for the rise of the civil rights movement.

The Civil Rights Movement

Christianity and the church community played a foundational role in the rise of the civil rights movement of the 1960s. Black civil rights leaders—Martin Luther King Jr., Ralph Abernathy, Bernard Lee, Fred Shuttlesworth, and many others—were also Christian clergy who drew both inspiration and support from the church. In addition to functioning as civic centers for Black Americans, Black churches provided the oratorical and organizational training necessary for the success of the civil rights movement. Protest and critique of Jim Crow laws, segregationist policies, and racist culture drew out of Christian teachings and interpretations about justice, God's love, and the dignity of all humans. Referred to collectively as the "Black Church," churches established by freed Black slaves during Reconstruction grew to become the backbone of many Black American communities.

Equally significant to understanding the role that Christianity played in the civil rights movement, however, is how some predominantly White churches understood that they too had a role to play to help to end segregation and promote racial equality. Martin Luther King Jr. in his *Letter from a Birmingham Jail* excoriates southern White Christian leaders for failing to take up the mantle of civil rights. King writes,

> I felt that the white ministers, priests and rabbis of the South would be among our strongest allies. Instead, some have been outright opponents, refusing to understand the freedom movement and misrepresenting its

leaders; all too many others have been more cautious than courageous and have remained silent behind the anesthetizing security of stained glass windows.[11]

Most White southern ministers and church leaders dismissed the civil rights movement as not being about morality, but rather politics, and they refused to take a stance against segregation. They failed to see segregation as driven by racist views. Indeed, they continued to view segregation and the subordination of Blacks below Whites as sanctioned by God. In short, many southern White churches did not simply adopt a stance of neutrality, they also actively fought against the struggle for racial equality.

In the years following the 1954 Supreme Court decision *Brown v. Board of Education*—a ruling that declared segregated schools unconstitutional—there was a rise in "segregationist folk theology."[12] Segregationist folk theology embraced a clumsy mix of cherry-picked Biblical literalism, White supremacy, and divine blessing confirmed by observations of social order and could be found throughout segregated society. Although this inelegant theology found little footing among the religious elite, segregationist folk theology proved immensely popular among some southern preachers. In addition to interpreting the "Curse of Ham," the "Table of Nations" (Genesis 10), and the "Tower of Babel" (Genesis 11) to justify the separation of races as divinely mandated, some would also attempt to explain away verses popular among integrationists such as Galatians 3:26–28:

> for in Christ Jesus you are all children of God through faith.[13] As many of you as were baptized into Christ have clothed yourselves with Christ. There is no longer Jew or Greek, there is no longer slave or free, there is no longer male and female; for all of you are one in Christ Jesus.

These verses, they explained, were—unlike other Biblical verses—not to be taken literally. God, after all, made women and men to be different from each other, so phrases like "there is no longer male and female" simply made no practical sense. Drawing on a parallel logic, segregationist preachers would argue that God likewise made different races that were meant to be separated.

Guy T. Gillespie, the president emeritus of Belhaven College and prominent Presbyterian pastor, authored *A Christian View of Segregation*, published by the Mississippi Citizens Council in 1954. *A Christian View of Segregation* enjoyed immense local popularity, although it was widely condemned outside of the state. In his composition, Gillespie praises Southern culture and proclaims White southerners' abhorrence of racial intermarriage as proof of their elevated status. Comparing segregationist culture to the superiority of purebred animals, Gillespie draws upon a kind of natural law to argue that the segregation of races was to be observed historically as the superior path of human development. Although he admits that the Bible does not specifically address the topic of segregation, he finds that one can infer from biblical passages that segregation is God's preference, and that integrated societies suffer God's wrath.

The Tower of Babel would figure prominently in Christian writings of the 1950s that defended segregationist ideals. Why, segregationists asked, would God have created separated languages if not to maintain differences between cultures? God, they claimed, set up linguistic barriers between peoples in order to preserve local freedoms. The fact that God separated people into different groups after the flood was proof that this was the way in which God wanted humans to live. This argument stemming from the story of the Tower of Babel would regularly emerge in religious literature to support segregationist views. Kenneth Kinney, a New York Baptist, argued that following the great flood, God, through his dispersion of peoples at the Tower of Babel, intended Noah's sons to maintain their individual family lines, and therefore intermarriage between the races—White, Black, and Asian—would violate God's intention.

One of the most widely reported instances of church members actively resisting integration took place in Jackson, Mississippi, when Charles Golden, a Black Methodist bishop, along with James Mathew, a White Methodist bishop, were turned away from Galloway Methodist Church, the largest Methodist church in Mississippi, on Easter Sunday, just before the denomination's 1964 General Conference. The *New York Times* reported that both bishops were turned away by ushers at the front of the church, and then turned away again when they attempted to enter from a side door. On that same Easter Sunday morning, seven White Methodist heads of seminaries and theology professors along with two Black college students attempted to worship at the Capitol Street Methodist Church, when a White usher called police to take them to jail. In that year, some 32 churchgoers were arrested for attempting to integrate worship services.

Not surprisingly, for White Christians in the deep South, "the scales of racial prejudice often fell from White eyes only well after African Americans appropriated their hard-won gains."[14] Surrounded by like-minded neighbors, and with their thoughts about segregation reinforced by newspapers, churches, politicians, and schools, they not only held firm in their beliefs about the evils of integration, but would have found it nearly impossible to dissent in a socially acceptable manner. While protests involving White clergy against segregation took place in states otherwise committed to segregationist policies, they were often initiated and largely populated by religious leaders visiting from northern states to provide support to Black citizens. Indeed, in many Jim Crow states, "communities met the religious challenge to white supremacy with brazen and near-unanimous resistance, demonstrating how patently absurd they regarded the notion that real Christianity demanded an end to white supremacy."[15] One should not, however, take this to mean that the clear majority of White Christians above the Mason-Dixon line protested against White supremacy and segregation. Unfortunately, the leadership of several White clergymen did not represent the views of many White northerners, who were in fact quite sympathetic to southern Whites' demands to preserve segregation.

With the passage of the Civil Rights Act (1964) and the Voting Act (1965), segregationists were forced to accept their defeat in the political arena. Their religious reasoning, however, did not shift. Still holding onto the belief that their version of biblical literalism was the truer form of Christianity, they attempted to discredit the political liberalism of integrationist Christians as too focused on civil rights rather than on the saving of souls. The more conservative strands of the Baptist and Presbyterian churches would eventually break off into their own communions.

Black Lives Matter

The Black Lives Matter movement began in 2013 after the acquittal of George Zimmerman, a White man who killed a young Black man, Trayvon Martin. Black Lives Matter was the brainchild of three Black American women, Patrisse Cullors, Alicia Garza, and Opal Tometi. A platform for organizing and protests, the Black Lives Matter movement describes itself as "ideological and political intervention in a world where Black lives are systematically and intentionally targeted for demise. It is an affirmation of Black folks' humanity, our contributions to this society, and our resilience in the face of deadly oppression."[16] The Black Lives Matter movement—commonly referenced with a social media-friendly hash-tag #blacklivesmatter or #BLM—gained momentum after the 2020 murders of Ahmaud Arbery, George Floyd, and Breonna Taylor. The spring of 2020 saw the largest social protest movement in American history, much of it orchestrated by Black Lives Matter.

While the Black church played a tremendous role in civil rights movement of the 1950s and 60s, for the Black Lives Matter generation, organized religion was much less significant. Millennials, those born between 1981 and 1996, are far less likely to attend church, and religious "nones," who declare adherence to no particular religious identity, are on the rise. One explanation for the shift in religiosity among younger Americans is that, for many, churches had not kept pace with changing views about gender and sexuality. "The church tradition has been very much focused on a singular male leader," Janaya Khan, international ambassador for Black Lives Matter, explained. "This movement that we have now in Black Lives Matter has been led by and informed by women, queer and trans people—you know, the despised of the despised."[17] Cornell West confirmed the Black Lives Matter critique of the Black church and its general stance toward gender and sexuality:

White supremacy [is] evil. The Black church historically has tried to hit it head-on and oftentimes has been magnificent. But male supremacy, homophobia and transphobia are evil too. They've got to hit those with the same level of intensity as they hit white supremacy. That's the challenge and the test of the Black church these days.[18]

Black Lives Matter supporters agreed with Christian leaders of the civil rights era that racism was a moral issue and not simply a political one, but they challenged the predominantly male, heterosexual, cis-gendered leadership of that movement. The critique of the Black church from within the Black Lives Matter movement, however, does not preclude their collaboration. The Reverend Al Sharpton, for example, delivered the eulogy for George Floyd. And younger activists look up to figures such as Sharpton, and to the late congressman and civil rights icon, John Lewis, for their hard-won expertise and knowledge.

The rise of the Black Lives Matter movement has, like the Civil Rights movement, garnered critique from Christians who disagree with the emphasis on Black Americans. Although supporters of the Black Lives Matter movement explain repeatedly that Black Lives Matter does not mean that other lives matter less—but, in historical fact, that Black people have counted as less than White people—White critics of the movement insist that the slogan is uncharitable toward people of other races. The refrain, "All Lives Matter," for example, has gained traction especially among conservative White groups that claim that Black Lives Matter is exclusionary. Predictably, conservative Christian churches that oppose gay marriage and transgender rights disagree with the inclusiveness of the Black Lives Matter movement.

Case Study: Reparations for Slavery

Ta-Nehisi Coates in his 2014 *Atlantic* essay, "The Case for Reparations," elaborates upon the practical damage that has been done—particularly in the form of lost generational wealth—to Black Americans and the moral debt that the United States owes the descendants of slaves. In this case study, we examine the 2016 decision by Georgetown University, a Catholic university in Washington, DC, to investigate the role of slavery in its past, to publish its findings, and to create programs meant to atone for having owned and sold human beings.

On September 1, 2016, Georgetown University released a report from the school's Working Group on Slavery, Memory, and Reconciliation. The report detailed the painful history of slavery at Georgetown, and specifically examined the university's notorious sale in 1838 of 272 men, women, and children. The sale, ostensibly to save the university from financial ruin, was notable for the large number of slaves sold and controversial because the Jesuit community was deeply divided about the morality of slavery.

Amidst fears about rising calls for abolition and the devaluation of slaves following an unstable market, the president of Georgetown at the time, Fr. Thomas Mulledy, S.J., and Fr. William McSherry, S.J., the Superior of the Province of Maryland, drafted the sale of the slaves to Henry Johnson, former governor of Louisiana, and Jesse Batey, a Louisiana plantation owner. In the end, Mulledy and McSherry sold the 272 slaves, listed by name in the "Articles of Agreement," for $115,000, or the equivalent of over three million dollars today.

Perhaps the most distressing aspect of the sale was the fact the Jesuits discussed and then rejected two other, more humane, options. The majority of Jesuits involved in the debate over the sale believed that it was a religious and moral obligation to keep the slaves with Georgetown; a minority argued for their emancipation; Mulledy and McSherry, along with other prominent Catholics, successfully argued for the sale of both slaves and Georgetown's plantations in order to finance Jesuit projects. When Jesuits in Rome became involved in the dispute, they initially argued that the slaves be freed, but eventually gave in to American pressure and agreed to the sale. They did, however, attempt to ameliorate the conditions of the sale by insisting that several conditions be placed on the sale:

> that families not be divided, that the continued practice of the Catholic faith by these baptized slaves be ensured, and that the monies raised from the sale be used for endowment, not for operating expenses or the paying down of debt.[19]

Not one of these conditions would, in fact, be met.

The Working Group concluded that the Catholic identity of the institution ultimately required that Georgetown issue reparations and apologies. Using the term "reconciliation," the Working Group would find guidance in

> the centrality of reconciliation to the mission of Jesus Christ, the moral imperatives of contrition and forgiveness, the virtue of hope as an inspiration to and precondition for reconciliation, and the specific commitment of Jesuit schools to a faith that does justice.[20]

With this understanding, the Working Group recommended that Georgetown University take a number steps, including:

1   Issue a formal apology from the president of the university and the superior of the Maryland Jesuits. No apology had previously ever

been issued for the university's complicity in slavery. An apology that admits wrongdoing, expresses regret, and promise for future action would begin to lay the groundwork for reconciliation. The apology should accompany, of course, symbolic acts such as changing the names of buildings named after Mulledy and McSherry.

2 Engage the descendants of the enslaved peoples by providing them admission and financial support to attend Georgetown University

3 Build a public memorial, place informative historical plaques, and make historical knowledge accessible.

Although these were first steps and hardly sufficient to compensate for the generations of the horror of slavery, Georgetown was one of the most prominent universities to make public its attempts to atone for its sins of slavery.

Questions:

1 What should an institution do with the knowledge that it was built with the labor of slaves?

2 How does one apologize on behalf of an institution for historical transgressions?

3 Should reparations be paid to the descendants of slaves? If so, how, and how ought reparations be paid to descendants whose ancestral history remains unknown?

Notes

1 Pew Research Center, "White Evangelicals."
2 Edgell, "Agenda for Research," 2.
3 Edgell, "Agenda for Research," 5.
4 Edgell, "Agenda for Research," 6.
5 Maldonado-Torres, "Race, Religion," 693.
6 Canon, "Christian Imperialism," 131.
7 Goldberg, Curse, 168.
8 Genovese, Consuming Fire, 4.
9 Genovese, Consuming Fire, 7.
10 Bennett, Religion and the Rise of Jim Crow, 5.
11 King, Why We Can't Wait, 78.
12 Dupont, Mississippi Praying, 80.
13 Haynes, "Distinction and Dispersal."
14 Dupont, Mississippi Praying, 231.
15 Dupont, Mississippi Praying, 181.
16 https://Blacklivesmatter.com/herstory/.

17 King, "From Bloody Sunday to Black Lives Matter."
18 King, "From Bloody Sunday to Black Lives Matter."
19 Georgetown University, "Report," 14.
20 Georgetown University, "Report," 26–7.

Bibliography

Bennett, James B. *Religion and the Rise of Jim Crow in New Orleans*. Princeton, NJ: Princeton University Press, 2005.

Blount, Brian K., Katie G. Cannon, Jamie Thompson, and Samuel L. Adams. "Exploring Race/Racism Past and Present: A Forum at Union Presbyterian Seminary." *Interpretation* 71:4 (2017), 371–97. https://doi.org/10.1177/0020964317716129.

Calhoun-Brown, Allison. "Upon This Rock: The Black Church, Nonviolence, and the Civil Rights Movement." *PS: Political Science and Politics* 33:2 (2000), 169–74. Accessed July 30, 2020. https://doi.org/10.2307/420886.

Cannon, Katie Geneva. "Christian Imperialism and the Transatlantic Slave Trade." *Journal of Feminist Studies in Religion* 24:1 (Spring 2008), 127–34.

Carter, J. Kameron. *Race: A Theological Account*. Oxford: Oxford University Press, 2018.

Coates, Ta-Nehisi. "The Case for Reparations." *The Atlantic* 313:5 (June 1, 2014), 54–71.

Cone, James H. *Black Theology and Black Power*. New York: Seabury Press, 2018.

Davis, Morris L. *The Methodist Unification: Christianity and the Politics of Race in the Jim Crow Era*. New York: NYU Press, 2008.

Dupont, Carolyn Renee. *Mississippi Praying: Southern White Evangelicals and the Civil Rights Movement, 1945–1970*. New York: New York University Press, 2013.

Edgell, Penny. "An Agenda for Research on American Religion in Light of the 2016 Election." *Sociology of Religion* 78:1 (March 2017), 1–8.

Eltis, David. "A Brief Overview of the Trans-Atlantic Slave Trade," Slave Voyages: The Trans-Atlantic Slave Trade Database. https://www.slavevoyages.org/voyage/about (accessed June 26, 2022).

Georgetown University Working Group on Slavery, Memory, and Reconciliation. http://slavery.georgetown.edu/history/working-group/report/ September 1, 2020.

Genovese, Eugene D. *Consuming Fire: The Fall of the Confederacy in the Mind of the White Christian South*. Athens: University of Georgia Press, 1998.

Gillespie, G. T. (Guy T.). *A Christian View on Segregation: Reprint of an Address Made before the Synod of Mississippi of the Presbyterian Church in the U.S.* Greenwood, MI: Association of Citizens' Councils, 1954.

Goldenberg, David. *The Curse of Ham: Race and Slavery in Early Judaism, Christianity, and Islam*. Princeton, NJ: Princeton University Press, 2003.

Haynes, Stephen R. "Distinction and Dispersal: Folk Theology and the Maintenance of White Supremacy." *Journal of Southern Religion* 17 (2015). http://jsreligion.org/issues/vol17/haynes.html.

Hulsether, Lucia. "The Grammar of Racism: Religious Pluralism and the Birth of the Interdisciplines." *Journal of the American Academy of Religion* 86:1 (March 2018), 1–41. https://doi.org/10.1093/jaarel/lfx049.

Jones, Robert. "The Challenge of Pluralism after the End of White Christian America." In *Out of Many Faiths: Religious Diversity and the American Promise*, edited

by Eboo Patel. Princeton, NJ: Princeton University Press, 2018. https://doi.
org/10.2307/j.ctvd58sn2 (accessed 24 July 2020).

Kaplan, M. Lindsay. *Figuring Racism in Medieval Christianity*. New York: Oxford
University Press, 2019.

King Jr., Martin Luther, and Jesse Jackson. *Why We Can't Wait*. New York: Signet
Classic, 2000.

King, Maya. "From Bloody Sunday to Black Lives Matter, the Role of Black
Lives Matter is Shifting." *Politico* (July 30, 2020). https://www.politico.com/
news/2020/07/30/the-role-of-the-Black-church-389180.

Lincoln, C. Eric, and Lawrence H. Mamiya. *The Black Church in the African-American
Experience*. Durham, NC: Duke University Press, 1990.

Lofton, Kathryn. "Religious History as Religious Studies." *Religion: The Study of
American Religions: Critical Reflections on a Specialization* 42:3 (July 1, 2012), 383–94.

Maluleke, Tinyiko. "Racism En Route." *The Ecumenical Review* 72:1 (January 2020),
19–36.

Mayeri, Serena. *Reasoning from Race: Feminism, Law, and the Civil Rights Revolution*.
Cambridge, MA: Harvard University Press, 2001.

Nelson Maldonado-Torres. "Race, Religion, and Ethics in the Modern/Colonial
World." *Journal of Religious Ethics* 42:4 (December 1, 2014), 691–711.

Nongbri, Brent. "New Worlds, New Religions, World Religions." In *Before Religion:
A History of a Modern Concept*, 106–31. New Haven, CT: Yale University Press,
2013. https://www.jstor.org/stable/j.ctt32bqx9.10 (accessed 8 July 2020).

O'Loughlin, Michael. "Reparations Georgetown Faces Up to Slave History."
America 215:7 (September 19, 2016), 9.

Pew Research Center. "White Evangelicals See Trump as Fighting for Their Beliefs,
Though Many Have Mixed Feelings About His Personal Conduct" (March 12,
2020). https://www.pewforum.org/2020/03/12/White-evangelicals-see-trump-
as-fighting-for-their-beliefs-though-many-have-mixed-feelings-about-his-
personal-conduct/.

Raboteau, Albert J. *Slave Religion: The "Invisible Institution" in the Antebellum South*.
Updated ed. New York: Oxford University Press, 2004.

Soyinka, Wole. *Of Africa*. New Haven, CT: Yale University Press, 2012. ProQuest
Ebook Central, https://ebookcentral.proquest.com/lib/gwu/detail.action?do-
cID=3421065 (accessed 22 July 2020).

West, Cornel. "Black Theology of Liberation as Critique of Capitalist Civilization."
The Journal of the Interdenominational Theological Center 10:1–2 (Fall 1982), 67–83.

West, Traci C. *Solidarity and Defiant Spirituality: Africana Lessons on Religion, Racism,
and Ending Gender Violence*. New York: New York University Press, 2019. https://
doi.org/10.2307/j.ctvwrm48n (accessed 20 July 2020).

Woodward, C. Vann, and William S. McFeely. *Strange Career of Jim Crow*. New York:
Oxford University Press, 2001.

Chapter 8

Who Are We? Diverse Voices in Religious Ethics

In the late spring of 2020, people all over the United States and around the world rose up in protest over the death of George Floyd and countless other Black Americans at the hands of police. Protesters condemned the systemic racism—racial discrimination that is reified through legal structures and accepted cultural norms—and structural violence that are perpetuated through the laws, organizations, and institutions of the society. Among these institutions are colleges and universities, which have been complicit in justifying and perpetuating racial injustices. One way in which we see this is by observing the demographic trends of students and faculty, including those who populate the halls of religious studies and theology departments.

Only until quite recently, religious ethics in North America and Europe was an academic discipline dominated by White, Christian—typically Protestant—men. This demographic is not surprising, given the history of exclusion of women and minorities, racial and religious, from higher education. Well into the twentieth century, colleges and universities denied women and people of color, as well as Jews, the opportunity to earn the requisite degrees necessary for entry into academia, where they could conduct research and teach undergraduate and graduate students. This demographic has fortunately begun to change, and the discipline over the last several decades has grown increasingly diverse in terms of gender, race, sexual orientation, and religious affiliation.

People, with their particular histories, viewpoints and agendas, create religious ethics. Religious ethics is the product of people affiliated with specific institutions within specific contexts in history. While the experience of reading about religious traditions and ethical theories may make the discipline seem as if it were a disembodied mass of ideas somehow separate and apart from its very human creators, nothing could be further from the truth. The purpose of this chapter is to help demystify the production of knowledge.

Below are responses from a diverse group of scholars about their personal and intellectual journeys into the discipline of religious ethics and their advice for students. Although not nearly exhaustive, the professors below identify with different genders, races and ethnicities, and religious traditions.

DOI: 10.4324/9781003350637-9

They come from a variety of backgrounds and now work at a range of institutions: public and private universities, small colleges, and seminaries, as well as different academic departments. They are established or emerging leaders in the field, have excellent reputations as scholars and teachers, and are actively involved in academic societies. My hope is that their candid narratives reveal the very human side of religious ethics and that in doing so, the work of ethicists becomes more accessible and less abstract. Books, essays, and articles—the written work that constitutes the bulk of what we study—are the products of people like these.

Jonathan K. Crane, PhD

Raymond F. Schinazi Scholar of Bioethics and Jewish Thought, Center for Ethics
Emory University, Atlanta, Georgia

How did you end up in the field of religious ethics?

I've always been fascinated with tradition and with what motivates people to change the world. If ethics is concerned with the latter, religions are definitely the former. Hence: religious ethics. For better and, sadly often for worse, religions motivate folks to do amazing and awful things. I want to understand how this happens and why. Religious traditions and Judaism in particular bequeath rich ways to engage with the world, and they offer many reasons to do so. This is why I think religious ethics is one of the most exciting fields to work in: it is always connecting with where civilization has been and reaching out toward the future. Religious ethics is relevant, if nothing else.

Can you list three of your favorite or most influential works that impressed you as a thinker?

Martin Buber's *I and Thou*
Daniel Quinn's *Ishmael, The Story of B, and My Ishmael*
Hermann Hesse's *The Glass Bead Game*

What are the main ideas or questions that guide your work?

What rationales are at work when people aim to persuade others? What's at stake here, really?

How can students best succeed in your religious ethics courses?

Knowing a religious tradition's or authority's position on a moral conundrum is nice but insufficient. How they reason to reach that conclusion—now that is where the action is at. I want students to be curious about how others think and justify their positions, so that, ultimately, they can formulate robust arguments themselves when facing life's many moral conundrums.

What do you believe will be the most important moral issues for the next generation?

Climate change poses not just existential challenges but moral ones: who pays attention (or not) to these issues; what values shape climate-impacting policies; who is invited to participate in such conversations? Technological issues, too, pose difficulties: privacy, artificial intelligence, cyber security, are just a few that merit moral deliberation. Biomedicine and health care is another complex arena, from genetic engineering to geriatric care and dementia, from access to care to payment for care, from discerning where therapy blurs into enhancement to prioritizing between individual and public health. The ethics of food and water will be central to most of these conversations.

Shannon Dunn, PhD

Associate Professor, Religious Studies
Gonzaga University, Spokane, Washington

How did you end up in the field of religious ethics?

I know this will seem shocking, but I was a nerdy kid who spent a lot of time with books, probably more time with books than peers. Some of this may be attributed to my shyness, but for a young person, I had an unusual sense of moral indignation and a proclivity for matters of existential concern. For context, my grandfather and father were both Protestant pastors, so these tendencies may have been inevitable, at some level. I became a religious studies major in college, focusing on Christian ethics and women's and gender studies. I was in a senior seminar on postmodern challenges to ethics on 9/11/2001, and at that point, it became obvious I needed to learn more about the Islamic tradition and international political relations.

In my graduate work, I had the opportunity to do work in both Islamic ethics and Christian ethics. I never felt a strong desire to become a Christian theological ethicist, although I found the study of Christian theology interesting at times. I was fortunate to find John Kelsay and the Florida State religion faculty, many of whom helped to shape my intellectual trajectory. They encouraged me to examine the ways in which religious communities interfaced with secular legal systems and norms, and the ethical questions and particular dilemmas that arise from such interactions.

Can you list three of your favorite or most influential works that impressed you as a thinker?

As for favorite works, I will focus on authors from three different genres, all of which have formed my thinking about gender and ethical agency. I love all of Toni Morrison's novels because of her ability to frame human agency and vulnerability in relation to American racism. I appreciate the work of Muslim feminism in religious studies and anthropology as a distinct body of work. Muslim feminists like Leila Ahmed, Kecia Ali, Saba Mahmood and others have raised questions that scholars of religious ethics need to be thinking about in terms of authority, dissent, and what it means to think from within, and at certain points against, authorities within religious traditions. Finally, Judith Butler's work continues to have tremendous influence on the ways I think about violence, otherness, and perception in ethics.

What are the main ideas or questions that guide your work?

Some of the main questions guiding my work pertain to identity, agency, and social environments. Generally, I am interested in how particular experiences, and the social construction of such experiences, engender or thwart the moral capacities of persons. What kinds of assumptions do we make in ethics and philosophy about who the normative subject is, and how might these assumptions mislead our descriptions of moral agency and freedom? In a more constructive sense, I am curious about the types of ethical traits and social environments which allow for reflective moral thinking in a postcolonial world, and which foster a more inclusive ethical imagination.

How can students best succeed in your religious ethics courses?

In my classes, success looks like: (1) Students participate in self-reflection as a part of their learning by evaluating the norms of the culture(s) of which they are a part, and work sincerely on understanding their own processes of determining good action in light of the norms available to them. (2) Students engage texts critically and closely, raise questions, and make connections between them. (3) Students leave the class with tools to better understand ethical problems, but also hopefully a desire to patiently continue this work with the knowledge that engaging in ethical inquiry is difficult but worthwhile.

What do you believe will be the most important moral issues for the next generation?

It's hard to predict the ethical issues that will figure prominently for the next generation. I suspect that we will need to encourage more creative and dedicated thinking on just war ethics, ethics and technology, and environmental ethics—to name just a few areas.

Nichole Flores, PhD

Associate Professor of Practical Ethics, Department of Religious Studies University of Virginia, Charlottesville, Virginia

How did you end up in the field of religious ethics?

I began my undergraduate years at Smith College with a desire to be a lawyer. I took lots of classes in the Government Department during my first year, thinking that they would prepare me for applying to law school. But along the way, I realized that the most interesting aspect of my politics course work was how religion played a crucial role in shaping political philosophy, public policy, and even law. I enrolled in a class on Christian women mystics which only confirmed my excitement for thinking about religion and ethics. I did end up majoring in government, but I ended up taking lots of classes in religion, philosophy, and ethics both in and outside of my major.

Can you list three of your favorite or most influential works that impressed you as a thinker?

Ada Maria Isasi-Diaz was leading the "turn to culture" in ethics decades before Richard Miller suggested it in *Friends and Other Strangers*. Isasi-Diaz's work remains as cogent and relevant as ever, especially given her attention to Latina cultural, economic, and religious practices as a source for ethical reflection.

Lisa Sowle Cahill, my own "doctor mother" [i.e., dissertation advisor], never ceases to inspire me through her work. She manages to balance the necessity of attending to particularity with the urgency of ethical norms in a society where human and creaturely dignity is constantly under attack. She also deftly navigates the distinctive conversations in religious ethics, Christian ethics, and Catholic moral theology without reducing them to each other.

Danielle S. Allen is a political philosopher, not a religious ethicist. But her work manifests the significance of religious understanding for excellent work in political theory. She is able to identify the influence of theology on the development of political philosophy. She also is able to bring her own religious experience into her writing without excluding other experiences.

What are the main ideas or questions that guide your work?

My work is primarily concerned with the relationship between justice and aesthetics. These interests were born from my practical experience of organizing with farmworkers to secure economic and human rights. This experience directed my attention to the significance of protest as liturgy to the success of a social movement. It also helped me to ask sharper questions about what justice means in the context of a global capitalist market that perpetually exploits human beings, especially those who are made vulnerable by their race, ethnicity, gender, and immigration status.

How can students best succeed in your religious ethics courses?

Students thrive in my courses when they are able to identify questions and concerns that are salient to their own contexts. Having a sense of their own particular social location allows them to better see the particularities of other contexts. I invite students to bring their own experiences and questions into the classroom—it helps us all ask better questions and imagine better responses.

What do you believe will be the most important moral issues for the next generation?

I think the meaning of truth and authenticity will be a crucial question for the coming generation. Being born, raised, and/or coming of age during the Trump presidency, as well as the #MeToo movement that has unveiled abuse and hypocrisy deep in some of our most trusted cultural and religious institutions, will influence the kinds of questions that the coming generation raises about the meaning of fact, truth, representation, and power.

Laura Hartman, PhD

Associate Professor, Environmental Studies
Roanoke College, Salem, Virginia

How did you end up in the field of religious ethics?

I came to religious ethics with an agenda. I knew I was concerned about environmental issues, and I knew that neither science nor politics was a good fit for me. I realized that religion has a big impact on culture, and culture has a big impact on how we treat the earth. So, I reasoned that finding ways to get religious people to care about the environment could be an effective way to make a difference. It was a very calculating approach. Thankfully, the more I studied religion the more I realized that there is value, beauty, and authentic insight in religious traditions: they have intrinsic value, not just instrumental value. I was able to temper my instrumentalist approach with a genuine appreciation for the traditions. I hope that has led to a respectful engagement that works with, rather than seeking to manipulate, religious thought.

Can you list three of your favorite or most influential works that impressed you as a thinker?

Sallie McFague's *Body of God* really got me thinking about metaphors and the ethical work that they do. This also got me thinking about gender and power as they relate to environmental thought. Wendell Berry's work taken as a whole, his essays such as those collected in *The Art of the Commonplace* and his fiction such as *Jayber Crow*, have to be on the list. Reading Berry allowed me to articulate an intuition I already had: that "preserving wilderness" is not the central task of environmental thought. Rather, we have to re-think how we work with land, how we produce and consume, what we think about work, how our communities form, and who we give our allegiance to.

I am always learning new things, so I have to mention my favorite recent work, Robin Wall Kimmerer's *Braiding Sweetgrass*. Kimmerer combines her training as a botanist with her Potawatomi heritage to sketch a compelling vision of deep reciprocity between humans and nature. I keep chewing on this statement of hers, which takes my breath away every time: "We are dreaming of a time when the land might give thanks for the people." This book is making me question all my assumptions; it's turning my world upside down!

What are the main ideas or questions that guide your work?

Two things: What are humans in relation to nature, and specifically how much power should we have? For this reason, I look into ecological restoration and climate engineering, asking if we are healers of the landscape, engineers of the atmosphere, destroyers, stewards, dominators, etc. I seek useful metaphors and models to help us see the possibilities for good human agency in nature.

Also, I want to know, in the words of Peter Maurin (who founded the Catholic Worker [Movement] with Dorothy Day), how to make a society in which it is easier to be good. For me, being good refers to living in an ecologically friendly way. Why is it so hard? Why must we swim upstream, go against the grain of society, just to avoid poisoning of the web of life? In answer to this question, I look into consumption and consumerism (my first book, *The Christian Consumer: Living Faithfully in a Fragile World*) as well as transportation. With transportation, I want to know why so many of us are stuck driving all the time, when we'd rather be able to walk, bike, and take the bus. I have a new project on church parking lots that asks, fundamentally, why have churches acquiesced to a culture of automobility, bending over backwards to facilitate it rather than fighting it?

How can students best succeed in your religious ethics courses?

The secret of success is attention. Students, your attention is a golden beam of sunlight that you can shine on whatever you choose. The world is competing for this attention. Advertisers want it. Your cell phone wants it. Social media wants it. Your roommate wants it. Everybody wants your attention. Your job is to steward that attention as best you can. Sleep well and spend time in nature so you can have the strongest light-beam of attention possible. And then use your attention for good. Read the readings. Write papers two days early so you can get someone to read them, sleep on them, and still revise them before the due date. It is such a gift to be in college. Give it your best shot by nurturing your beam of light and shining your attention on the things that really matter.

What do you believe will be the most important moral issues for the next generation?

Aldo Leopold, famous for articulating "the land ethic," sums up basically every generation when he writes, "the oldest task in human history [is] to live on a piece of land without spoiling it." We're still working on that one. The climate crisis looms large and its human justice dimensions are very compelling. Biodiversity loss is just as upsetting; many species are already basically on hospice care and large numbers of others are as good as gone. And don't get me started on toxic substances and how they affect all of us—but especially the poor! We are entering a time of grief, as coral reefs and ice caps slip away, but also a time of action, as people wake up to the urgency of the situation. Fundamentally, we need to find a way to create well-being for humans without spending the well-being of the planet or poisoning each other in the process. Greater human equality would help, but we also need a willingness to learn from, and be guided by, natural processes.

Anything else?

Environmental ethics is not for the faint of heart. I have to face bad news every day. Many forms of applied ethics are like this: sexual ethics often means thinking about sexual assault and other terrible topics; ethics of war means facing atrocities and death.

I think that a religious ethics approach is extremely useful for applied ethics because it gives us extra tools to handle all the bad news. For one thing, religious thought recognizes a role for emotion. It gives me permission to have feelings about my topic. I know those feelings are an expression of truth, and I know that denying them is unhealthy. For another, religious thought helps me think about healing: feeling guilty? There's a ritual for that. Ready to make amends? There's a ritual for that. Need to lament? There's a ritual for that. Need some perspective? There are prayers and scriptures for that. Religions have all these spiritual technologies that are intended to help us patch up wrongs. They're so helpful in handling the bad news of applied ethics! Finally, all religions tell stories about situations that seemed to be the end of the world, but turned out to be a new, miraculous, holy phenomenon. When I worry about melting permafrost or cancer rates or dying coral—which I do, often!—I need those stories to remind me that tragedy is not the only way to interpret life's problems.

Terrence L. Johnson, PhD

Professor of African American Religious Studies
Harvard Divinity School, Cambridge, Massachusetts

How did you end up in the field of religious ethics?

This is a difficult question to answer. I guess I stumbled my way into the field. In graduate school, I was trying to find a way to answer the question W.E.B. Du Bois raised at the turn of the twentieth century, "how does it feel to be a problem," and I discovered in my coursework that a single discipline could not provide an adequate answer. I needed many tools and different texts to shed light on the varying ways the "problem" emerged in modernity and during the rise of American slavery. In light of Black religion's longstanding role in grappling with freedom, justice, and liberation, religious ethics seemed like a good starting point for piecing together the broad scope of antiblackness and addressing how best to tackle the problem. The interdisciplinary framework of religious ethics opened a new window through which I imagined Du Bois's haunting question. I turned to political theory, Africana existentialism, aesthetics, and literature to dive more deeply into how antiblackness operates within our moral and political beliefs.

Can you list three of your favorite or most influential works that impressed you as a thinker?

It seems like a severe injustice to limit one's intellectual heritage to three works but I will try. (And I must say that this list will change depending on the day I am asked the question!) I'd like to list three authors who played a critical role in my overall formation as a human being, teacher, and scholar: Cheikh Anta Diop, W.E.B. Du Bois, and James Baldwin. My mentor, Ketu Oladuwa, introduced me to these thinkers when I was a junior or senior in high school. But my formal introduction to them happened at Morehouse College, where I studied as an undergraduate. In different ways, all three thinkers opened unknown worlds to me, where human passion, sorrow, and joy (to borrow from Du Bois) emerged without fear or concern of the normative white gaze (Cornel West). Of course, they were responding to white supremacy and the ongoing implications of antiblackness, but their works pointed to the epistemic traditions and blueprints for ways of being I had previously not known, dismissed or discounted.

In a narrow sense, they compelled me in college to 'trouble' standard narratives of African slavery, Christianity, and Western civilization. Diop's *The African Origin of Civilization: Myth or Reality* turned my eyes away from America as the starting point for Black life to a world and civilization where human existence in Black thrived, flourished, and succumbed to ebb and flows of life. I imagined the possibility of a world prior without Black enslavement. And if this were possible, how might I think about Black life in and beyond the boundaries of antiblackness, slavery, and white supremacy?

Du Bois's *The Souls of Black Folk* is without question his major gift to the world and to the study of Black life since African enslavement, but I encountered Du Bois's political and "ethical" imagination in another work, *The Autobiography of W.E.B. Du Bois: A Soliloquy on Viewing My Life from the Last Decade of Its First Century*. Through his musings on communism, Black liberal politics, and empire, I discovered the strange and contradictory ways ideal theories clashed and collided with the Negro problem. Du Bois' narration of liberalism and socialism, for instance, uncovered new sightings of human agency, racial solidarity, and democratic aspirations.

James Baldwin reinforced what I could only intuit as an undergraduate: religion was not simply a resource communities relied on to reinforce their faith commitments, but it was also an expression of a community's lingering fears, aspirations, and doubts about a world from which they were excluded and denied human dignity. His semi-autobiographical novel, *Go Tell It on the Mountain,* introduced me to the inventive ways Black Pentecostals grappled with Black subjugation through themes of sexuality, gender, poverty, and racism. But one of the most enduring themes of the novel unfolds in the expression of the Black body, specifically the performative ways Black religion reimagined blackness. The characters transform their 'sinful' bodies, albeit momentarily, into radiant and holy-filled vessels for their God. The move echoed the Nation of Islam's call for Black people to redeem blackness by reclaiming their 'true nature' through self-love. In other words, Blacks possessed an interiority that could be recovered for generative purposes.

From behind the Du Boisian veil of blackness, Diop, Baldwin, and Du Bois grappled with the moral and political dilemmas of a people embroiled in an ongoing effort to fight against claims of Black inferiority as they pursued political rights, economic equality, and social justice.

What are the main ideas or questions that guide your work?

Questions related to human agency, freedom, truth, and interiority animate my research and scholarly writings.

How can students best succeed in your religious ethics courses?

I encourage my students to see themselves as conversation-partners with the authors we are reading. This is a necessary step in envisioning themselves as young intellectuals who have something important to contribute to the debate at hand. I also encourage them to claim their traditions and practices as justifiable starting points for engaging the material. By doing so, they can often make connections to texts that others have never considered, and the engagement creates the conditions to join in or push against existing debates on the subject matter. That being said, I expect my students to allow the text to speak back to them. They cannot assume their starting points will remain adequate or sufficient as they dig deeper into the material. When arguments contradict, or push against their norms, they are obliged to wrestle with the points of tension. With this framework, students generally feel confident enough to think through some of the major concerns regarding social justice, normative commitments, and moral agency.

What do you believe will be the most important moral issues for the next generation?

Many of the concerns the next generation will face are, unfortunately, abbreviated or extended forms of what we are facing now: racism, xenophobia, misogyny, classism, and heterosexism. One such issue stems from the refugee crisis: how will world leaders handle the displacement of peoples caused by war, poverty, and climate change? In addition, the growing wealth inequality will exacerbate unless transnational efforts emerge to address how social welfare can play a bigger role in wealth creation, management and distribution. Even a weak understanding of socialism may avert an inevitable clash and/or war between the elite and working classes.

As we deal with the lingering implications of global pandemics, technology and how it is used to monitor, track, and predict health crises, will compel us to address broader questions around big data: how it is used and who owns it? Undergirding my concern with technology is the racialization of data. We must ask ourselves: will race continue to be the determining factor in how we deploy technology and track data? Will governments and corporations use new technological resources to eradicate health, economic, education, and social inequality?

Lastly, institutionalized religions will remain a vital part of many communities, but how we understand the divine and/or the good in relation to aesthetics, human agency, and community will continue to loom large as religious 'technologies' such as meditation, conjure, and divination extend and expand within our rapidly changing societies.

Aline Kalbian, PhD

Associate Dean, College of Arts and Sciences
Professor, Department of Religion
Florida State University, Tallahassee, Florida

How did you end up in the field of religious ethics?

I had been a religion major as an undergraduate, but mostly interested in biblical studies and the ancient Near East. In fact, I never took an ethics course as an undergraduate. After college, I worked for about eight years in DC for two non-profits and became really interested in the intersection of religion and politics. The program at the University of Virginia seemed like a possible fit for me, but to me honest, I didn't really know much about the field. My first semester there, I was exposed to three phenomenal professors who really influenced my decision to stay beyond an MA and get the PhD in Religious Ethics.

Can you list three of your favorite or most influential works that impressed you as a thinker?

The Fragility of Goodness by Martha Nussbaum was one of the first books I read in graduate school. It took my breath away and convinced me that I wanted to be a scholar who thought about ethics. *Moral Understandings* by

Margaret Urban Walker helped show me how to think about feminist themes and ideas in the context of my study of a particular religious community; and the *Summa Theologiae* by Thomas Aquinas challenged me incredibly (it still does), but it helped me see the beauty and poetry of Catholic moral theology, which made me a better reader of the tradition.

What are the main ideas or questions that guide your work?

How do religious communities change and adapt to the world and culture around them while remaining true to their essential teachings? How are attitudes about gender shaped by theological ideas and how do theological ideas shape attitudes about gender?

How can students best succeed in your religious ethics courses?

Do the reading!! Be open to ideas that challenge their own beliefs. Listen to what others in class have to say.

What do you believe will be the most important moral issues for the next generation?

I think it has become increasingly evident that climate change and environmental destruction will be the most important issues. Sadly, I think the next generation will have no choice but to face the consequences of what humanity has done to the planet and try to come up with viable and sensible solutions to slow down the damage.

Anything else?

One thing that has sustained me on my intellectual journey as a scholar has been my love of good fiction. I encourage all students to cultivate a similar love. Fiction can open your eyes in ways that you would never imagine.

Grace Kao, PhD

Professor of Ethics
Claremont School of Theology, Claremont, California

How did you end up in the field of religious ethics?

The story of how I ended up in religious ethics is connected to how I decided to pursue a professorship in philosophy/religious studies/theology as a career path. I was raised in a conservative, monoethnic Taiwanese evangelical church, where the site of my ethnic identity coincided with my spiritual formation. By the time I reached junior high, I was reading "Christian apologetics" and some entry-level philosophy and world religions books on my own because I had a deep desire to know—as idealistic as this sounds—if what my pastor and church elders was telling me about the world and the nature of God and so forth were true. For the most part, in high school, I remained comfortably situated in the evangelical world.

The questions I had about truth wouldn't escape me, however, so I decided to major in philosophy and religious studies in college. Some of my elders in my church community warned me that I might "lose my faith" if I did. I didn't, to be clear, but the Christian faith I ended with upon graduating was not as it was when I began. I also ended up writing an undergraduate honors thesis on the classical Confucian concept of filial piety; what was at stake for me is whether this virtue—one so important in East Asian Confucian-based cultures—could hold appeal for contemporary Westerners if properly demythologized.

While it was the search for truth that brought me to the study of philosophy and religion, I soon found that I was most interested in practical matters — i.e., what is good, just, right, virtuous, morally required or supererogatory, etc. With the guidance and encouragement of my undergraduate thesis advisor, I applied to graduate school to continue the study of such matters and the rest is history.

Can you list three of your favorite or most influential works that impressed you as a thinker?

It was my encounter with the pseudonymous Kierkegaard—Johannes de Silentio's *Fear and Trembling* (1843) that rocked me to the core as an undergrad and exposed me to something I previously hadn't encountered before—a Christian philosopher wrestling with the relationship between the particular demands of faith and the requirements of (universal) morality. Frankly, in my work on human rights and public theology, I've been working on versions of this question ever since. The second would be Delores Williams' classic, *Sisters in the Wilderness* (1993). Today the book is rightly heralded as a classic in womanist theology; for me the power of the book lay in her exposing me to what we would now categorize as postcolonial and contextualized scholarship. That is, prior to reading her book, I hadn't realized that I had been taught a colonial form of Christianity—one that would have me "side" with the story of biblical Sarah and not the foreign and enslaved Hagar (and subsequently with the movements of the ancient Israelites and not the various peoples the Bible records as them having conquered). The third would be Margaret Farley's *Just Love: A Framework for Christian Sexual Ethics* (2006). This is a book I deeply appreciate and regularly assign in my Intro to Christian Ethics course. The book displays careful scholarship, accessible writing style, and seven norms at the end that do not just lead readers to a rejection of traditional Christian sexual ethics or taboo morality ("fidelity in marriage [between a man and a woman], chastity in singleness"), but rather a constructive framework for person to reconstructive a healthier, more justice-oriented sexual ethic.

What are the main ideas or questions that guide your work?

I approach all questions or issues with a feminist consciousness. I'm also always mindful of the question whether the norms and values I have concluded are good and right for everyone or if they are to be esteemed for only a particular group (e.g., Christians). Recently I've been developing with several of my colleagues a uniquely Asian American approach to the study of Christian ethics, so I am also attentive to the ways our experiences as persons of Asian heritage in the U.S. give us a unique vantage to approach the field of study.

How can students best succeed in your religious ethics courses?

Students ideally should come with an open mind and be willing to be persuaded by the force of the better argument. They should also come to terms with what assumptions or orientation (etc.) they already bring to the texts or issues under study and then be willing to name them and have them challenged.

What do you believe will be the most important moral issues for the next generation?

I would name three. The first is, hands-down, climate change. Environmental scientists and other thought leaders have been telling us that it is too late to avert a catastrophe—all we can do its minimize or ameliorate its impacts. So, we will need more than individuals acting virtuously in their own lives (e.g., recycling, reducing their consumption)—we will need states, corporations, and other entities (in addition to people of goodwill) to coordinate action for the common good.

The second is tangentially related. As environmental consciousness grows, we are increasingly asking ourselves questions about the boundaries of the moral community—that is, whose interests or welfare "count" and on what basis? In the language of philosophical or religious ethics, this is essentially a question of moral status or standing. We have seen the boundaries of the moral community stretch over centuries to include segments of the human community previously excluded (e.g., women, slaves, particular ethnic or racial groups, queer folks, persons with disabilities, etc.) Increasingly, philosophers and religious ethicists have made a case—persuasively in my view—that the moral community must be extended to include other than humans—for instance, non-human animals and, as I would say in my Christian tradition, other elements of the created world (e.g., plants). It is one thing to argue that we should "save the Amazon" or "save the rainforests" for future generations to take joy and/or benefit from them (e.g., for medicines that can be harvested from certain plants or for indigenous cultures who rely upon them). It is another thing to say that we should do the same not just for current or future generations of human beings, but for the sake of non-human nature itself. There is, to be sure, no worldwide consensus on this, but I anticipate questions of moral standing only increasing (not deceasing) in urgency in the decades to come, particularly as we wrestle with human overpopulation and habitat encroachment.

The third is how current generations reconcile themselves—and one another—with the past. It's been argued that the 1990s was the "age of the apology," as several foreign dignitaries, congressional or parliamentary bodies, religious leaders, and heads of corporations acknowledged what gross human rights abuses the institutions they now represent took part in and apologized for it, in some cases by offering reparations. I do not see calls to address historical grievances and provide intergenerational justice dying down; if anything, I see them ramping up. In the US, this has mostly taken the form of how the US will deal with its genocidal (with Native Americans) and slavery past (with African Americans). The concerns may be different in other contexts, but the basic concern is the same—survivors or surviving generations are keeping the memory of the atrocities alive and are pressing for those either responsible or complicit in it to make amends.

John Kelsay, PhD

Distinguished Research Professor, Department of Religion
Florida State University, Tallahassee, Florida

How did you end up in the field of religious ethics?

Mine is a story of the way things turn out differently than expected. My passions growing up were baseball and music. I was not very good at the former, but had some success with the latter, and I began college as a music major. For a variety of reasons, however, I became increasingly interested in Christian theology. Having studied mostly on my own, I decided to attend Columbia Theological Seminary, a Presbyterian school located in Decatur, GA, beginning in the fall of 1976.

At the time, students at Columbia were debating a number of issues related to gender, sexual ethics, and the like. And I found myself fascinated with the different ways people argued for their views. The study of ethics seemed a good way to pursue that interest, and as it turned out, the graduate program at the University of Virginia provided training that helped me to develop skills in describing Christian and Muslim arguments related to a variety of issues. I continue to think that this type of study—that is, of the arguments people make about right and wrong, or good and evil—is one of the most interesting ways to come at the study of religion.

Can you list three of your favorite or most influential works that impressed you as a thinker?

I read the two volumes of Reinhold Niebuhr's *Nature and Destiny of Man* as a student at Columbia Seminary, and I have returned to them throughout my career. As a graduate student, I discovered Max Weber's work, and his programmatic essay on "The Social Psychology of the World's Religions" lays out an approach that informs all of my teaching and research. More recently, Robert Brandom's *Making It Explicit* helped me to think about the connections between normative reasoning (that is, ethics) and social life, especially in connection with the ways groups of people try to deal with moral change.

What are the main ideas or questions that guide your work?

As Max Weber put it, one of the most characteristic things people do with religious ideas involves the description and justification of social order. His term for this is legitimation. In discussing this notion, Weber's focus was on the "big picture," in the sense of the ways power and other goods are distributed in society. The idea also applies to smaller issues, however, as in discussions about the rights and wrongs of war, or questions about sexual ethics. I would say that this idea animates most of my work, along with another idea from Weber: that is, that when we think about the role of religion in human life, we should expect disagreement and even conflict, not only between adherents of different faiths, but also (and perhaps even more) among those who share a common faith and set of sources. So, we anticipate disagreement between Christians over normative issues, even as we also expect disagreement between Christians and Muslims.

How can students best succeed in your religious ethics courses?

I tell students that the road to success is very simple. First in importance is regular attendance, since I present a lot of material in lectures and class discussion. A second step is to do the reading ahead of time, with the idea of returning to it after class. And the third step involves writing and rewriting papers, since I require students to respond in writing to questions that allow them to demonstrate that they have understood and are able to analyze the material presented in lectures and readings.

What do you believe will be the most important moral issues of the next generation?

The issues related to war and international politics are not going away anytime soon, and I expect religious rhetoric to play an important part in this. Environmental issues will grow in importance, as will questions related to justice in economic life.

Anything else?

From my perspective, the study of religious ethics provides a unique window into the things people care about. The work requires a broad combination of the analytic skills valued by philosophers, knowledge of various types of theology and religious thought, and historical and ethnographic work—which means that there is always something more to learn!

Charles Mathewes, PhD

Carolyn M. Barbour Professor of Religious Studies
University of Virginia, Charlottesville, Virginia

How did you end up in the field of religious ethics?

I think like a lot of people I was influenced by accidents and by deep impulses. Accidents include who I took classes with and when. I ended up taking a series of classes with a teacher who was an ethicist and who thought about ethics in a capacious sense, sort of as addressing who we are as creatures, and how we flourish. I found her classes and the questions driving them totally gripping, and I've been doing it ever since.

But there were also deep impulses from my past. My family lived overseas when I was a kid, and I was exposed to a lot of ways of life, and I never took any particular one for granted, or as the "natural" one from which all others were flawed copies. Then we lived in a place of some political and religious precariousness, so we paid attention to the world and what was going on in ways that kept us alert to the complexity of events and the actors within them. Finally, my parents were foundational to my mind, and gave me a powerful impulse to ask questions, and different—and quite rival—senses of what you could call a "tragic sense of life." So, from the scale of international geopolitics to intimate domestic matters, questions of meaning and moral order, of plausible forms of normativity and the different ways people can inhabit and/ or experience the same phenomena, shaped me from the beginning.

Can you list three of your favorite or most influential works that impressed you as a thinker?

Well there's a lot! I would say certainly Augustine of Hippo—his *Confessions* is actually incredibly hard to understand, but in a devilishly subtle way; I recommend students start with the far more massive *City of God*, whose difficulty is at least visible from the first page. Second probably would be Hannah Arendt, whose liberty of mind and intelligence and fearlessness still amazes me; her *The Human Condition* is perhaps her most wide-ranging book, though I have to say I think *Eichmann in Jerusalem* will stand the test of time as the most aesthetically powerful work she ever wrote. I still find it incredibly moving. Third? A philosopher, GEM (Elizabeth) Anscombe; her essay "Modern Moral Philosophy" is the toughest piece of philosophical beef jerky I ever chewed. But it is, in its own, ingrown, Oxbridge way, a quiet masterpiece.

Beyond those three, I would recommend two American writers, Reinhold Niebuhr and James Baldwin, who have both written the kind of non-fiction prose that seems to me still necessary for thinking and living today, for the academic discipline of religious ethics but for anyone who wants to be conscious in our world; I'd recommend Niebuhr's *The Children of Light and the*

Children of Darkness and Baldwin's *The Devil Finds Work*. Many other books and thinkers have been powerful for me, but from those, a lot of other stuff has been organized.

What are the main ideas or questions that guide your work?

There are two descriptive sets of questions that occupy me, one about the nature of the different ways distinct human communities have imagined what it is like to be human and live in this world, and one about, well, what is going on in the world? What is happening to us? I think that, ever since I would sit at lunch in the fourth grade and listen to the AP (or UPI?) world news with my mom, I've been somewhat obsessed with figuring out what was about to happen, and why. We needed to know it to figure out if we should flee the country where we lived (long story), but even as the rationale for it has changed, the serious urgency has stayed with me.

More normatively, I think, I am interested in a couple questions: what does it mean to be a human agent in this world? and, why do I feel that the world is fundamentally good, despite all the evidence that weighs against that judgment, and what does that goodness entail about the cosmos and my response to it? I think the mystery of what humans are is a matter of humans "in motion," in action; and I think the languages we have for thinking about ourselves as actors are really quite thin right now, and not likely to get much thicker. And—maybe like the filmmaker Terrence Malik, and behind him Arendt, Heidegger, Augustine, Aristotle, a lot of people—I find the sheer wonder of the world remarkable, truly remarkable.

How can students best succeed in your religious ethics courses?

The virtues most immediately demanded are patient attention, bordering on devotion, to the object of study and to your own reactions and responses to the object of study; careful listening to the arguments of those with whom you think you agree and those with whom you think you disagree; meticulous scrutiny of those arguments; and honesty about the strengths and weaknesses of those arguments; and a willingness to explore the weaknesses of positions you think you agree with, and the insights of positions you think you disagree with. All of these virtues need to be developed intentionally; we are not naturally reflexive beings, and such hesitation as this entails does not confer any evolutionary advantage on us.

Once we begin, we have different questions to ask and it will be important to know the questions. There's a normative task in "religious ethics" and an ethnographic task. Normatively, we have a lot of questions that are more or less "immanent criticism" of the positions we study. What do we think is the right thing to do? How should we achieve our aims, and what should our aims be, and why? What is decency? What is immorality? What is inhumanity, and what is generosity? These are all questions we will find in religious ethics, and we cannot avoid them. They may be questions we ask in an instant, and only for ourselves, or in the context of a class, but they are real questions.

Ethnographically, we have to ask: How are the traditions and communities we study (when we study them) organized? What intuitions or insights do they build upon or appeal to for legitimacy? What do they affirm? What do they deny? In this ethnographic dimension, and maybe even in the normative one as well, I think of ethics as about intimacy and estrangement. It is about becoming familiar enough with a position to feel its "grip" upon your understanding of why and how people act, so that you can begin to inhabit, intellectually and perhaps empathetically, an overall stance or worldview—so in this way it is about gaining intimacy with ways of being human. But it is also about recognizing that there are different "grips" and each of them can be as compelling to those susceptible to them as any other is as compelling to you—so that the world is maddeningly susceptible to different construals that all seem sufficiently plausible and inhabitable to their various adherents.

What do you believe will be the most important moral issues for the next generation?

I think of three big things.

First, issues broadly around "the politics of recognition." How will we manage to recognize, and honor, difference? This is obviously roiling our world. Religious difference is a big one, but racial, ethnic, cultural, gender, sexual difference—this is all a huge challenge.

Second, issues broadly around agency. What kinds of creatures are we, and how do we understand our actions in the world, how are they prompted/ provoked by our environment, are we "ex nihilo" actors, are we driven/ determined, what? This is broadly a question of moral and religious anthropology, I think.

Third—somewhat more indirectly—the question of our relationship to our past. Walter Benjamin said, "There is no document of culture which is not also a document of barbarism." The resources of my teaching—of "humanistic" teaching more generally, I think—are broadly historical resources. Can we learn from documents and artifacts that we think are deeply morally compromised, perhaps utterly corrupt? Can we inhabit institutions we find to be morally terribly compromised? In my tradition: once we have begun to see the depths of sin, what then?

Anything else?

We live in a world of enormous technical accomplishment and tremendous human ignorance. We in religious ethics, like we in the humanities as a whole, are working on the final clause of that sentence. We should never let ourselves, teachers and students, forget that what we do matters, matters desperately. I think the questions we are asking are descendants of questions humans have asked for millennia, and we need to honor that and also recognize we may be able to learn from the past, but we also need to find the answers that help us today. Reiterating what others knew is not likely to be of great benefit. And on the other hand, our technical knowledge will only be as good, or as bad, as our humanity enables it to be.

Aaron Stalnaker, PhD

Professor, Religious Studies
Indiana University, Bloomington, Indiana

How did you end up in the field of religious ethics?

I stumbled into religious ethics after deciding that math and physics were not as fascinating as I had expected once I got to college. Really it was the result of inspirational teaching combined with increasing intellectual fascination. The tipping point was being allowed to take a graduate seminar on "Character and the Good Life" taught by Lee Yearley when I was a sophomore. I was in over my head, but it was great! This was my first serious encounter with classical Confucianism, via reading the Mengzi (i.e., Mencius); with Aristotle's *Nicomachean Ethics*; and with two astounding (to me) recent works of philosophy: Alasdair MacIntyre's *After Virtue*, which argues that the modern West has gone fatally wrong by leaving behind the Aristotelian tradition of the virtues as the core paradigm of ethics, and Bernard Williams's *Ethics and the Limits of Philosophy*, which takes some very different lessons from the ancient Greeks, including the idea that the "modern morality system" built around an interlocking scheme of duties is a form of mental slavery that we should reject. All of it was electrifying, and both Mengzi and Aristotle made more sense to me than many of the elements of Protestant Christian ethics I had been taught growing up, even if other parts seemed wild and wrong.

As I went further, the field seemed more and more like it was my destiny, as corny as that sounds. My parents divorced when I was seven, and lived rather different lives: my dad was a gay artist and professor who devoted enormous energy to aesthetic pursuits; while my mom had the temperament of a literarily inclined monk or nun, despite being Protestant, and was a very serious intellectual Christian. (The heroes in our house were Martin Luther King, Jr., and Dietrich Bonhoeffer.) They both were living good lives, and loved me in ways I am deeply grateful for, but they were not following the same codes or seeking exactly the same goals, so it would have been wrong to try to homogenize them into one archetype of "the good life." Comparative religious ethics seemed for me a way to explore the varieties of good lives that I had already begun to experience growing up.

Can you list three of your favorite or most influential works that impressed you as a thinker?

To return to the previous question, I've been wrestling with MacIntyre ever since I first encountered him as a sophomore, because he articulated a very demanding program of cross-tradition philosophical/theological comparison which appealed to me strongly enough that I essentially signed up for it, learning classical Chinese and Latin to write my dissertation on the early Confucian Xunzi and the early Christian thinker Augustine of Hippo. What made Mengzi so amazing was, first, his claim that human nature naturally tends toward goodness and mutual sympathy, rather than sinful depravity, as Calvinists contend; and second, that he was simply not that worried about God, and so sidestepped all the classical philosophy of religion questions about the problem of evil and free will that were bedeviling me at the time, and which seemed inescapable, insoluble, and deeply worrisome. But here was a text, which became the basis in some ways for all of later East Asian civilization, which proceeded in a quite different direction, and articulated an attractive and ethically appealing vision for life. My horizons were much expanded.

One other book that's meant a lot to me is Pierre Hadot's *Philosophy as a Way of Life*. This book reads ancient Greek and Roman philosophy as more or less like a family of religions, animated by shared commitments to spiritual exercises. These exercises, according to Hadot and the ancient thinkers he studies, transform aspirants so that they move gradually from foolishness and suffering to wisdom and a superior form of happiness. This was an appealing way to approach not just ancient philosophy, but a whole host of religious and philosophical movements, with attention to how ideas related to the practices of everyday life. I organized my first book around these ideas (a rewrite of the dissertation).

What are the main ideas or questions that guide your work?

The main ideas that guide my work are first, how do people become good? I usually cash this out in terms of what practices should we engage in to cultivate our virtues and purge our vices. And second, I focus on how to grapple with religious diversity through careful comparison across cultures and traditions. Just how similar and different are various ethical teachings from different religions and philosophies? How do we handle situations where different issues are highlighted by different traditions? How important is ethical theory, anyway, to living the good life? You can see how the basic questions quickly generate further research possibilities.

How can students best succeed in your religious ethics courses?

Students can best succeed in my classes by really doing the reading and thinking about it before coming to class, so that they get the most out of both lectures and discussions. By "thinking about it" I mean carrying on an imagined dialogue with the assigned text, where you ask it whatever questions you have about things that seem mysterious, baffling, or wrong as you read, and then really try to figure out how the author of the text might intelligently respond to your questions. And then, students should carry over this level of engagement to writing their essays. They should make some claim they believe in and that is significant enough to be worth arguing about, and write sensitively in favor of their view, with full awareness that ethics is complicated. In other words, when there are disputes, there are almost always real considerations on both (or multiple) sides of an issue, and they should write accordingly.

What do you believe will be the most important moral issues for the next generation?

I think the most important ethical issues for the next generation stem from the social and environmental problems caused by climate change. We are only getting a taste of what's to come right now. What we owe to needy strangers and refugees, and how we should help them, if we should (I think we should), are going to only become more and more pressing questions as millions of people's home habitats become unlivable. A lesser set of problems, but still pressing, concern the proper aims of government and what should be done, if anything, about massive accumulations of wealth and the rapidly increasing stratification of wealth. As far as specifically religious questions, I think comparative theology and comparative philosophy of religion will only grow in importance as more and more people have direct personal experience with strangers and neighbors practicing unfamiliar ways of life, which tends to raise questions that can't be easily dismissed about the rightness of one's own way of life.

Bibliography

Ahmed, Leila. *A Quiet Revolution: The Veil's Resurgence, from the Middle East to America.* New Haven, CT: Yale University Press, 2011.

Ali, Kecia. *Sexual Ethics and Islam: Feminist Reflections on Qur'an, Hadith, and Jurisprudence.* Expanded & revised edition. London: Oneworld, 2016.

Allen, Danielle S. *Talking to Strangers: Anxieties of Citizenship Since Brown V. Board of Education.* Chicago, IL: University of Chicago Press, 2004.

Anscombe, G. E. M. (Gertrude Elizabeth Margaret), Mary Geach, and Luke Gormally. *Human Life, Action, and Ethics Essays.* Exeter: Imprint Academic, 2005.

Arendt, Hannah. *Eichmann in Jerusalem: A Report on the Banality of Evil.* New York: Viking Press, 1963.

Arendt, Hannah, Danielle S. Allen, and Margaret Canovan. *The Human Condition.* Second edition. Chicago, IL: University of Chicago Press, 2018.Aristotle, and Hippocrates George Apostle. *Nicomachean Ethics.* Grinnell, IA: Peripatetic Press, 1984.

Augustine, and Henry Chadwick. *Confessions.* Oxford: Oxford University Press, 1991.

Augustine, Jand J.W.C. (John William Charles) Wand. *City of God.* London: Oxford University Press, 1963.Baldwin, James. *The Devil Finds Work: An Essay.* New York: Dial Press, 1976.

Baldwin, James. *Early Novels and Stories: Go Tell It on the Mountain; Giovanni's Room; Another Country; Going to Meet the Man.* New York: Literary Classics of the United States, 1998.

Berry, Wendell. *Jayber Crow: A Novel.* Washington, DC: Counterpoint, 2000.

Berry, Wendell, and Norman Wirzba. *The Art of the Common-Place: The Agrarian Essays of Wendell Berry.* Washington, DC: Counterpoint, 2002.

Brandom, Robert. *Making It Explicit: Reasoning, Representing, and Discursive Commitment.* Cambridge, MA: Harvard University Press, 1994.

Buber, Martin, and Walter Arnold Kaufmann. *I and Thou.* 1st Touchstone ed. New York: Touchstone, 1996.

Butler, Judith, and Sara Salih. *The Judith Butler Reader.* Edited by Judith Butler and Sara Salih. Malden, MA: Blackwell Publishing, 2004.

Crane, Jonathan K. *Eating Ethically: Religion and Science for a Better Diet.* New York: Columbia University Press, 2018.

Diop, Cheikh Anta. *The Cultural Unity of Black Africa: The Domains of Patriarchy and of Matriarchy in Classical Antiquity.* London: Karnak House, 1989.

Du Bois, W. E. B. (William Edward Burghardt). *The Autobiography of W.E.B. Du Bois: A Soliloquy on Viewing My Life from the Last Decade of Its First Century.* Oxford: Oxford University Press, 2007.

Du Bois, W. E. B. (William Edward Burghardt). *The Souls of Black Folk.* Oxford: Oxford University Press, 2007.

Dunn, Shannon. "New Directions in Theorizing Moral Injury and Just War." *Journal of Religious Ethics* 49:3 (2021), 438–41.

Farley, Margaret A. *Just Love: A Framework for Christian Sexual Ethics.* London: Continuum, 2008.

Flores, Nichole M. *The Aesthetics of Solidarity: Our Lady of Guadalupe and American Democracy.* Washington, DC: Georgetown University Press, 2021.

Hadot, Pierre, and Michael Chase. *Philosophy as a Way of Life: Ancients and Modern: Essays in Honor of Pierre Hadot.* Edited by Michael Chase. Hoboken, NJ: Wiley, 2013.

Hartman, Laura M. *The Christian Consumer: Living Faithfully in a Fragile World.* Oxford: Oxford University Press, 2011.

Hesse, Hermann. *The Glass Bead Game: Magister Ludi.* New York: H. Holt, 1990.

Isasi-Díaz, Ada María. *Mujerista Theology: A Theology for the Twenty-First Century.* Maryknoll, NY: Orbis Books, 1996.

Johnson, Terrence L. *We Testify with Our Lives: How Religion Transformed Radical Thought from Black Power to Black Lives Matter.* New York: Columbia University Press, 2021.

Kelsay, John. *Arguing the Just War in Islam.* Cambridge, MA: Harvard University Press, 2007.

Kierkegaard, Søren, and Bruce H. Kirmmse. *Fear and Trembling: A New Translation.* Translated by Bruce H. Kirmmse. New York: Liveright Publishing Corporation, 2022.

Kimmerer, Robin Wall. *Braiding Sweetgrass: Indigenous Wisdom, Scientific Knowledge and the Teachings of Plants.* Minneapolis, MN: Milkweed Editions, 2013.

MacIntyre, Alasdair C. *After Virtue: A Study in Moral Theory.* 3rd ed. Notre Dame: University of Notre Dame Press, 2007.

Mahmood, Saba. *Politics of Piety: The Islamic Revival and the Feminist Subject.* Princeton, NJ: Princeton University Press, 2011.

Mathewes, Charles T. *The Republic of Grace: Augustinian Thoughts for Dark Times.* Grand Rapids, MI: W.B. Eerdmans, 2010.

McFague, Sallie. *The Body of God: An Ecological Theology.* Minneapolis, MN: Fortress Press, 1993.

Mencius and Bryan W. Van Norden. *Mengzi with Selections from Traditional Commentaries.* Indianapolis, IN: Hackett Publishing, 2008.

Miller, Richard Brian. *Friends and Other Strangers: Studies in Religion, Ethics, and Culture.* New York: Columbia University Press, 2016.

Morrison, Toni. *Beloved: A Novel.* New York: Penguin, 1998.

Niebuhr, Reinhold. *The Children of Light and the Children of Darkness: A Vindication of Democracy and a Critique of Its Traditional Defense.* New York: Scribner, 1949.

Niebuhr, Reinhold. *The Nature and Destiny of Man.* Louisville, KY: Presbyterian Publishing Corporation, 2021.

Nussbaum, Martha C. *The Fragility of Goodness: Luck and Ethics in Greek Tragedy and Philosophy.* Revised edition. Cambridge: Cambridge University Press, 2001.

Quinn, Daniel. *Ishmael: A Novel.* New York: Bantam/Turner Books, 1992.

Quinn, Daniel. *My Ishmael.* New York: Bantam Books, 1997.

Quinn, Daniel. *The Story of B.* New York: Bantam Books, 1997.

Stalnaker, Aaron. *Mastery, Dependence, and the Ethics of Authority.* New York: Oxford University Press, 2020.

Thomas, and Peter Kreeft. *A Summa of the Summa: The Essential Philosophical Passages of St. Thomas Aquinas' Summa Theologica.* San Francisco, CA: Ignatius Press, 1990.

Walker, Margaret Urban. *Moral Understandings: A Feminist Study in Ethics.* New York: Routledge, 1998.

Weber, Max, Hans Heinrich Gerth, and C. Wright Mills. *From Max Weber: Essays in Sociology.* Abingdon: Routledge, 2009.

Williams, Bernard, A.W. Moore, and Jonathan Lear. *Ethics and the Limits of Philosophy.* London: Routledge, 2011.

Williams, Delores S. *Sisters in the Wilderness: The Challenge of Womanist God-Talk.* Maryknoll, NY: Orbis Books, 1993.

Conclusion

Although we do not hold crystal balls, we can make educated guesses about topics that will become increasingly important for the future of religious ethics. Certainly, climate change and the environment will continue to be pressing topics. Sexism and racism will also likely continue to be challenges for societies to face. We will also likely see ethical dilemmas arise in relation to new medical advances. There are, in addition, several issues that will pose novel ethical quandaries. In this conclusion, I would like to suggest three areas to ponder for their impact on religious ethics:

1 The increase in the population of religious "nones"
2 The rise of religious nationalism
3 The impact of artificial intelligence

Religious "Nones"

In 2021, the Pew Research Center reported that the number of Americans who have no affiliation with organized religion was at an all-time high. Approximately 30% of Americans identified themselves as atheist, agnostic, or belonging to no religion in particular—these groups constitute what pollsters are labeling "nones." This number is about 10% higher than reported a decade previously. In 1972, only 5% of Americans reported not having a religion. This indicates a growing trend away from organized religions that appears to be accelerating over time.

Most people in the US who are leaving organized religions are leaving Protestant sects of Christianity. Much of the European population, too, does not identity with any particular religion. About 30% of the population in France and Spain, and over 40% of the population in the Netherlands, Norway, and Sweden are religious nones. The *absolute* number of religious nones in North America and in Western Europe is expected to increase over time, but as a *percentage* of the world population in the future may likely decrease. This is because religious nones tend to have fewer children than people who identify with particular faith traditions.

DOI: 10.4 324/9781003350637-10

The two main reasons reported by nones for lack of religious affiliations are (1) questioning of religious teachings; and (2) disliking the position of churches on social and political issues. With the exception of atheists, many nones still report, however, believing in spirituality or in the possibility of the existence of God. If fewer people continue to belong to organized religions, then those religions may also eventually cease. Religions require membership, and if no one is there to attend services, to lead rituals, and to carry out the work necessary for the day-to-day operations of religious organizations, then religions become not "living" institutions, but dead. Their artifacts may be preserved and their histories recorded, but with no one to participate in these religions, traditions will pass.

The impact of nones on religious ethics, in particular, would seem to parallel the impact on religious organizations. Religions with larger populations are generally more influential in culture and politics, and religions with few members are unlikely to be heard. As such, when religions hold particular stances on ethical matters—whether it be climate change or women's reproductive rights—the most influential stances often come from the most popular religions. This is a general rule, however, and the translation of religious views on controversial ethical issues into policy, law, and culture is not straightforward. Many Protestant Christian denominations, for example, hold more liberal views on abortion than some American politicians and judges, who take deeply conservative positions on abortion that appear to reflect their own Christian values.

On a more basic level, the unfamiliarity of many nones with any religious tradition will likely mean a decrease in religious literacy. Even if a large minority of populations chooses not to affiliate with an organized religion, religions have played a significant role in world history. Religions will also likely continue to influence global politics. Because an informed population is critically important for participatory democracies, the lack of religious knowledge could have detrimental effects reflected on the policy level. People who know little about religions may not be able to make educated decisions about issues that involve religion.

Religious Nationalism

Religious nationalism, or the fusion of religious identity with state patriotism, is on the upswing around the world. Although many in the twenty-first century tend to equate religious nationalism with fundamentalist Islam, we are also seeing a rise in nationalist movements associated with other religions, such as Hinduism, Judaism, Christianity, and Sikhism. While each instance of religious nationalism is borne out of a unique context, all seem to attract followers who believe that religious identity should be the central value that guides a state. Supporters of religious nationalism are dissatisfied with the modern promises of a secular state.

Religious nationalism may or may not be associated with violence. As Mark Juergensmeyer notes, religious violence tends to erupt in regions where defining the nation state has proven difficult. In these areas, people are unable to overcome religious differences despite repeated attempts to form a unified government. Israel-Palestine, the Punjab, and Afghanistan are areas where disputes over land and power reflect religious conflict and have at times turned violent. The conflict between Jewish Israelis and Muslim Palestinians in the West Bank, Sikhs and Hindus in the state of Punjab, and between the Taliban and Shi'a Hazaras expose deep rifts in these communities that fall along religious lines.

In many nations, religious nationalism is found in attempts to change laws or culture to reflect the preferences of the dominant party. Political groups vying for influence in these regions utilize religious identity as a means to generate loyalty among supporters. Rather than emphasizing the common territory and values shared by multiple religious groups, religious nationalists attempt to assert power based upon the religious identity of their group. In the United States, evangelical Christians, who overwhelmingly voted for Donald Trump, support policies that limit immigrants and refugees from Muslim countries. Christian nationalists in the US and other countries may also encourage prayer in school, discourage the extension of rights to gay and transgender peoples, and support the display of the biblical verses or the cross in public spaces. In Israel, the 2018 Nation-State Law affirms that the "right of national self-determination in the State of Israel is unique to the Jewish people"; Israeli citizens who identify as Muslim and Arab, however, are concerned that their rights as equal citizens of the state are undermined by the language of this law. Attempts to link religious identity with state power can also be found in India with the Bharatiya Janata Party (BJP), one of the major ruling parties that has espoused Hindu nationalism over and against Indian Muslims.

The dangers of religious nationalism to secular democracies are apparent: increased polarization, decreased toleration for diversity, and the threat of violent conflict. Religious nationalism, however, may also pose dangers to religions themselves. The fact that religious nones are turning away from organized religions because they disagree with the political views of religious organizations suggests that overt attempts by religions to influence politics are repellent to a growing number of the population. Given that the number of nones is highest among the younger generations further suggests that religious nationalism is an ineffective strategy for attracting new and younger members to aging religious organizations. At the same, however, conservative religious movements appear to be attracting a different segment of the population that is dissatisfied with the offerings of secular governance. One possible outcome is the realignment political communities, if not entire nation states, along religious lines.

Artificial Intelligence

In 2018, Akihiko Kondo made headlines around the world for marrying a holographic robot. The affable Japanese businessman married Hatsune Miku, a computer-generated popstar with turquoise hair. Manufactured by the technology company Gatebox, Miku engages in conversation much like a wife or girlfriend might, albeit in holographic form. In one Gatebox commercial, a young man at work reads a text message from his holographic girlfriend reminding him of their "three-month anniversary" and proceeds to hurry home to prepare a special celebratory dinner with his beloved.

The wedding between Kondo and Miku was attended by 39 people, mostly strangers and one Member of Parliament. There was no religious officiant. Although Kondo is a member of a growing community of "fictosexuals," that is, those who profess love for fictitious humans, most people hesitate to legitimize relationships between real and imagined humans. Nonetheless, the marriage between Kondo and Miku is just one of thousands for which Gatebox has provided "marriage certificates." This phenomenon raises profound questions about the ethics of artificial intelligence (AI). Questions abound regarding the proper role of AI in human life, as well as the creation of AI algorithms that reflect—for better or for worse—the values of their human creators.

AI refers to the ability of a computer to perform tasks that would normally require human intelligence. Some common examples of AI in our everyday lives would be language translation, speech recognition, or face recognition. A computer-generated player in a video game would be an example of AI. AI is used to create digital assistants such as Siri (Apple) or Alexa (Google), which when asked, will tell us the time or the weather report, play a song, or provide driving directions. Social media platforms, such as TikTok, Instagram, Facebook, and Twitter, use AI to engage with users by presenting them with options that appeal to their interests based on online histories. Online shopping, banking, and travel booking all use AI to perform tasks that would have, in the past, required human assistance. There is even a robot Buddhist monk in Japan and a robot Catholic priest in Poland that give sermons, answer questions, and lead prayers.

Many of us cannot imagine a world without AI. However, ethical issues raised by AI lead us to scrutinize how and by whom AI is created, and the impact of AI on our lives and on society. Algorithms are generated using data sets that are selected by people, and therefore these selections reflect people's biases, whether intentional or not. For example, data sets used to develop facial recognition software have lacked sufficient gender and racial diversity. Facial recognition software has been found to be most accurate when identifying lighter-skinned men and least accurate for darker-skinned women. Because one potential use of facial recognition software is the identification of criminals, the algorithms need to be highly and equally accurate across categories such as race and gender. Including more diverse and comprehensive data sets would likely increase the accuracy of such algorithms.

During the COVID pandemic, incorrect information about vaccines that was perpetuated through AI-generated algorithms on social media platforms prevented people from receiving life-saving inoculations. Because AI in social media is designed to prioritize entertainment and engagement rather than education, millions of users were repeatedly exposed to information that was not medically sound. This tragically contributed to the loss of untold numbers of lives due to COVID. Along similar lines, democratic governments are extremely concerned about algorithms that exacerbate the spread of false information about elections. Because so many people rely upon social media to learn about candidates and elections, social media plays an important role in ensuring that voters receive accurate information. Unfortunately, events such as the insurrection at the US Capitol on January 6, 2021, during which Trump supporters violently interrupted the counting of electoral votes that would have formally recognized Joseph Biden as President, result from mis-information campaigns that are allowed to run unchecked on social media.

As AI becomes an even more integral part of our daily lives, religions will invariably take a stance on its creation and its limits. AI reflects human values, desires, and dangers; and religious thinkers will increasingly need to consider its proper place in a good life. Religious thinkers will also need to probe further the question of what it means to be human. If, in the future, a church ordains a robot priest, then ought that church also permit a human to marry a hologram? The value of human beings might lie not our biology, but in our functionality within society and our ability to build relationships to other human beings.

Religions both influence and are influenced by the humanity. The growing number of religious nones, the rise of religious nationalism, and the rapid proliferation of AI technologies are important issues that religious thinkers will continue to grapple with in the years ahead. The study of religious ethics can hopefully help us to better understand—and perhaps even to guide us through—these complex dilemmas of our world.

Bibliography

Burdett, Michael S. "Personhood and Creation in an Age of Robots and AI: Can We Say 'You' to Artifacts?" *Zygon* 55:2 (2020), 347–60.

Burge, Ryan P. *The Nones: Where They Came From, Who They Are, and Where They Are Going.* 1517 Media, 2021. https://doi.org/10.2307/j.ctv17vf41v.

Campbell, David E., Geoffrey C. Layman, and John Clifford Green. *Secular Surge: A New Fault Line in American Politics.* Cambridge: Cambridge University Press, 2021.

Dooley, Ben, and Hisako Ueno. "This Man Married a Fictional Character. He'd Like You to Hear Him Out." *New York Times.* April 29, 2022. https://www.nytimes.com/2022/04/24/business/akihiko-kondo-fictional-character-relationships.html.

Juergensmeyer, Mark. "The Global Rise of Religious Nationalism." *Australian Journal of International Affairs* 64:3 (2010), 262–73.

Index

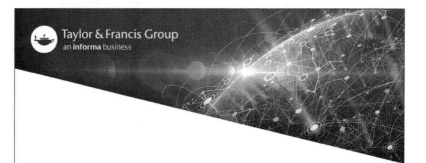